BEST NEWSPAPER WRITING 2003

WINNERS: THE AMERICAN SOCIETY OF NEWSPAPER EDITORS COMPETITION

Featuring
Community Service Photojournalism Award
and Companion CD-ROM

EDITED BY KEITH WOODS

The Poynter Institute
and
Bonus Books

07 06 05 04 03   5 4 3 2 1

International Standard Book Number: 1-56625-210-5
International Standard Serial Number: 0195-895X

The Poynter Institute for Media Studies
801 Third Street South
St. Petersburg, Florida 33701

Bonus Books
875 North Michigan Avenue, Suite 1416
Chicago, Illinois 60611

Book design and production by Billie M. Keirstead,
Director of Publications, and Vicki Krueger, Publications
Assistant, The Poynter Institute

Cover illustration by Anne Conneen, Design Editor,
The Poynter Institute

Photos in the Community Service Photojournalism section were
provided by the photographers. Photos of winners and finalists were
provided by their news organizations. Photos that accompany "The
Seekers" series were provided by *The Star-Ledger*, Newark, N.J.
Photos that accompany "Along Martin Luther King: A Passage to
Black America" were provided by Newhouse News Service.

Printed in the United States of America

To Jim Naughton, who launched Poynter
boldly toward a future in cyberspace
while never forgetting
the enduring value of words on paper.

'You bet I'm trying to sell newspapers'

MAY 2003

When I was 16 and had the great good luck to get a part-time after-school job at *The Painesville Telegraph* in my Ohio hometown, they'd occasionally trust me to read proofs in the composing room. I'd sit amid huge, noisy Linotype machines as they belched and clanked and spat lines of type formed from molten lead. The lines were arrayed on galley forms, inked, then pressed against narrow sheets of newsprint to produce long columns of type. These were read—usually by a matron with thick eyeglasses—and, if necessary, corrected, a new line of type inserted for the one bearing an error.

When, thanks to the dedicated work of innumerable nuns at St. Mary School, I found a mistake in spelling or grammar, my contribution to the newspaper was to occasion a virginal, silvery line of type being set amid the lines smudged by ink. I was, in effect, the newspaper's last word on accuracy. I was terrified by the responsibility—and loved it.

Half a century later, I have Jim Smith, executive editor of the *Record-Journal* in Meriden, Conn., to thank for reminding me how glorious it was to sit amid the Linotypes. Smith's passion for journalism made him the recipient of a 2003 ASNE Distinguished Writing Award. As you'll see when you get to that section, Roy Peter Clark was curious about the source of Smith's passion.

"First of all," Smith said, "it's renewed almost every day. Every time some public official says, 'No, you can't learn that,' I say, 'Yes, we can, and it's our obligation to let the public know.' On the other hand, I think it goes way back. One of the jobs my father had was as a Linotypist, and he took me to work one day when I was 7 or 8 years old. He sat down at that Linotype machine and typed out my name. That piece of lead sits on my desk today. So I think way back in my own memory I got molten lead and printer's ink in my blood."

I used to carry a stick of lead with my name on it and would pull it out of my pocket to show dubious citizens that I was, in fact, a reporter and photographer. Unlike Smith, I hadn't the wit to hang on to the lead byline all these years.

You never know what delectable recollection may be stirred or delicious insight occasioned by *Best Newspaper Writing*. For 25 years, such editors as Keith Woods, who's responsible for the volume in your hand, and their Poynter colleagues have had the audacity to ask the most admirable journalists in America to explain themselves. There are lessons to be learned in how the Jim Smiths of our craft did their honored work. That is why very senior leaders of news organizations have gathered each February at Poynter to spend two intensive days examining the kinds of stories and images reproduced in this book and on the accompanying CD.

This year, led by Rich Oppel, editor of the *Austin American-Statesman*, the judges were:

Andrew N. Alexander, Cox Newspapers,
　　Washington, D.C.
Jim Amoss, *The Times-Picayune,* New Orleans
Caesar Andrews, Gannett News Service,
　　Washington, D.C.
Gerald M. Boyd, *The New York Times*
Gregory Favre, The Poynter Institute
G. Maria Henson, *Austin American-Statesman*
Deborah Howell, Newhouse News Service,
　　Washington, D.C.
Ed Jones, *The Free Lance-Star,* Fredericksburg, Va.
David A. Laventhol, Committee to Protect
　　Journalists, New York
Pamela K. Luecke, Washington and Lee University
Walker Lundy, *The Philadelphia Inquirer*
Tim J. McGuire, Plymouth, Minn.
Skip Perez, *The Ledger,* Lakeland, Fla.
Madelyn A. Ross, *Pittsburgh Post-Gazette*
N. Don Wycliff, *Chicago Tribune*

They were aided in selecting the photojournalism award by Carolyn Lee of *The New York Times* and three other experts:

Ken Geiger, *The Dallas Morning News*
Naomi Halperin, *The Morning Call,* Allentown, Pa.
Kenny Irby, The Poynter Institute

All of the work these journalists selected is worthy of emulation. So is Jim Smith's passion. You know that throwaway question we journalists ask: "Is there anything we left out?" Unlike most interview subjects, Smith told Clark that there was something: He was concerned our legitimate focus on credibility might be making journalists too timid.

"We allow the phrase, 'They're just trying to sell newspapers,' to be pejorative," Smith said. "My response to that is, 'You bet I'm trying to sell newspapers, because the more newspapers that are sold in this society, the better off society is!'"

Amen, brother, amen.

Cheers,
Jim Naughton, President
The Poynter Institute

Acknowledgments

The publication of this book is the highest note in a yearlong celebration of the *Best Newspaper Writing* series' 25th year. So thanks are due not just to those who wrote and edited, photographed and sketched, but to those, past and present, who helped place an exclamation point on this anniversary year.

First, though, thanks to the journalists who produced the winning work and to the American Society of Newspaper Editors judges who chose the stories we publish here. Special thanks to publications director Billie Keirstead, who has overseen the production of all but two books in this series and who contributed mightily to our efforts to mark this silver anniversary. Thanks to Vicki Krueger, whose sharp editing eye should comfort anyone who aims for perfection. Helping to edit the text were proofreaders Sarah Kennedy, Dan Puckett, and Kathleen Tobin. Thanks also to ASNE executive director Scott Bosley and publications assistant Suzanne Martin, who make it easier each year to collect materials and speed up the time it takes for the book to reach the public.

The book is better because of Poynter faculty members Roy Peter Clark, Aly Colón, Kenny Irby, Pam Johnson, Kelly McBride, Bill Mitchell, and Christopher "Chip" Scanlan, whose cheerful help with interviews in these increasingly demanding times magnifies the value of their contributions. Scanlan's work continued online for Poynter as he created "Brown Bag" workshops based on the work of previous ASNE award winners.

Poynter's design editor Anne Conneen designed this book's cover and logo and the CD-ROM presentation, with multimedia editor and Flash-master Larry Larsen providing essential technical expertise. Poynter Online news editor Julie Moos and producer Robin Sloan gave the BNW@25 celebration its online presence. Marketing manager Ola Seifert and program assistant Cary Peréz Waulk found creative ways to get word out that BNW was having a big birthday. Others from Poynter gave time and talents to the book, including library director David Shedden, program assistant Jeannie Nissenbaum, and office assistant Rita Estrada.

Finally, thanks to Eugene Patterson for starting the ASNE Distinguished Writing contest and launching the book, and to Roy Peter Clark, who imagined, edited, and nurtured this series from the start as a tribute to great writing and a gift to those who aspire to such things.

Contents

"LEAP Year"

"Enrique's Journey"

"Chasing Hope"

"The Seekers: Faith's Place"

"The Seekers: Genesis"

"The Seekers" Illustrated Glossaries

"Along Martin Luther King: A Passage to Black America," Parts 4–6

"Along MLK" Photo Slide Show

25 years of excellence:
How do you get here from there?

BY KEITH WOODS

"How do I get in that book?"

An old friend put the question to me a year ago when he got his copy of *Best Newspaper Writing 2002*. It's a question I've heard more than a few times, and it's dispatched easily with a short answer: Win a prize.

A longer answer would delve into the minds of the American Society of Newspaper Editors judges when they gather at contest time. The fullest answer would begin with the story idea and wend its way through reporting and interviewing strategies, ending with nouns, adjectives, and verbs.

But I'd rather start with Eugene Patterson.

He's the one who used the pulpit of his ASNE presidency to launch a contest that would reward "distinguished" newspaper writing. And he was the one who thought it would be a grand idea to publish the winning works, pull the stories apart, and, with the aid of the writers, talk through what made them winners.

That would make him the father of *Best Newspaper Writing*.

His baby turns 25 this year.

So, in the spirit of celebrating that journalistic milestone and in pursuit of an answer for my friend, I asked Patterson a slightly different question: What did he have in mind when he envisioned the contest that begot the book?

In each of the categories, he replied, judges are looking for writers "who understand the lilt and the loveliness of the English language....That's what the writing awards seek to foster, and it's what they recognize."

The "lilt and the loveliness" of the language. What is that, I wanted to know? Patterson, a Pulitzer winner who wrote daily columns for eight years as editor of *The Atlanta Constitution* and led both the *St. Petersburg Times* and The Poynter Institute, has given the matter some thought.

It is a directness, he would say, propelled by active

verbs. It is evocative. "It stops you in your tracks," he told me. It is writing that asks this question of every sentence: Why can't I do this better?

Said Patterson: "It's clarity, grace, brevity. But clarity above all.

"It would be easy to write ordinary stuff and send it in," he said. "Extraordinary is the way to go. You apply those rules even if you have 15 minutes to write. You should be on a quest for something better. You should be demanding that the language answers to you."

In Patterson's plan, that's what would distinguish the ASNE awards from the Pulitzer Prizes, which, he says, "reward various other aspects of journalism." That sort of literary grace, that quest for something better, would be the engine that would elevate the quality of writing over a quarter century. That craftsmanship would be fueled by a book that seeks to understand why some writing has lilt, while too much writing, Patterson says, "just comes out and lies there and looks at you. It has no spirit, no vigor, no force to it."

As the first of five editors of *Best Newspaper Writing*, Poynter vice president and senior scholar Roy Peter Clark started the search for the "loveliness" that Patterson hoped could be found in the ASNE winners. Clark created the structure of the book 25 years ago, adding the interviews and the "Writers' Workshops" that are so helpful to students of the craft. Affiliate Don Fry and Dean Karen Brown Dunlap guided the book through its middle years before National Writers Workshops director Christopher "Chip" Scanlan took over, adding the finalists' "Lessons Learned" essays to the book's repertoire of writer introspection.

Today, professionals, professors, and aspiring writers can search "The Journalist's Toolbox," an index constructed to take readers directly to passages that explore writing's winning elements: finding story ideas, reporting with purpose, using details and quotes effectively, sharpening focus, embracing revision, and working with editors. Since 2001, the book has included a CD-ROM containing the winning work from the Community Service Photojournalism competition.

It's all in pursuit of the lilt. The loveliness. The solution to the puzzle embedded in the question, "Why can't

I do this better?" Turn these pages, and you'll find some of the answers. You'll see how Andrew H. Malcolm, writing offbeat editorials for the *Los Angeles Times*, meets Patterson's challenge by looking for one "small, telling detail" in every piece he writes. You'll learn from *The Star-Ledger*'s Amy Ellis Nutt that the power of an elementary writing tool, the analogy, lies in its ability to wrestle something as huge as the universe into an image accessible to all readers. You'll find in the interview with Newhouse News Service's Jonathan Tilove a lesson in how humility and reporting preparation can make great writing possible.

The winners in this book carry forward a tradition of constructive deconstruction that is forever chasing the perfect sentence, the quintessential quote, or the detail far greater than itself. They do justice to Eugene Patterson's vision, now 25 years old, of a collection that would help students and professionals "study what excellence truly is."

That's how you get better. It's how you get the best from this book. And it may well be how you get your byline into the next one.

ABOUT THIS BOOK

Through recorded conversations, follow-up calls, and e-mails, members of the Poynter faculty produced the interviews that follow the stories honored in this book. For the sake of clarity, flow, and brevity, some of the answers have been compressed and reordered and some questions have been edited or added.

Electronic versions of the winners' and finalists' stories were provided to Poynter by ASNE for publication in this book. They may differ slightly from the stories that originally appeared in print.

Best Newspaper Writing editors made minor changes in stories for style and grammar. Where editors found errors of fact, those were corrected after consultation with the writers.

Best Newspaper Writing 2003

Andrew H. Malcolm

Editorial Writing

Andrew H. Malcolm likes the little things.

With good reason.

Doing the math on the path that has shaped his career and sustained his family (wife, Connie, and four children), he adds up thousands of stories—and the little things at their core. He estimates he has written more than 12,000 articles during his nearly 30 years' combined tenure at *The New York Times* and the *Los Angeles Times*.

"I think every one of them contains at least one… small, telling detail," Malcolm says. "It's the power of the relevant detail to tell the story."

Malcolm, 60, gets those little things working overtime—for himself, as he plots his reporting, and for the reader, as he crafts what he writes.

A little thing Malcolm recalls from his Cleveland childhood is the occasional trip he'd make with his dad to an observatory telescope to see the planets. Nearly half a century later, a story about a solar system called 55 Cancri prompted Malcolm to contact Geoff Marcy, the leader of a team searching for planets like ours elsewhere in the universe. Thinking of his trips to the Cleveland observatory, Malcolm got Marcy to trace his childhood interest in astronomy.

"I said to myself, 'That's the lead,'" Malcolm recalls.

Malcolm attributes some of his devotion to detail to an encounter with actor Hal Holbrook at Culver Military Academy. Malcolm was a student there from 1958 to 1962, and Holbrook (Culver, '42) invited him backstage before one of his performances as Mark Twain. Malcolm watched as Holbrook applied 75 age spots to each cheek.

"Now, Andy, no one but you and I will know that. But I'll know it when I'm Mark Twain," Malcolm recalled Holbrook saying. "And that's the power of small details."

A few years later, studying journalism at Northwestern, Malcolm discovered the sociological research tool known as "Unobtrusive Measures." For Malcolm, it meant trying two approaches to articles about Chicago's Museum of Science and Industry.

First, he interviewed the director, got a tour, and collected documentation on the most popular exhibits. That produced a traditional story about the 25-cent train ride through a simulated coal mine. According to the documentation provided by ticket sales, that was the most popular exhibit.

Then he interviewed the janitors using unobtrusive measures and asked about little things: where the rugs and doors wore out first, where the windows were dirtiest, and where the trash cans filled up the fastest. That yielded a story indicating that an egg-hatching exhibit in a free area of the museum was drawing even bigger crowds. Since there were no tickets to count, it took unobtrusive measures to find a story otherwise obscured.

One other thing about little things. They're a big help when you're writing short. Malcolm's editorials, described by ASNE judges as "graceful, clever, evocative, humorous," almost never exceed 500 words. He relies on those small, telling details to convey by implication and suggestion what might otherwise consume another leg of type.

—Bill Mitchell

A thesaurist leaves, exits

MARCH 3, 2002

Regrettably, unfortunately, lamentably and mournfully, Robert L. Chapman is deceased, demised, departed and dead at 81. The son, boy and male offspring of a West Virginia typewriter mechanic, Chapman once drove trucks, then studied poetry and medieval literature before editing the timeworn, antiquated, irreplaceable Roget's International Thesaurus.

He transformed, altered and caused the transmutation of the stuffy, dull, ill-ventilated compendium of synonyms and antonyms into a hip, cool, with-it collection of words and associations, not only piquing the intellects of language lovers but saving the behinds, fannys and GPAs of countless late-night collegiate essay writers (see also Indolent, Slothful, Procrastinating). With their new shoes, underwear and a Webster's, college-bound juveniles have long packed a Roget's, hoping to sound more educated while getting there.

Before (Slang) cashing in his chips and giving up the ghost, Chapman quietly shaped the way we speak and think of words and idioms as tools to effectively communicate to each other the multi-toned richness of the human experience (see Feeling, Knowledge). You know how people in 19th century photographs posed as if nailed to boards and never smiled? Today's photographers encourage relaxed and open. Same difference for thesaurus editors.

A doctor and Londoner despite his French name, Peter M. Roget produced in 1852 more than a mere alphabetical listing of similar and dissimilar words. He also created categories such as Kindness, Benevolence to suggest enlightening linguistic links likely to be missed by word seekers. The goateed Chapman was engagingly subversive in his academically rooted but pragmatic, populist approach to chronicling and improving how English speakers speak and write. His computers also tracked word usage to update and expand categories and words for new times, inserting

AIDS, Scud, hacker, fax, ecosystem, even new dog breeds and slang and modern phobias (i.e. Fear of Flying, not prominent in 1850). Roget's perusers find themselves wandering the distinctive wordways of Chapman's lexicon, encountering new meanings, associations and phrasings through serendipity, an increasingly rare modern commodity and a delicious entry that needs no synonym. As things eventuated, credit goes to Robert Chapman, who has no synonym.

All decisions, all the time

FEBRUARY 23, 2002

Thanks a lot, Judge Greene.

He was the well-meaning, earnest fellow who, in 1984, decided the nation couldn't live with one telephone company. His decisions implemented AT&T's breakup but seemed to unleash a cascade of theoretically beneficial competition, confronting millions of innocent Americans with a compounding surfeit of overwhelming daily decisions.

You can now blow an entire Saturday deciding stuff.

We used to have it simple—a number for the phone, Social Security and license plate. We survived on one species of M&Ms and two choices about toilet paper, rolling off the top or the bottom depending on maternal tradition. But now, what phone company for local service? What company for long distance? DSL? Unlisted? Messaging? Forwarding? Call waiting? Line insurance? What Internet company? By the hour or unlimited? Cable TV or satellite? Which satellite? Which movie package? Which news channel—the one with Larry King in suspenders or the one with short skirts? You know going in that no packages compare. Same for cell phones. How to figure if the 7 p.m. minutes plan is better? How many are out of state? Or region? What region? Do you want a vanity auto license? Also, decide right now: If you die on the 101, can some strangers have your organs?

Once, passwords were only for childhood clubhouses. Now, grown-ups need one at work. "Your password expires in four days. Do you want to change it?" Aging minds must choose—numbers, letters, capitals?—how to jumble old passwords to remember new ones without psychiatric care? Same for PINs. Is this ATM worth $2 or wait for the free one near home? $40, $60, $80? Which PIN is it—birthday or anniversary? Need checks? What style?

Movies used to show one film; 17 now playing. At the grocery store, brand name or generic? Grande or venti? How many apple varieties do we really need? Sodium-free crackers? Reduced fat? Even Cheerios require decisions now. And then: Paper or plastic? Lottery ticket? Club member? Four ways to pay. Need help to your car? Gas low? Several grades to pick. Pay inside or out? Credit or cash? Want a receipt? Car wash? Tire treatment? Wax? Need a snack? Is drive-thru always slower than walk-in? Regular or diet? Supersize? What sauce? Here or to go? Cold in the car? What fan speed and where to blow—windshield, mid-level, floor or combo? Same for passenger side? Now, about your sprinkler settings....

As for Harold Greene, he retired, then died two years ago of a cerebral hemorrhage. May his selection of heavenly golf courses and plaid pants be many.

Wish I may, wish I might

JUNE 23, 2002

One day many years ago in a valley not far away, Geoff Marcy's parents gave him a used 4-inch telescope. At night he would unlatch his bedroom screen and climb onto the patio roof with his new toy. There, for countless hours, the boy toured the solar system and Milky Way. Marcy recalls feeling very small but strangely connected to something much larger and grander as he studied Saturn's rings, monitored the movements of Jupiter's moons and wondered whether anyone or anything was out there looking back at Granada Hills.

Marcy grew up and defected to Northern California, to a planet called Berkeley. He's taller now but still feels small as he scans the skies with UC Berkeley computers, $5-million spectrometers and telescopes with 33-foot mirrors. Marcy leads one of several global teams quietly collecting intriguing evidence of earthlike planets orbiting stars. While we obsess about really important things such as budgets, secession and soccer and a few things of somewhat less galactic import like songs and thongs, these isolated bands of men and women spend their nights atop mountains imagining what might be in places far away.

Because their work does not involve blowing anything up, these astronomers get little attention. Until the other day, when they announced the discovery of a solar system, 55 Cancri, with planets possibly positioned like ours. This could create the conditions for evolutionary life "just" 41 light-years away.

It took years to find the first such planet. Now, seven years later, Marcy and others have plotted more than 90 planets orbiting stars like our sun; most are like Goldilocks' porridge—too hot, too cold or too hot and then too cold. Because the host stars are so bright, Marcy doesn't actually see these planets; that awaits a new generation of telescopes. He can, however, infer a planet's presence by the minute wobble of its star, as the unseen planet's gravity tugs during orbits. Big tugs equal big planets. Star movements appear as shifting colors in a spectrum as starlight passes through telescopes.

If you think your house is big or your commute long, here on this summer solstice weekend are some numbers the 47-year-old Marcy confronts daily: In 15 years, they've examined 1,200 nearby stars. In our Milky Way, there are about 200 billion stars like our sun. Probably half of those stars harbor orbiting planets. And there are an estimated hundreds of billions of other galaxies like ours. Today's rockets travel 20,000 miles an hour. But light travels 186,000 miles a second. Which means the telltale wobbling starlight recently transiting Marcy's huge telescope left 55 Cancri right about the time the young boy with the little telescope was peering up from that patio roof in Granada Hills.

The master and his human

NOVEMBER 25, 2002

Some smart humans with pleasant scents and a largely incomprehensible vocabulary have determined that over thousands of years their species, through domestication and interaction, changed the genetics of what would become canines. The scientists, who have only two legs, just reported their serious findings in the journal *Science*. They believe that humans changed wolves—rescuing them from a cold forest life of surviving paw to mouth—by bringing these canny creatures into the warmth of a house as domesticated dogs with their own toys, soft beds and biscuit treats they needn't share.

The *Science* research suggests it was humans' idea to serve meat in a bowl to former wolves who once had to chase dinner. Now, this retired wildlife sleeps around the house whenever it wants. The scientists say dogs have learned to read human looks, gestures and sounds; even puppies know how to do this from birth.

We can report exclusively here that this news—considered hilarious in dogdom—is traversing the globe through bouts of coded barking from one backyard to another. Although dog dialects and accents differ by region, the rough translation of these canine messages is: "It's still working perfectly. They think they're training us!"

Humans' uncanny ability to learn from dogs was, like many important advances, discovered by accident. Legend says that thousands of years ago a portly dog seeking a workout one cold morning delivered a stick to an idle human. Instantly, the human knew the trick. He tossed the stick away. The dog brought it back. The human threw it away. Again and again. Even when the dog fetched a different stick, the human knew to toss it.

Since then, other animals have deciphered human learning patterns. Even illiterate ducks have successfully trained humans frequenting parks. The ducks walk up, ask for bread and tilt their heads, waiting. Well-trained humans know to stop and drop large quantities of bread crumbs.

Training humans requires time—and patience. Sure, all it took was little puppy licks for humans to learn baby talk. But generations of whimpering passed before humans finally began cloaking cold floors in carpets. Humans encountering each other still don't get the sniffing protocol. And despite centuries of example by all breeds during morning and evening walks, humans still haven't learned where to do their business, though most know now to clean up after the dog.

A growing cadre of conservative canines holds that humans, though adorable when children, are stubborn and quite simply untrainable as adults. According to this orthodox interpretation of the stick-tossing legend, the dog who discovered humans' apparent capacity for learning was not seeking exercise. He was cold in the cave and intended the stick for the fire.

Saddams everywhere

OCTOBER 2, 2002

More good news from the Middle East: Germany's public television network ZDF reports there's not just one evil Saddam Hussein. There may be at least three evil look-alikes, plus, of course, the evil original. The look-alikes appear for security reasons or perhaps because Saddam hates missing Angels games. ZDF experts studied 450 recent photos of Saddam, identifying doubles or triples only by tiny details.

In fact, ZDF said, the real Saddam hasn't been filmed since 1998. The other guys are genuine phonies—the Saddam shooting his gun straight up, the Saddam waving a bent arm at unseen crowds, the Saddam standing stiffly in windowless rooms giving pathetic handshakes to lackeys. No wonder he looks insincere; it's the 12th take and he isn't paid that much. Some Saddams were surgically adjusted, ZDF suggested, to more closely resemble the bad guy with the bushy Hitler-like mustache and several mistresses but no gray hair at age 65.

Duplicate Saddams could complicate Bush's Iraq plans. Will we need four regime changes with matching assassination teams? If one Saddam gets nailed, will the others quickly shave and retire? Wouldn't it be easier if the CIA hired its own Saddam? He could tell Larry King he's joined Greenpeace and regrets almost everything— the wars, invasions, oilfield fires, gassings, executions, missiles, everything except the mistresses.

This is priceless material for lovers of conspiracy novels by Robert Ludlum, who reportedly died last year. And imagine doing scheduling for four identical dictators—the days off, the big hats and medals, the different salary withholdings, always having a Saddam handy for rally-waving without another appearing simultaneously across town at the tank races.

Do several Saddams augur other human replicas? Only one Gray Davis and Tony Blair, of course, but might there be two Gerhard Schroeders—one pro- and one anti-U.S.? We've seen several Al Gores speak, a couple of Tom Daschles and, judging by his pre-injury play this fall, at least two Kurt Warners. Are rumors true that Mayor James Hahn's disappearances involve training as a Jackie Mason look-alike? Is the original 99-year-old Sen. Strom Thurmond retiring this year or is that Strom Thurmond Version 9.9? Will Osama bin Ladens pop up everywhere now, waving to crowds like all those circus clowns emerging one after the other from the tiny car?

Few recall that the mother of all celebrity look-alike businesses is Elvis Presley. He tired of fame, trained countless clones in Las Vegas and returned to Mississippi to drive trucks and sing in karaoke bars. We all knew there were two President George Bushes. But there's only one likely explanation for how George W. Bush could appear at so many fall fund-raisers in two states on the very same day.

A conversation with
Andrew H. Malcolm

BILL MITCHELL: When people ask you what kind of editorials you write for the *Los Angeles Times*, what do you say?

ANDREW H. MALCOLM: Feature editorials that don't look like editorials. One of the great values of growing up is that you don't get lectures from Dad anymore. If people are like me, they're tired of being told what to do in life. They almost resent it. The sense of lecturing and woulds and shoulds and this faceless, nameless writer telling me what I ought to think—that's the old-fashioned editorial. I've never wanted to be in the business of telling people what they ought to think. Now I might try to lead them there through the writing, but everyone should feel that they came to the conclusion themselves.

I got into this business in high school when I heard a journalist speak and was fascinated by his description of traveling through Africa during the revolutions. I thought it'd be great to travel on somebody else's money and then get my name in the paper. And to tell stories. I think a lot of people get into the business now because they want to fix society. I didn't do that. I wanted to tell stories.

And over your career you've done a lot of story-telling.

Indeed. I think there were more than 12,000 stories in *The New York Times* over 26 years and then there have been about 300 editorials here at the *Los Angeles Times*. A large majority of them are stories being told through a particular person with some small detail. I think every one of them contains at least one—many have a lot more—small, telling detail. It's the power of the relevant detail to tell the story.

Traditionally, editorials are aimed at provoking readers to do something. What are you looking for in terms of reaction?

I'm looking for readers to think about things they haven't thought about, to think about things they *have* thought about but think about them in different ways, to learn things. As we get back to these small details, there'll be little pieces of trivia in there. I'm fascinated to learn things. A lot of people I have encountered in this business get tired. It's understandable. It's a brutal business. You come in all excited about a story and they say, "Well, somebody else is doing it" or "Somebody else did that" or "We don't have space tonight" or "You don't have enough time to do it, maybe for the weekend," and then it gets squeezed out after the first edition. It's a brutal process that beats down enthusiasm and excitement. I vowed early on that I wasn't going to let that happen to me and, on most days, that's the case.

How do you sustain the enthusiasm, the excitement?

Well, I think it's an innate thing. One, I really want to tell stories. It's part of my being. But most important is the curiosity. I went through some fairly serious dental surgery yesterday and even with my mouth in a very strange position, I'm saying to the dentist, "What are you doing now?" And then all the time I'm thinking, "How would I write this?" Things don't happen in my life officially until I've written them down.

Curiosity is why I went into government for a while to see how it worked inside. I'd been running around outside for all those years trying to jump up and peek in the window and listen. It was very humbling because I had thought that on my best days of reporting, I would know 70, 75 percent of what was going on. And I now know that on the best day it might have been 35 percent. And so when I came back to journalism, I came back with much more humility than I had before.

What about the significance of small details in editorials about policy or about things like the discovery of a new solar system, for example?

My editorials typically involve a person. When I read about astronomers discovering that solar system, I just knew there was some human detail to that search. These people had been looking for so long. So I got hold of the team leader, and the first thing I asked him was, "Where did your interest in astronomy start?" And he told me about going out onto the porch roof with his used telescope.

Let me read the lead of that editorial: "One day many years ago in a valley not far away, Geoff Marcy's parents gave him a used 4-inch telescope." What a wonderful storytelling lead. Tell me how you got to that lead.

Like Geoff Marcy, I've always been fascinated by space. I don't want to go there because it's too cold, but I have always been intrigued by the size and the scale. My dad and I used to go to an observatory in Cleveland once a month, and they would have this huge telescope focused on some particular star or something, and we'd look at it and you could actually see Saturn's rings. I found it very exciting, so I guess I was looking for something like that when I got hold of Geoff Marcy. As soon as he told me the story, I said to myself, "That's the lead."

I have a question about the kicker: "And there are an estimated hundreds of billions of other galaxies like ours. Today's rockets travel 20,000 miles an hour. But light travels 186,000 miles a second. Which means the telltale wobbling starlight recently transiting Marcy's huge telescope left 55 Cancri right about the time the young boy with the little telescope was peering up from that patio roof in Granada Hills." You packed a lot of math in with that storytelling.

It's a way of getting at the scale without saying it. If you tell a joke and you start out by saying, "Boy, is this a funny joke; this is the funniest joke you've ever heard," and then you tell the joke and then you tell them why it's funny, it's not funny.

That's why newspapers have such a problem with humor. They think they have to explain it for all the fourth-graders reading. But the 10th- and 11th-graders are insulted. So you may draw in two fourth-graders but you lose a lot of other people. It's really boring and insulting. For instance, in the "Saddams" editorial, we refer to Kurt Warner. In the news pages they would explain who he is. Our editorials don't belabor those kinds of points.

This is my "lingerie theory" of communications: You are always more intrigued by what you *can't* see than by what you *can* see. Newspapers want to tell you what they saw, but literature writes like peripheral vision. It writes about things that are off on the side, in your consciousness, and that's where the power comes. It draws you into your imagination. It's like a Japanese garden. The crucial element in Japanese gardens is that part of every single item in that garden must be hidden. A rock must be partly buried, covered by a bush; a tree has to have another tree growing in front of it; a pond has to curve around so you can't see it all from any one place. It's the same thing with lingerie.

So you're consciously holding back in an effort to tantalize the readers a little?

At least the way I do it, I imply strongly but I don't say it. Now if you do it right—and I don't always do it right—there's only one way that they can take it. But they think they got there themselves.

I wonder if the kicker of your "Saddams Everywhere" editorial is an example of what you're talking about.

That one began with a short wire story. A German TV network hypothesized that there were several Saddam Hussein look-alikes for security reasons. So right away I wanted to go against the grain of pompous editorials. I wrote a lead that said, "More good news from the Middle East." It's not a complete sentence; and this is why I thank heaven for the editors I have, because they're receptive to what on the surface could be a seemingly zany idea. We're going to prompt our readers to think about something they hadn't thought about. And I knew it was going to be fun.

What sense do you get from readers about how they're reacting?

Hardly any, because the editorials are not signed. I hear from editors and the publisher that people inquire about the "new" editorial writer, but nothing personally.

Not signed, no mug, no e-mail address at the bottom. Do you long for some reaction, some feedback?

They asked me that when I came to work here. They said, "How do you think you'll be able to handle having no bylines?" And I said, "Well, one, I've got 12,000 or so in another paper; two, I've just spent eight years writing speeches that everybody thought were somebody else's."

My assignment—when *L.A. Times* editor John Carroll hired me—was, one, "You will have no beat"; two, "You will write whatever you want to write, as long as I would never expect to see it on the editorial pages of the *Times.*" And I said, "Well, that'll be great. I can do that."

How do you generate these ideas? Do you go to the editorial board meetings?

I'm a full member of the editorial board, but we do more talking about other editorials than we do about mine. It's very hard to say, "Look, I'm working on a joke about there being several Saddam Husseins." What is an editorial board going to contribute to that? Now, they might say, "Gee, Andy, that's not funny." I say, "Well, let me work on it and you guys can see it." So, it's not like hashing out a policy on the potential for war in Iraq. I mean, this isn't rocket science. And it's something that is personal in the sense that it's my strange mind at work. I don't claim that it's always good. But it's almost always different and, hopefully, gets people to think about things in a different way.

You're part of this group, but you're clearly doing something that the others aren't.

As a foreign correspondent you're a lone wolf, and alone is a hard life for a wolf. It's a hard life for humans as well. But when you're on a team, as I was in a governor's office or a political campaign or an editorial board, it's different; everybody has their thing. One or two of our people are really, really good at writing foreign affairs and, I suspect, have no interest whatsoever in trying to write anything funny. And my thing is to write things funny, which, hopefully, people enjoy, but hopefully then they read the other stuff. So we all attract different audiences who then enjoy the mix in the paper. I have a very serious journalism background, but I also love to tell jokes and I love to tell stories—and so you put the three of them together. I'd say probably two-thirds of the ones I write have an element of humor.

Also, it comes from what I hope is a powerful sense of observation. For instance, the day my father died, I flew to San Diego and while I was waiting for the bags to come down, there was a man and woman in front of me and their bags were obviously coming and the man stepped forward toward the conveyor belt. As he was doing so, without looking, he put his right hand with his briefcase back behind him, and, without looking, his wife took it. Now that's a detail I will use sometime.

Do your editors edit what you do much?

They don't change much. I think there have been three of my editorials that haven't made it into print. I do not turn in overspaced writing. If the assignment is 68 lines, that's what you're going to get. You will never get 69 or 70. First of all it's a discipline (I went to a military school), but it's an intellectual discipline as well. It's part of the teamwork deal. Having been an editor, I know that it's going to create problems if I write long. Somebody else is going to have to give, and if I've agreed to 68 lines, I ought to live with 68. Also, frankly, I want to be in control. If I wrote 70, they might take out my two favorite lines. So I made it clear that I like to be involved. Every word is picked with pretty much precision, and I've thought about it, trying to make each word do the work of two or three. I may have missed something and I'm always happy to consult on it, if there's a better way of saying it or clarifying why I said it, and we do that a fair amount.

Let's talk about the writing.

Okay. That's the fun part.

The ASNE judges said your winning columns played language like a musical instrument. Do you do that consciously?

Yeah, yeah.

You told me you played the drums as a kid. Is it anything like that?

I love playing the drums because I love the syncopation and the rhythm. I always have. I try to make it like music. Here's the process. Like the "Saddams" editorial, I'll have the premise in mind, probably during my commute. I have a notebook and my wife just gave me a keychain that's got a little tape recorder on it. A lot of my editorials could begin, "Has anyone else noticed…?" I'm going to write one soon, "Has anybody else noticed that the usage of the word 'absolutely' has increased absolutely and exponentially as well?" Everything is "absolutely." And then I'll do some riffs on what the meaning of "absolutely" is in some examples.

My Poynter colleague, Roy Peter Clark, has written about how we depend on music for metaphors of writing: voice, audience, rhythm, cadence, tone. You just described doing a riff.

Real writing is very much like music. But newspapers haven't permitted many riffs. Music doesn't talk to us about explicit things. Music implies. You haven't traditionally been able to write, especially in editorials, about wind and music and feelings. But that's what connects with people now. That's why the wink is so powerful; that's why a politician going on *David Letterman* and making a self-deprecating joke is powerful. It's human. I've often thought about these things as peripheral vision. You know something's there, but if you turn your head and look over there, it's gone; it's moved over to the other side. When you turn to the side, you can't see it. So to me that's kind of what writing is on newspapers.

I wanted to ask you the secret of making readers smile, and I think you've already helped me in that regard by concealing a bit, implying, suggesting...

A little sarcasm, a little irony. "More good news from the Middle East." When's the last time we heard more good news? I wrote one earlier this year that began (they always dump mine down at the bottom of three or four other editorials), "Now that you got through all that serious stuff..." That was the beginning of it, sort of poking fun at the business.

I wrote about ad placements in movies and TV shows now and how it's increasing. You know, where they'll have a specific Coca-Cola can there and the guy keeps drinking from it and stuff like that, and the last paragraph of that was full of other Tribune-owned items. If they keep doing this stuff, they'll turn off readers.

You've written your share of long stories through the years. How does it feel to write never more than 500 words?

I love it, I must say. Ted Bernstein of *The New York Times* used to say, "I don't have time to write short" and it's true. It takes more time. Jack Fuller and I worked in college together and he told me, when he was writing editorials for the *Tribune,* about the satisfaction that he found in writing short. I know when I'm at 468 words.

Do you?

Oh, I just have a feel, and I'll have the thing counted and it'll be 472 or 460. I just know. It's a rhythm, you know? It's like going out and doing a show in a nightclub. You know about how long, you know when it's clicking with the audience.

People's attention spans today are a lot shorter and, frankly, if I did 800 words I don't think it would work. Get a good premise and two or three examples, you're off to the races.

You mentioned that your government experience has made you a humbler reporter and writer. How so?

Well, I'm more aware. In the past, I fear I may have gone into some stories—on state government, say—with a sense of cynicism, basically assuming that they're all crooks or they're all loafers in state government. Change state government to Asians or Hispanics or blacks, could we say that? No. And you could never even imply it, because it's stereotyping. But we still accept it in other areas. All politicians are crooks. Some are, and guess what, some journalists have been, too.

I'm more open now about what I'm doing. I go in right away and say, "I'm Andrew Malcolm. I'm writing about this. I understand this part of it. I don't understand this part and I don't want to screw it up and get it wrong and make life harder for you. So could you help me or steer me to somebody who can explain this to me, how it really works?" And when you do that, it then makes it to their advantage to help you, which my father always told me was the best possible position to be in. Make it to somebody's advantage to help you. And I don't go in thinking, "I'll bet there's a crook in here and I'm going to find him." There's a role for those kinds of people. It doesn't happen to be what I am.

What are you working on now?

I'm writing one for this Sunday on the study they've done on the common cold, except I'm calling it the very common cold. They say the common cold in the head costs Americans a fortune. I write the editorial as if my nose is all stuffed up.

How are you conveying that in the editorial?

By spelling words wrong. "So now dere, D-E-R-E, is dis ting called da common code, C-O-D-E, that costs the country $39 billion." And we go on that way.

How many plates do you have spinning at any given time? Are you saving a lot of string?

I have two files; each one of them is five or six inches thick of clippings, news releases, studies, notes to my-self. I'm probably actively thinking about four or five at any one time. And then all of a sudden I'll think of a great phrase for one I want to do on chocolate, and so that'll cause me to move it up on the list.

I realized as I started writing the "Our Town" columns in *The New York Times* that most of my ideas came from the paper's regional sections. I had the clerks there keep a cardboard box by their desk and all of the news releases the editors threw out as unworthy of news, they sent to me, and that's where all my column ideas came from, little ideas. You would read through 50 and you might get one idea. And for every 10 ideas, you might end up doing one of them. And as you go through that process you begin to look at each idea as just the germ, the premise. You just take that and run with it and imagine it, and then write it in a journalistic way, except that it's hopefully a little bit funny but makes you think about the event in ways that you hadn't thought of before.

You say you've got two files. What's in one and what's in the other?

They're both the same. They just accumulate, and I don't want to throw them out. It's just intriguing stuff. It's not unlike a dresser drawer, you know, the top dresser drawer where you keep all these little things. You open it up and suddenly something that was just interesting last week connects because there's something in the news—like the Saddam Hussein thing. The trick is to bring the reader along with you. To me, this is exciting. When I hang up the phone, I'm going to write the rest of this editorial on colds, and I'm excited. I can't wait to do it to see what comes out.

How do you go about constructing an editorial that takes so many unexpected turns?

As you're writing it—back to the lingerie theory—you hold something out at the beginning and then drop it in later. I mean the newspaper instinct would be to put all your good stuff at the top, and I sprinkle it throughout. The trick is how to balance the funny with the serious. You know what, folks, this isn't all funny because X, Y, and Z. And then in the end have a kicker that is a little bit off to the right or the left that you didn't really expect. So the people go away saying, "I didn't know that," and maybe it'll cause them to think about something more, something different. Also, one thing I do is read these editorials out loud to myself to see how they sound.

I purposely don't outline because I don't want people to feel that they're walking through a blueprint. I want people to think that they're on a serendipitous journey with this mind. For better or worse, it's a little bit strange, and we don't know where it's going to go in the next paragraph. On traditional newspapers you want them all comfortable, where they've been and where they're going. I want people to wonder: Is he going to fall off or not? Is he going to pull this off?

I don't do a lot of rewriting, but I do a lot of tweaking. I'll write the first paragraph, the second paragraph, the third paragraph; then I'll move the paragraph down and that'll become the end usually. I'll fill in the middle, then I'll go back over my notes to see what I didn't get in that I really wanted to get in.

I'm much more disciplined now than I was in the old days. And so I try to be more rigid about making it relevant. And then I'll get up and walk away. I'm a Diet Coke-aholic, so I'll have another, walk away, and maybe get a cookie or something and come back, and probably go back into it five or six times until I'm not making any changes.

This sounds like it might be quite different from the kind of work you'd done on deadline previously, where most of your time would be consumed in the reporting and then you'd be in more of a scramble for the writing?

Yeah, I've done that. I enjoyed being able to do that. Sometimes I'm asked how I handle writer's block, and I say I've never had it. You can't go up to the editor and say, "You know what, those 84 trucks out there in the street, you're going to have to have them wait because I'm having writer's block." You can't do that. It's a luxury that I haven't been able to give myself.

Sometimes I will postpone the writing almost because

it tastes too good in anticipation. I had one the other day that I purposely waited and didn't start writing until about 2—it wasn't for that night—because I just wanted to sit down and have fun with it.

Every once in a while an editorial doesn't seem to count right. Then I'll go through and take out widows and other stuff. Or change it from a compound verb and cut out two words there and that saves you a whole line. I really enjoy that. And then at the end I'll realize that thing I cut, I really want that, so something else has to go. It's just important for the rhythm and I do it—that's why I read it out loud. It's got to sound good to me before I turn it in. And so there's a rhythm to the prose.

When I was in high school, they had us read all different kinds of writers, and I didn't realize it then but, of course, you're absorbing little bits of their different styles from Hemingway to the first Thomas Wolfe and those lush, long sentences about North Carolina springs and you copy that for a while. So now you can drop them in. You can have a long, lush sentence and the whole point of the sentence is to create a feeling of a long, lush thing.

At least in your winning editorials, you don't use many direct quotes. How do you decide when to use a quote rather than to paraphrase? Let me read an excerpt from your editorial "All Decisions, All the Time" about the proliferation of choices confronting us these days. "Once, passwords were only for childhood clubhouses. Now, grown-ups need one at work. 'Your password expires in four days. Do you want to change it?' Aging minds must choose—numbers, letters, capitals?—how to jumble old passwords to remember new ones without psychiatric care…At the grocery store, brand name or generic?…How many apple varieties do we really need?"

Take the quote, "Your password expires in four days." That's a direct quote so that it would ring bells. It's not a paraphrase because I wanted it to ring bells with people and then you say "aging minds," which implies maybe you're getting older. Then you call in the things that most people use to make up a password and then you throw in the grocery store thing—you know they allow me to do fragmented sentences. "At the grocery store, brand name or generic?...How many apple varieties do we really need?" That's a little grumpiness. That's hopefully funny. It's a different tone. If you didn't have different tones in each one of these, people would give up, right?

Your range of tones is fascinating. It never seems to get into the anger zone, though.

No, no. I don't want it to be. There's enough anger in the world. In fact, I turn off the TV when there are angry people on there. My idea of the end of civilization is *Crossfire* on CNN, which is basically a verbal food fight. Now there's entertainment in all these editorials. There has to be because we're competing. But hopefully there's a little bit of substance there. And being forced to write short forces me to say you're not going to get everything in here. I want people to think that this guy's a character; he's sort of kindly but he can get a little grumpy. But what he's grumpy about I'm grumpy about, too, if I thought about it. That's all. It's fun, it's fun. The fun is back in journalism.

Writers' Workshop

Talking Points

1) The ASNE judges said Andrew Malcolm's writing "set a different tone from all the other entries" in the editorial writing category. One judge described his piece on the death of the editor of Roget's Thesaurus as "dazzling." What makes this editorial so unusual?

2) Malcolm says he tries hard to find common experiences that many, maybe most, of his readers can relate to. See if you can determine the "common experience" in each of his editorials. Are they common to your experience? Did they help you relate to the editorial?

3) One of the secrets Malcolm shares with readers of this book is his "lingerie theory" of journalism. What do you understand the theory to be? Do you find it an effective technique?

4) In addition to common experience, Malcolm tries to include at least one small and telling detail in everything he writes. Can you pinpoint such a detail in each of his editorials?

Assignment Desk

1) Write a letter to the editor on a topic you care about and, were you working for a newspaper, might have published as an editorial. Try to get your letter published in your newspaper's letters section or op-ed page.

2) Try standing news on its head, as Malcolm does with his editorial about dog training. Have fun letting your imagination get a little carried away.

3) The judges said Malcolm "played language like a musical instrument." Try writing a couple of paragraphs as if you were playing a musical instrument. How is it different from the way you usually write?

4) Take another look at Malcolm's editorial on the deceased editor of Roget's Thesaurus. Then try your hand at an obit-editorial about someone whose life story might lend itself to similarly whimsical treatment.

David Barham
Editorial Writing

David Barham was born in Baton Rouge, La., the son of baby boomers whose idea of a Democratic president was John Kennedy. Republican? Richard Nixon. Barham says he grew up with Jimmy Carter and Ronald Reagan shaping his view of national leadership, a heritage that helped shape a different brand of Barham politics.

Married with three children, Barham has his own family now. When the whole clan gets together, the talk is usually about hunting, fishing, and grandkids.

Barham finds political kinship on the job, where he writes editorials that ASNE judges say are packed with "personality, impact, and character."

Barham, 35, got his start in journalism in high school. After graduating from Southern Arkansas University, he joined the *Bastrop* (La.) *Daily Enterprise*.

There he covered a governor's race that gave him a

grounding in Southern politics on display in the editorials he writes today. In 1992, he joined *The News-Star* in Monroe, La., where he covered courts, cops, and politics. The editorial page editor's job opened up in 1997, and Barham got it.

"I had covered politics in Louisiana for so long that I loved the sport of it," he says. "So I began writing editorials that just came naturally to me."

What didn't come easily was forging acceptable opinions among an editorial board of colleagues and citizens with strikingly divergent politics.

"It just comes out all watered down," Barham says, when they would try to agree.

Then, last year, Paul Greenberg hired him onto the *Democrat-Gazette* in Little Rock, Ark. The give-and-take became less about politics ("Paul hires conservative writers to write conservative editorials.") and more about writing. Greenberg, a 1968 Pulitzer Prize winner who won a Distinguished Writing Award for Commentary in 1981, "edits pretty heavily," according to Barham.

"It makes for better editorials," Barham adds. "We go back and forth…and we really try to work together."

Barham says Greenberg pushes him to take his editorials to a "second level" that readers will find irresistibly engaging and unpredictable.

One of the pieces that won Barham his ASNE prize touted the benefits of an immigration-driven increase in Arkansas' Hispanic population—certainly not a predictably conservative position.

"I've been thinking a long time about" people who immigrate to the United States, Barham says. "Who would do something like that? Well, somebody who's braver than I am, and those are the types of people you want living in your community."

When the former president of the Southern Baptist Convention denounced the founder of Islam as "a demon-possessed pedophile," Barham denounced the Baptists for putting up with such "brotherly hate." Not surprisingly, given his collaborative style, Barham can't recall the origin of one of the editorial's more memorable lines. But you can hear the exasperation—along with the personality, impact, and character—in the voice behind the words: "Sweet Jesus."

—Bill Mitchell

Brotherly hate: How to lose a war—and our souls

JUNE 20, 2002

Hate can be useful when giving a war. All sides use it. Not excluding ours. Gentle Reader may remember 1991, when Bush I had to enrage an entire nation against his erstwhile ally—Saddam Hussein—before going to battle. It wasn't hard, given the target.

But then you have useless hate, callow hate, hate directed against an entire culture or people, hate for hate's sake—stupid, destructive, even suicidal hate. Like poison gas, hate can drift back into our own ranks, sickening, confusing and dividing us. Look at what happened to Americans of Japanese descent during the Second World War. Unfortunately, that kind of hatred bubbled over again last week, and at a place where some of us might not have expected it:

Islam was founded by Muhammad, a demon-possessed pedophile who had 12 wives—and his last one was a 9-year-old girl. And I will tell you, Allah is not Jehovah either. Jehovah's not going to turn you into a terrorist that'll try to bomb people and take the lives of thousands and thousands of people.—The Rev. Jerry Vines, former president of the Southern Baptist Convention, in St. Louis last week.

Sweet Jesus.

While we appreciate people who call 'em like they see 'em, and while we know the PC Police have increased patrols after September 11th, we have to wonder whatever good the good Reverend hoped to accomplish by that kind of ugliness. Just change the name of the religion and the prophet, alter a phrase or two, and his statement could have come straight out of one of the more hate-crazed Arab dailies on the subject of Jews or Christians. Are we now going to overcome our enemies by imitating them? God forbid.

There are some obvious flaws in the Rev's logic—God or Allah or Jehovah, they are but different names for the Unnamable, and He scarcely directs terrorists to do His bidding. All that sounds more like the work of a fallen angel, the Old Boy in red socks. But the Reverend Vines didn't seem out to make a theological case, however poor, but just to insult and inflame.

What other purpose could there be for such comments? To educate? To convert? To persuade? To reason? Surely not to love. No, a simple insult it was. Nothing more. And therefore, unworthy of a man of the cloth. Or any man.

We've read belittling remarks like this before, words meant only to humiliate or to stir up hatred against whole peoples, whole religions, whole races. Oftentimes, we've seen them in the Arab media. You know, the benevolent Saddam Hussein keeps the Great Satan at bay…Israelis plotted the 9-11 attacks to frame the Arabs…Another young boy goes to Paradise after blowing himself up near Tel Aviv.…

Americans have just shrugged, been outraged, or even laughed off such drivel. But we wonder what the reaction will be when the Reverend Vines' comments make it to Jordan, to Syria or to Saudi Arabia, where there is already so much hate, if of an opposite-but-equal brand. We doubt many will yawn at this insult. More likely it'll be one more excuse to take to the streets, shouting slogans, hating Americans.

This much is certain: It's a tactical error to insult a fifth of the world's population. That's why the commander-in-chief has been at pains to emphasize that this is a war against terror, against evil-doers, not a matter of Us versus Them. The prospect of a U.S. vs. Entire Islamic World fight is exactly what the September 11th terrorists were hoping for. Those who would turn this conflict into a religious war, a crusade, a jihad, are doing just what the enemy wants.

American leaders were smart enough, after a verbal slip or two, to find a synonym for Crusade to describe this war on terror. Why would freelancers like the Reverend Vines want to sabotage all that diplomacy? We can't think of any reason except the brief, putrid satisfaction of hate.

Think of the reaction of our Muslim allies in the Middle East and Asia to the Rev's comments. In Turkey, for example. Or in Egypt or Pakistan, whose governments have pledged to help in the war against terror, at least formally. Why add to their already beleaguered leaders' problems by insulting Islam?

It won't be any easier to prosecute this war, and the war ahead with Iraq, without allies nearby. And bases. More rhetoric like this from the good Reverend, *et al.*, will only increase the pressure to shut down those American bases, or maybe to bomb a few more American embassies.

As if the Reverend Vines' invective weren't bad enough, what's also sure to be reported in the Arab press is that the current president of the Southern Baptist Convention didn't condemn the Rev's strange views. And by their silence, all those at the Baptist convention seemed to give consent. What were those delegates thinking, or were they?

We haven't even mentioned our fellow Americans who share the Islamic faith—our neighbors, our colleagues, fellow Americans. Many of them stand on guard this very hour, rifle in hand, or at their battle stations. We remember them among the nurses and interns treating the injured on September 11th. And if our fellow Americans are insulted, we are all offended. Or should be.

But beyond all that, certainly beyond the tactical error of slighting our allies, and even beyond the moral offense of insulting our countrymen, a more important question arises:

Where was the brotherly love at the Southern Baptist Convention?

WWJD?

If we remember our Bible School lessons, and we do, didn't this Jesus of Nazareth preach love and peace, even and especially toward those despised by the world? Whatever name your God goes by, it has been said that God is Love.

Hispanics? Sí. Because the enterprising come here

OCTOBER 18, 2002

The spinners tried to make good news from our poll. We didn't see it in the same rose-colored way.

A survey the *Democrat-Gazette* paid for and published this week showed that 46.8 percent of Arkansas residents think the Hispanic influx in the state has been a good thing.

That's mighty white of us.

Hispanic leaders praised the numbers. Said they're making progress, etc., etc.

But we're more worried about the 35.6 percent who said Hispanics are a problem, and we're worried about those who didn't know or wouldn't answer. When those who say Arkansas newcomers are doing the state good don't get even 50 percent in a poll, we have to worry.

What's the problem? Is it that them Hispanics are taking away jobs from good old Arkies who've been here forever? Or at least since the Indians were pushed out?

No, that can't be it. These immigrant workers have been flowing toward the increase in jobs and some of those jobs are not the kind others want.

Maybe Hispanics are putting too much pressure on schools and other public services....

But who would complain about that if the immigrants were from, say, Mississippi, Louisiana, or Germany? Is a booming economy—one that attracts workers, and their wives and children—a bad thing? We can't imagine many would prefer the alternative.

Those of us who have been here a while—as the song says, "Red and Yellow, Black and White"—might pause and consider the defining characteristic of any American immigrant: They're *immigrated*. They've freely chosen to be here. Because their hopes and dreams and ambitions match ours. That's why they left their land and came to America. In a way, they were American even before they left—in their minds, hearts and hopes.

The lazy, unimaginative, self-satisfied aren't about to leave the comforts, or even non-comforts, of home.

Englishmen didn't brave the dangerous sea to move here because they were lackadaisical. Italians didn't leave their families to move here because they were dullards with no dreams. Chinese and Japanese folk didn't uproot their families and move to a strange land with strange customs because they were unindustrious.

And dreamers who move here from Mexico or Honduras don't strike out on their own because they are unambitious or don't want to work. On the contrary, they're looking for work. They may not know the phrase "American Dream," but they've dreamed it. Just like so many of our pioneering forefathers.

These new Americans have a better life here, working on farms and washing cars. They hope, too, that their children will get a better education in America, and they want their children's future to be bright. So the Hispanic immigrant will gut chickens for slaughter at midnight because he can make more money here than he can across the Rio Grande. And, yes, he'll wash dishes and mop restaurant floors and do all kinds of jobs others will not.

These migrants aren't the only folks moving around, either. These days, your daughter may live on the west coast, and your son on the east coast—of Australia. Travel is easier these days, and uprooting and replanting is a way of life, all over the globe.

But still, like always, *it is the ambitious who do it.*

Those who are content—no matter how poor their circumstances—stay on the same hill they were raised on. Whether that hill is in France, Mexico, or Drew County.

Many immigrants, thankfully, have chosen to call Arkansas home. We had one of the fastest-growing Hispanic populations in the nation during the 1990s, with a 337 percent increase. That's a more than three-fold increase in a group known for its appetite for work, religious fealty, and its dream of a better life.

We should be proud.

We're definitely better off.

Collared: One strike and that's it

JUNE 13, 2002

*Because of the great harm done by some priests…
the church herself is viewed with distrust, and
many are offended at the way in which the
church's leaders are perceived to have acted in
this matter. The abuse which has caused this crisis
is by every standard wrong and rightly considered
a crime by society; it is also an appalling sin in the
eyes of God.—Pope John Paul II*

Some 300 Catholic bishops are meeting this week in
Dallas to discuss the recent—well, the recently publi-
cized—allegations of sexual abuse of children by priests.
What some of us can't understand is why there is any
need for so solemn and extended a debate among the
revered bishops about what to do. Looks like an open-
and-shut case to us:

Pedophiles should be in prison, not in the pulpit. Any
questions?

Abusive priests—like abusive parents or abusive
teachers—are nothing new. But the sheer number of
complaints that have been newspaperized in the last 12
months has given the American public a collective
pause about the priesthood.

Boston. Baltimore. St. Paul. New Orleans. This week,
another bishop resigned in Kentucky amid a cloud of
similar accusations. One story after another after another
after another. The dirty tide grew so powerful that even
the Pope had to call a meeting about it in April. To a lay-
man innocent of gnostic interpretations and Clinton
clauses, what he said there didn't seem to leave any
room for debate.

The American bishops seemed to see it that way, too:
Priests (in name) who molest children should be kicked
out of the church when they're outed. But the men of
God are less clear on what should happen to those who
committed such crimes in the past.

If a priest, they ask, committed this crime 10 years

ago, should that propel him from the ministry?

Our considered theological conclusion in response to that question is: Hell, yes.

Priests should be held to the highest standard because they're like teachers and police officers—no, we take that back. Priests are more like parents. Priests are supposed to be protectors, instructors, guides—*fathers*. They're supposed to be people whom children can trust, utterly. They have God on their side. They carry all the symbols of authority that the young and impressionable are taught to respect and follow.

Is a one-strike policy—no matter when that strike occurred—a harsh punishment? Of course it is. And should be. Priests should be held to a higher standard than other miscreants because they have a higher calling. Priests vow before God that they will be spiritual guides, that they will be examples for others (especially the children of the church), and do the right thing even when no one is looking. No one mortal, that is.

Priests are human, certainly, but a different kind of human: They are to be men who walk this earth concerned not with making themselves rich, not with obtaining political power, not with conducting war, building businesses, erecting bridges or making scientific breakthroughs. They are called to an even higher purpose: to save souls.

Not scar them.

The implication to be found in certain Vatican newspapers—that American culture is to blame for this predicament—is unworthy of the church. Is there more nudity on American TV than in, say, Europe? Is there more prostitution in American big cities than in, say, Hong Kong? Is there more drug use in Miami than in, say, Bogota? You might as well blame the American press for devoting so much space to this story, though no more than some of the Vatican journals do.

Here's one proposal being kicked around: Priests caught abusing children after the new policy is in place would be defrocked. So far, so good. It just doesn't go far enough. By this wobbly standard, a priest who molested a child in the past could remain in the priesthood if he (a) underwent psychological treatment, (b) had been declared no longer a pedophile by the grace of science, and

(c) had the backing of a church committee which interviewed, among others, the victim.

This won't do. Psychological standards have proven all too elastic. (Ask the parent of a child who's been abused—or worse—by a pedophile out on parole.) Besides, most psychologists will tell you that pedophiles don't change easily, if at all.

Yet the church now seems prepared to embrace yesterday's psychology rather than adhere to its own ever relevant doctrine and discipline. Just as earlier, by paying hush money and weighing the legal odds, the church aped the worst of the corporate culture rather than the best of its own. Rather than revere and uphold its own mysteries, the church went to lawyers for the latest secular cures for what ailed it; now it's turning to shrinks. It is time for the church to return to that old-time religion, to be renewed, and to renew others by its example. Instead, the bishops will hold a solemn convocation in Dallas to debate pros and cons. Why not just keep the faith?

The bishops seem to be debating about what is best for its priests, or for the church's image. But someone else is involved here. Jesus loves the little children, goes the simple old song, all the children of the world. What about them?

The bishops would be wise to announce a one-strike policy, and not waver from it. These men of the church should also vote to report each allegation to secular authorities for review. If they have any doubts about that, they might note what a priest named John Paul has just said: Child abuse is rightly considered a crime by society. And society is about to make reporting these abuses a law, anyway. The church should be taking the lead—not trailing behind bearing a briefcase full of up-to-date reservations and escape clauses. Not when victims must live with the shame and horror of their abuse for the rest of their lives, instead of fond memories of visits to the zoo or favorite Christmases.

Besides the young victims, there are others who have suffered harm: the Catholic laity and the vast majority of priests who are good stewards. They all have been unjustly tarred by this sweeping brush. The bishops can lift this shame from all by taking an uncompromising stand against this crime—this sin.

Although the word of the Pope carries no small weight among Christians, Catholic or otherwise, at Dallas the bishops would do well to note the words of someone of even higher rank:

Then little children were brought to Jesus for him to place his hands on them and pray for them. But the disciples rebuked those who brought them. Jesus said, "Let the little children come to me, and do not hinder them, for the kingdom of heaven belongs to such as these."

Libertarians are coming!
Hide the women and liquor!

OCTOBER 21, 2002

Oh, the humanity.

We're told that there are actual *Libertarians* behind this proposal to remove sales taxes from food and medicine. What's next? Aliens from Neptune making an endorsement, too?

APPLES, which stands for something or another besides regressive taxes, is the group behind the effort to keep the tax on the books in Arkansas. Its argument: Government needs the money.

And, apparently, this as well: *Libertarians are on the other side*. (Look! I saw one peeking from behind a pine tree!)

We'll admit that the Libertarian Party isn't exactly mainstream. Some ideas Libertarians float are indeed strange, not to mention unworkable. But then again, those ideas have a snowball's chance in South Mississippi to ever make it into law, anyway.

Libertarians can be something to see, and hear—when you can find one. There aren't many lurking about these days. But America needs 'em, few as they are, bless their anti-government hearts. They pull starboard even when Republicans are moving port. If the Greens and the Communists and the militant environmentalists are lobbying bombs at the two major political parties from the extreme left, Libertarians are on the opposite side of the fight—lobbying bombs from the extreme right.

Most of the time.

You see, right and left mean little to Libertarians. The glue that binds them together is a belief that government is best that governs the very, very least. They can make Republicans look like socialists. And sometimes they can make Democrats look like arch conservatives.

Their position on the issues? Sometimes on target, sometimes foolhardy—like every political party.

On legalizing drugs: America can handle it. Big government should have little to say in this matter.

On education: Let the market and local communities

run education. Big government should have little to say in this matter.

On gun ownership: Guns protect us from tyranny. Big government should have little to say in this matter.

On foreign policy: The United States should bind together to defend these shores. As for stationing American troops all over the world and playing cop, this big government should have little to say in this matter.

You may like some of their stands, adamantly disagree with others. But you have to hand it to the Libertarians, they are consistent: *Big government should have little to say.*

When Democrats are anti-choice on education but pro-choice on abortion, and Republicans are pro-government interference on protecting the flag, but anti-government interference when it comes to gun registration, you get a little hungry for consistency.

Other fringe groups want government to get involved in more parts of our lives. So it's refreshing to hear about Personal Responsibility and Limited Government from at least one quarter. You can rely on the Libertarians to scream *hands-off!*

Yeah, the Libertarians are off in right field on some issues, left field on others. Legalizing drugs? Stationing American troops on our own shorelines waiting for the inevitable? Come on. Sometimes a little government is useful, like when the country's been attacked. And may soon be attacked again.

But malcontents have always been a part of American politics.

And every once in a great while the Libertarians—like anybody in the professional antagonist class—are right.

For example, like now. Now, when a bunch of them want to ax the food tax, and take this burden from the least among us.

It's the right thing to do. Libertarians happen to be standing on the humane, and workable, side of this issue.

Just because you might not agree with the Libertarians on some of their notions is no reason to take it out on the working poor. On the food tax, the Libertarians—like it or not—are right.

Ax the food tax.

UnSATisfied: Essays reveal more, trust us

JULY 3, 2002

To the horror of high school students everywhere, there comes word from the SAT industry that essays will become a part of that national college entrance exam and ordeal.

Let us explain this for our high school readers: Essays are written sentences, linked together in paragraphs, that reflect a thought or tell a story—and, by the way, grammar counts. When taking an essay exam, there are no little bubbles to blacken, there are no multiple choice questions, there are no true/false guesses. You have to (we can feel you shudder) *explain* an idea using the English language. Like, write or something.

No matter how many young subscribers we may lose saying this, we tend to look with favor on the change in the college entrance exams, sterile and unavailing things as they may currently be. Writing reveals understanding, or the lack thereof, in a way no multiple choice exam can.

Logic. Transition. Confidence. Imagination. Humor. All these things are difficult to measure when answers are T/F or (a), (b), (c), or (d). (Ever notice it's almost never (e)?) Any pocket calculator can add and subtract, but it can't *think*, no matter what fans of AI (artificial intelligence) believe. Essays are the best way to measure what separates us from the computers.

After educators in California noted their interest in putting essay questions on the SATs, the SAT's rival—the ACT—began looking into it. It's a done deal for the SAT, starting in 2005. Will the ACT follow?

There are hurdles ahead. Because computers cannot yet grade essays (yippee!), officials are wondering what the cost will be of lining up another kind of judge—they're called humans—to grade the essay questions. But can they be fair to students who express a view different from their own? How many graders would read each essay? How subjective might the process become? How long would the essays be? What happens when the grader, like some teachers, turns out to be less literate than the student? And can the manufacturers of the tests survive the piercing pother from unhappy high schoolers everywhere? Problems await, which means the lawsuits will proliferate.

Where find Americans still capable of judging the written word? They've grown steadily rarer over the years. The telephone replaced the posted letter long ago, and with the letter went writing, at least for most Americans. And writing hasn't made a comeback, no matter the instant message you just answered. E-mail may be closing in on the phone as the first choice of communication among the young crowd, but it's telegraphic, halfway telepathic. E-mailing hardly qualifies as prose. That's not writing, as Truman Capote said of Jack Kerouac's stuff, it's typing. And soon even the primitive lingo of e-mails may be displaced by voice messaging.

The telephone reduced the spoken word to "uhs" and "whatevers," replacing "I said" with "I go," and e-mail completed the process by replacing language with a kind of pidgin shorthand. (Who cares how u spell stuff on e-mail? Speed iz whut counts.) Telephones made communication lazy; e-mail has made it atrocious.

Yes, more essays! For posterity's sake, more essays! Educators can counter the evil of smiley faces created with colons and parentheses by assigning good, old-fashioned, eraser-smudged, thought-provoking compositions. Where will the judges come from? Draft retired English teachers, the kind who never showed the slightest interest in administration, the sort whose title included the honorific Old, as in Old Mrs. Smithers. Her vanishing breed is needed more than ever.

Yes to capitalization. Yes to punctuation. Aye to alliteration. Poe would never write: "bird at doorway. only says nevermore. LOL." Today's younger generation may not appreciate writing because it's never had to undertake it—like the couch potato who pooh-poohs the golf he sees on television, never having had to take back a seven iron with water on the left. Shakespeare? Wasn't he one of the Ninja Turtles? Samuel Clemens? Didn't he pitch for the Yankees in '78? Emily Dickinson? Isn't she one of the night vee-jays on MTV?

Just think of the classroom fallout once essay questions start popping up on the SATs. If teachers really do teach the test, and they have reason to, they'll soon be handing out loose leaf paper and No. 2 pencils like Ritalin pills and condoms. Teachers will find themselves being forced to do what many of them went into the business to do: Teach. Enlighten. Broaden horizons. Push students with the absorption and dedication we may now see only in certain high school coaches. And the results may extend far beyond the SATs. To write well is to think well, and feel more deeply. This could be the start of something great.

"If there's a writing test that helps kids get into college, then schools are going to spend more time writing, which can't be a bad thing," says Professor Eva Baker of UCLA. "The change could be profound if it had the impact that we hope it would have on the high school." We are encouraged by her prediction, mainly because it doesn't use impact as a verb.

We give the idea a B-plus. Not an A-plus because we can just see the job of grading these papers handed over to the kind of educantists who write those unintelligible Ed.D. theses. They all sound like Alan Greenspan on a foggy day. But if we could just find educated people to grade these essays—not the kind of "educators" who just censored the great writers on New York's Regents Exam—well, writing could be back in business.

:)

A conversation with
David Barham

BILL MITCHELL: The ASNE judges point out that you managed to break the usual rules of editorial writing in winning this award. They accuse you of writing long, using big quotes, even enjoying what you're doing. I'm afraid you're going to have to explain yourself.

DAVID BARHAM: People ask if I write editorials, and I say that I start some of them. Editorials are the newspaper's opinion, not a personal column. Assistant editorial page editor Kane Webb gets first look at anything I write. He adds, subtracts, suggests, etc. Then Paul Greenberg, our editorial page editor and the big dog on the porch, does the same thing, only more so. The finished product is very much a combination of writers and editors. Paul and Kane allow me to take chances, to write long, as they say, and to enjoy what I'm doing. That's the secret to writing editorials. You read editorials from around the nation, and it seems to me that most editorial writers hate what they're doing because it's just very boring stuff.

What's the key to enjoying what you're doing?

Well, I don't have an editorial board to deal with.

You don't?

No. I've worked in two different situations. I've worked for an editorial board that could have eight to 10 members on it, and I don't have one now. It allows a lot more freedom the way I'm doing it now. Paul hires conservative writers to write conservative editorials, so I do. I send it up the chain and, if he likes it or the publisher likes it, it goes in the paper. If they don't, they say, "No, it's not going into the paper. Try again." That is a beautiful way of doing it, because I have worked for editorial boards before, and they kill good ideas; they kill a lot of good writing. Paul likes to say there aren't but two works ever written by a committee that are worth a dime—the U.S. Constitution and the Bible. And both were inspired by God. I don't get the impression God will inspire an editorial board to write about the newest transportation project in Arkansas.

The discussion kills good writing, good ideas?

Well, not necessarily a discussion itself, because we have some very good discussions among ourselves. But, for example, you have an editorial board where the publisher is a Pat Buchanan fan, dyed-in-the-wool Republican, and you have a managing editor who, like P.J. O'Rourke said, is a dyed-in-the-hair-shirt Democrat, and an executive editor who probably agrees with the publisher on everything he's ever said, and a newsroom representative who's way to the left. So the board lurches left and right, left and right.

I used to work for Gannett, and since Gannett cares more about diversity than good writing, I had to go out into the community and get three so-called community representatives to serve on the editorial board, and these people changed every three months. Now imagine getting a white guy from the banking industry who lives on the north side of town, a black female from the south side who's a public defender, and try to put them in the same room with the other members of your editorial board and try to come to an aggressive, strong position on anything. We even had to go out and get a college student to serve on the editorial board so we could say we were getting youth into our newspaper. Well, this college kid doesn't know a political party from a rave party, and you try to get all 10 of these people in the same room and try to have them agree on anything, and it just comes out all watered down.

You have a group of editorial writers. You just don't have an editorial board.

Right.

How many editorial writers are there on the *Democrat-Gazette*?

Four: Paul Greenberg, Kane Webb, George Arnold, and me. I'm very much the low man on the totem pole. I just started in June of 2002.

Who else appears on your page?

We have several different columnists who write on our editorial page every day and those are as diverse as you can get. We have folks like George Will on one side to Maureen Dowd on the other side. But when it comes to the editorial section of the editorial page, that's when you need to say something and quit all this "on the one hand this, on the other hand that" nonsense that appears in so many editorials in the nation today.

What kind of reaction do you get from readers?

I love getting calls from little old ladies who say, "That was just a very biased editorial in today's paper." I think to myself, "Well, thank you." The problem with editorial writing in the United States today is that there's too much *unbiased* editorial writing. Diversity of opinion among the editorial writers and decision-makers is killer. Sure, have your liberal columnists and your conservative ones. But when you write an editorial, the opinion of the paper, don't water it down by putting a liberal and a conservative in a room and try to make them agree on something. That's how too many editorials are written in this country. And that's why so many editorials are wishy-washy and bland. We want our opinion to mean something.

If my math is right, you became an editorial page editor in Monroe, La., before you were 30 years old. What brought you to the world of opinion at such an early age?

Actually, it was just a situation where I had an opportunity. The editorial writer for the paper I was working for switched jobs, and they asked me if I would like to try my hand at it, and I said sure. I had covered politics in Louisiana for so long that I loved the sport of it. So I began writing editorials that just came naturally to me.

Do you recall your first exposure to the idea of an opinion as opposed to a fact? I'm not sure how far back we should go, but I'm wondering if great editorial writers are born or whether they're developed. What's it been like for you?

It's been a developing process, I think. Of course, when I first started—I go back now and look at some of the stuff that I wrote just five or six years ago when I first started writing editorials, and I think, "Oh, God, how terrible." So sometimes, even today, when I write an editorial I think, "Oh, God, how terrible." It's not always great stuff. But at this newspaper we try to make it great stuff all the time. My boss brought me into his office one day and handed me an editorial I'd written. He looked me in the eye and said—and this is Paul Greenberg—he said, "This is good enough for *The New York Times*, and it's good enough for *Newsday*. It's just not good enough for us." I love that attitude.

What did Paul mean that it was good enough for them and not for you, for your paper?

I think that you could take the *Democrat-Gazette*'s editorial page on any day of the week, just pick it out at random. You may not agree with it, but you'll be interested. You'll read it to the very end, even if it's long. But now go to any of the bigger newspapers in the United States and pick the best editorial of the week and compare it to the random ones you picked from our paper. Ours are just so much better. Our standards are so much higher.

The standards are higher in what regard?

It must be interesting. It must hold the reader's attention. It must take it to a second level. Paul's always talking about "taking this to a second level." We have a personality. There are so few editorial pages that have a personality. You could take the editorial that was written in today's *Washington Post* and switch it with the one in *The New York Times* and switch that one with *USA TODAY*, and I don't think anybody would know the difference.

Let's talk about the nature of opinions for a minute. Who or what has helped shape yours?

I'm a big fan of P.J. O'Rourke, and I have been for many years. I love that style of writing. I like to read books. The first books I really began reading that had anything to do with newspapers were Lewis Grizzard's books. Lewis Grizzard was a great writer and he was an opinion writer and a feature writer. His stuff was so funny that I knew after I started reading him that that's what I wanted to do.

Have you ended up with opinions that for the most part are similar to those of your parents and other family members?

No, probably just exactly opposite.

No kidding!

Yeah, my parents are baby boomers and I am definitely not. When they were growing up, their idea of a Democratic president was Kennedy and a Republican president was Nixon. My Democratic president was Jimmy Carter, and Ronald Reagan was my Republican president. We grew up totally different and have totally different opinions when it comes to politics, most of the time.

The heart and soul of much of your work appears to be more about observation than recommendation. Is that fair?

I guess it's fair.

Tell me how it's turned out that way for you.

I guess working in Louisiana has had a lot to do with that. When you work down there, it's not enough just to tell a story. You have to give really interesting tidbits. That's why Edwin Edwards was so popular down there, because he could say things that made people smile. You know, you go to a Mardi Gras and you watch a rainstorm pass over the crowd and you notice how everybody covers their…drinks, and you add that to a story and it helps.

The judges used the word "pungent" to describe your editorials.

Oh, great! They couldn't have used "piquant"?

Tell me how you make an editorial "pungent."

I guess you add some spices to it and you stir it up and make a good roux. A newspaper is like a good meal. You have your steak and potatoes on the front page, you have your vegetables on the local pages where you're getting everything you need, your sports would be dessert, and "Dilbert" would be like a red wine that makes you giggle a little bit. And the editorial page in most newspapers is the glazed beets of the meal. If you were at a buffet, you would not have put these on your plate. Somebody went to all the trouble—you don't want to be rude, they may make you regular, and you know they're good for you—but they're just awful. They're just very boring, and our newspaper doesn't want editorials to be the glazed beets of the meal.

Tell me how your style has developed. It's quite distinctive and very conversational. Is it different from the other three people writing editorials on the page?

No, we all try to write that way. Paul demands the conversational style, and he edits to make sure that everybody understands that. He doesn't like noun phrases with four or five nouns in a row. The city prosecutor, the Nevada County city prosecutor, etc., etc. He likes "the prosecutor from Nevada County who dah, dah, dah." Very conversational. We use the word "ain't," we use sentence fragments, anything that helps make it clip along like you're talking to someone.

How about walking us through one of your winning editorials? I was thinking of the editorial on the decision to include essay questions in the SAT. That's a delightful essay about the denigration of language in American life. Do you look for pegs like that to get stuff off your chest or did this one really start out as an editorial about college testing?

No, it really started out as an editorial on college testing. I very rarely look for reasons to get things off my chest. I come in in the morning, open the newspaper or read newspapers on the Web and find something that jumps out at me, and I grab it and use it as a news peg.

Tell me the process. Did it come up in a meeting of the editorial writers?

No, it was in our paper one day that the SAT was thinking about going to an essay format in places, and I thought, "This is great." This is what our children need because it makes you a deeper thinker to write essays than it does to blacken some box and take a guess at some question. You get a so much better grasp of what a person knows or doesn't know if you have that person write about it.

Tell me about the writing itself. How much time did you spend thinking about this thing, researching it, reporting it, writing it, and then revising it?

Well, it probably didn't take more than an hour or so. I read the story and immediately knew what I wanted to say. So I started typing and typing, typing and typing until I got everything off my chest into the computer, and then I went back and organized it and rearranged it, and then I shipped it over to my officemate, Kane Webb. He looked it over, made a few suggestions, took something out here, nip and tuck there, and then we sent it up the chain to Paul. He edits pretty heavily.

Does he?

Yes. Which is great. It makes for better editorials. And we go back and forth, back and forth, and we add this and take away that and we really try to work together.

Do you recall his edits on this one?

Yeah, a couple of them. The thing about his edits is that you never feel slighted. He always kind of makes you smile. When you read it you think, "God, I wish I had thought about that." Let's see. "Retired English teachers, the kind who never showed the slightest interest in administration, the sort whose title included the honorific Old, as in Old Mrs. Smithers." That was good. I enjoyed that sort of thing. He also made the point that e-mailing hardly qualifies as prose. He inserted that it's "not writing, as Truman Capote said of Jack Kerouac's stuff, it's typing." Little stuff like that, little sentences that just make the whole editorial better.

What was the transition like for you from news to editorial?

Well, there wasn't much of a transition. I was called in to see if I could do it due to the situation where the job was empty, so I jumped in and I could.

What newsroom habits have you found useful on the editorial page?

A lot of editorial writers don't like to use reporting skills, but I do.

How so?

You do your own reporting sometimes. You don't want to take a story, look at it, and say, "Representative So-and-so said this on the House floor yesterday, so we're going to take an arrow and shoot it through his backside." You may want to pick up the phone and call Representative So-and-so and say, "Did you really say this? Is this a fair thing that was taken out of context? Were you talking about something else, or was our reporter just simply wrong?" And if he says no, well then it's time to take your quiver and your arrows out. But every once in a while, and let me say that has not happened here since I've been at the *Democrat-Gazette*, but in my previous job, several times I'd pick up the phone and say, "Is this true?" and they'd say, "No, it wasn't true." Of course I was working with reporters who were very much right out of college in my last job, at a much smaller paper, and I found myself several times saving our editorial page from having to print corrections by picking up the phone and making a phone call.

Tell me what you're trying to accomplish as an editorial writer and how it differs from what you were trying to do as a reporter.

We want people to pick up the *Democrat-Gazette* and turn to the editorial page to see what we're saying next. Whether it be about our congressman visiting Cuba, whether it be about our mayor who's not taking a stand on much of anything at city hall. We want people—whether they agree with us or not—to smile, to shake their heads, pound their fists on the kitchen table, whatever, but we want them to turn to us first.

Where do your editorials usually get their start?

The newspaper or on the Web sometimes. If I can't find something to write about in the newspaper, I'll get on the Web and go to Fox News or CNN or *The New York Times, The Washington Post*. Just look at the stories from around the nation until I find something.

How has the Web changed the nature of your job?

I don't know because I started in 1997 when the Web was just beginning. You'd have to ask somebody who has 20 years of experience doing this and I've got barely five, nearly six. So the Web's always been around for me. I don't see how people wrote editorials without it. I don't see how they did research without it. Just the other day I looked up Internet sales taxes and how much the states were losing to Internet sales, as far as sales taxes went. That was at my fingertips. I didn't have to call each state's sales tax person. It's right there at your fingertips and it's amazing. I don't see how people lived without the Internet. Of course, I don't see how people used typewriters, either.

Most traditional editorials seek to provoke action, whether it's voting for a particular candidate or defeating a particular tax hike. Your editorial on the food tax ends with a very specific recommendation. But there's a pretty unusual editorial sandwiched between your lead, "Oh, the humanity," and your

kicker, "Ax the food tax." Can you talk about why you wrote it the way you did? How did it come to be an editorial largely about Libertarians?

Well, the Libertarian Party here in Arkansas came out against the food tax, and the argument of the people who are trying to keep the food tax on the books was: "Look, the Libertarians are for this! How could you possibly be for something the Libertarians are for?" And that made me laugh. It was sort of funny that this was their best argument so far. So after I wrote the headline, "Libertarians Are Coming! Hide the Women and Liquor!," it just took off from there. It was just funny. It wrote itself. At the end of it, I was disappointed that I didn't have anything else to say.

Are you writing to a particular length?

No. We write to no set length here. When the editorial stops, that's when you stop. If an editorial goes over 40 inches, well, you may have to cut back some in order to get it to fit the maximum space that we have on the page. But if it comes up a half-inch too short, you don't write to fill it in. We'll put in a one-sentence editorial on the bottom of it. We never write to space.

In the fourth paragraph of your editorial about Hispanics, you wrote, "Hispanic leaders praised the numbers. Said they're making progress, etc., etc." So how do sentence fragments like these square with your call for a return to respect for the English language the way we were taught in school in your SAT editorial?

I think there's a difference between those two subjects. It's like the old saying: English and journalism aren't the same things. And the SAT story was more like, "Let's get an essay on the test so we can find out how smart or how dumb these kids are who are taking the test. Let's get to the true meaning of it. Let's get down to brass tacks, if you will, to find out more about the kid and not necessarily about not using the word 'ain't' and grammatical style." I bet if you go back and look in the

SAT editorial, you'll see sentence fragments, too.

I thought the Hispanic editorial was especially interesting in terms of the notion of the enterprising people who immigrate to this country. How did that emerge in your thinking about immigration?

I've been thinking a long time about it. It doesn't matter if you're from rural Arkansas or if you're from Mexico City or if you're from Beijing. If you're unenterprising and you have no desire to do better, you stay where you are. The scariest thing in the world to me would be to go to a foreign land where I can't speak the language and have no job, have no opportunities, few opportunities anyway, to start washing dishes and trying to learn the language. Who would do something like that? Well, somebody who's braver than I am, and those are the types of people you want living in your community.

Is it fair to say that this would surprise, if not confound, some conservative critics of immigration?

Certainly.

Tell me how you think about surprising or jolting reader expectations. Do you set out to try to show people a new way of looking at things?

We always try to set out for that second level. We never want to take the Republican Party's stand on anything just because we're Republicans, and we don't. We often disagree with our conservative brothers and sisters in the Republican Party. We don't want anybody to pick up our newspaper and think we're a knee-jerk reaction newspaper like so many on the other side are. Our page is devoted to deeper thinking than that. We like to say so anyway.

Let's look at the other editorials among your winners. How about the "Brotherly Hate" editorial? Tell me about that one.

I picked up the paper and here was this guy screaming bloody murder about Islam, and I'm thinking it's not a very good tactic to insult so many in the world. And the second level that we were talking about here is, "What would Jesus do? Is this how Christians are supposed to act?"

Let me be sure I'm understanding the second level here.

Whenever you finish an editorial, you sit back and you think about it some more. You can almost always take it to a different level, always crank it up a notch.

Personality really seems to be at the heart of what you're trying to accomplish. Does the personality sometimes come in at that stage or does that need to be there from the start?

When you start writing, you start writing to get your idea across. And then you go through in the editing and rewriting process and try to add the personality to it.

As I listen to you describe the process of sitting down and writing, writing, writing, as you put it, I had a sense that the personality was flying onto the page at that point.

No. For example, the "Brotherly Hate" editorial. We wrote it and we wrote it and we wrote it, and almost on the very last edit, after the quote from the good reverend, we put "Sweet Jesus." Little things like that add personality, add to the tone of the editorial, add to the conversational style, and sometimes they're done very lightly.

It's a pretty interesting close for a piece that's on an editorial page you describe as certainly conservative. "Where was the brotherly love at the Southern Baptist Convention? WWJD?" Did you get any reaction from the Baptist community?

Nope. Not a word. Which is strange. I guess it's because they either agreed with it or were ashamed by it. I don't know, because they aren't the type of folk who are afraid to say what they feel.

How do you gauge whether you're having an impact in terms of persuading people of your point of view? Does the page get much feedback in the way of calls or letters?

We get letters all the time telling us that we're full of it. And we come out at election time for different things that are on the ballot, and you can tell if you're making an impact that way. Of course, I haven't had much impact yet. I've only been here a few months.

What part of your job are you trying to get better at these days?

Thinking deeper and trying not to start writing on first blush. I read a story in the paper and I think, "How dare they?" and I start writing and writing, and then I don't give it that extra bit of thought that would help me see it from another point of view.

Writers' Workshop

Talking Points

1) The ASNE judges said David Barham breaks the usual rules with his prize-winning editorials: He writes long, he uses big quotes, he seems to have fun writing them. Did you have fun reading them? Why or why not?

2) Barham talks about moving his editorials to a "second level." What do you understand him to mean by that? Can you pinpoint the second level in his winning editorials?

3) The judges described Barham's editorials as "pungent." Do you agree with that assessment? Why or why not?

4) Do you find his editorials persuasive? What are some of the keys to his persuasive technique? How might he make his editorials more persuasive?

Assignment Desk

1) Discussing his editorial on immigration, Barham notes that regular readers of the *Democrat-Gazette*'s editorial page might be surprised by the page's take on this issue. Write an editorial that would surprise readers who think they know you.

2) Try something similar in adding personality to your persuasive writing. In your first draft, just get your ideas and arguments down. Then come back and throw in whatever it takes to add your personality.

3) Paying attention to the techniques you pinpointed above, write a brief editorial that you believe will successfully persuade readers to reconsider their position on a policy or practice in your community.

4) Using the Internet, find editorials in today's *Democrat-Gazette, New York Times,* and *Washington Post.* Barham says he believes people are more likely to read to the end of *Democrat-Gazette* editorials than they are to the end of editorials published in the *Times* or the *Post.* What was your experience?

Mark Mahoney

Finalist, Editorial Writing

Mark Mahoney, 39, is the editorial page editor at *The Post-Star* in Glens Falls, N.Y. He started his print journalism career as the paper's night general assignment reporter 15 years ago. He soon moved into local-government reporting and editing before shifting his focus to editorial writing.

In addition to writing all of the newspaper's local editorials and political endorsements, Mahoney administers the paper's political candidate debates.

He still edits daily news copy, which helps him maintain a strong connection to the readers, the reporters, and the local issues covered by the newspaper. He began writing editorials for *The Post-Star* in 1994 and has since won nine state awards. The ASNE award is his first national honor.

Prior to working at *The Post-Star*, Mahoney was a legislative correspondent for a year at the state capital in Albany, N.Y. He began his career as a radio reporter at WEOK-WPDH in Poughkeepsie, N.Y.

A native of Wappingers Falls, N.Y., Mahoney is a 1985 graduate of Ithaca College in Ithaca, N.Y., where he received a bachelor of science degree in communications management. He lives in Glens Falls and is the father of three daughters—Caitlin, 10, and twins Christa and Chelsea, 7.

His editorial, "Leaf Pickup Should Be Adjusted," uses an issue as mundane as a town's leaf cleanup to demonstrate how city officials can become estranged from the citizenry.

Leaf pickup should be adjusted

OCTOBER 26, 2002

The doctor walks in to see his patient, who's covered from head to toe in bandages, his right arm in a sling, his left leg raised in a strap attached to the ceiling.

"How'd you hurt yourself?" the doctor asks.

"I was raking leaves," the patient groans through the tiny mouth hole in his bandages.

"How on earth did you do this kind of damage to yourself just raking leaves?" the doctor asks in amazement.

"I fell out of the tree," the patient answers.

Don't laugh.

If you live in Queensbury and you expect to have the town pick up your leaves this year, that guy in the hospital bed could be you.

The town of Queensbury—where officials shoot themselves in the foot so often they should be issued bulletproof loafers—has done it again. This time, they've blown a hole in a genuinely beneficial public service by refusing to adjust the town's leaf-pickup schedule to coincide with this year's late autumn. The schedule is the schedule, they say. And if the leaves they were supposed to pick up are still on the trees when they came around, that's your tough luck. They've gone on to other things.

It's not like they weren't warned. State tourism officials said early this month that the fall foliage season was at least a week behind schedule. Heck, all you had to do was look out the window in September and notice how green the leaves were to know that they weren't going to be falling anytime soon.

So you'd think a town like Queensbury could hold off a week or two on the leaf cleanup until there was something to actually pick up. Several other area communities, including Hudson Falls and Lake George, saw the forest through the trees and postponed their pickup weeks. Glens Falls officials have been cruising the city looking for leaves by the side of the road, but haven't found many yet. They said they'll keep cruising. But not Queensbury.

"We're too busy preparing for winter and we can't backtrack," said the deputy highway superintendent, whose boss made leaf and brush pickup a campaign promise. Town Supervisor Dennis Brower defended the decision not to change the schedule, saying, "The Highway Department has got to set up some kind of schedule for these guys, and I think they're being reasonable."

No they're not.

Busy preparing for winter? Doing what, gathering nuts? Does it really take a month to attach a snowplow to a dump truck? Why can't they just plug away at their winter preparations now and then set the work aside for a week or two to pick up brush and leaves?

Smaller communities—with older and fewer pieces of equipment and fewer highway employees to do the work—have found a way to do their winter preparations while waiting for the leaves to fall. But the best-equipped, best-staffed highway department in the region's most populated and lowest-taxed town can't pull it off.

It's ridiculous.

The only thing saving Queensbury officials is that this isn't an election year. If it was, you can bet there'd be a lot more highway workers on the road and a lot fewer residents in the trees.

Lessons Learned

BY MARK MAHONEY

My aunt used to be very heavily involved in partisan politics in the Washington, D.C., area.

I remember one time shortly after I started writing editorials, she asked me to describe my newspaper's editorial philosophy—expecting me to say something like "liberal" or "conservative."

I thought about her question for a second and responded, "We write about whatever ticks us off."

These days, I'm still angry. But I've broadened my approach. If asked the same question again, I'd answer, "We write about what people really care about."

At first, I was slightly amused that of the five editorials I submitted to this prestigious national contest, the one chosen for publication was an editorial on such a completely grassroots issue—literally—yard waste pickup. But the selection made perfect sense. This was an issue in which a newspaper could actually play a role in bettering its readers' lives.

■ **Listen to people and learn their concerns.** What people care about doesn't necessarily happen in Washington or New York or Europe. They care about how they are going to pay their property tax bills, how well their children are being educated, how their community looks and feels, and whether their local politicians are responsive to their needs. Local newspapers, through their opinion pages, can make a tangible difference in people's lives by understanding those concerns, choosing the right topics for editorials, putting the facts into perspective, articulating the issues clearly, and being passionate advocates for change.

■ **Make a connection with readers by choosing the appropriate approach.** To connect with readers, you have to select an approach that will inspire them first to read what you're writing and then to act. If you want to stir people up, you write it angry. If you want to inspire them, you appeal to their sense of duty or community. And if you want to shame a government into changing, you point out the absurdity of its actions. Use any experience or memory or writing style in your arsenal to hook them. In this case, the town's stubborn stance cried out for dripping sarcasm. It was silly, and I was having fun. But I knew everyone would get the joke, and it fit perfectly with the point I was trying to get across.

■ **Make your case with strong, fact-based arguments.** As great as your lead might be, you can't have an editorial if you've got no compelling argument to support it. In this case, I called up notices from the state tourism department predicting a late foliage season. I checked with other municipalities to find out whether they were canceling their fall pickups to prepare for winter. I asked around to find out how long it really takes to convert equipment for winter use. I also reminded readers that the town has a history of this kind of behavior, establishing this measure as the latest in a pattern of anti-citizen maneuvers. For good measure, I reminded readers that taxpayers had ensured that the town was neither underfunded nor understaffed.

■ **Address the other side.** If you pretend the other side doesn't exist, it takes away from the credibility of the editorial. I made sure to quote town officials justifying their decision, then pointed out how that thinking was flawed.

■ **Recommend action.** I hate what I call "*Seinfeld* editorials"—editorials about nothing. They just present the facts and state that people should be "concerned" or "vigilant." They don't make any arguments, don't take any position, don't advance the discussion, and don't demand action. This editorial shamed the town into action by pointing out the absurdity of its position.

A week later, the town changed its mind and rescheduled the leaf pickup.

■ **Have fun.** I wrote this editorial several months ago. But I still get a chuckle remembering how much of a kick I got, first out of writing it, then later out of actually seeing the town scramble to change its position.

I believe newspapers still have the power to make a difference in their communities. Editorials should always strive to make people think, make people act, and make things better.

Amy Ellis Nutt
Non-Deadline Writing

Amy Ellis Nutt is a feature writer for *The Star-Ledger* in Newark, N.J. She became a journalist in 1988 after a brief career teaching ethics and the history of ancient and modern philosophy at the University of Massachusetts and Tufts University. Starting out as a fact-checker at *Sports Illustrated*, she worked her way up to writer-reporter and won two national writing awards from the Women's Sports Foundation and the Golf Writers Association of America. She co-authored *A Good Swing Is Hard to Find* with professional golfer Helen Alfredsson.

At *The Star-Ledger,* her stories have ranged from AIDS orphans, teenage gambling, and ex-mobsters to the history of the Post-it Note. In 1991, she won a first-place writing award from the National Mental Health Association for an article about electroshock therapy and in 2001 received a first-place prize from the Newswomen's Club of New York for a series of essays. Nutt is a graduate of Smith College and received a master's degree in philosophy from the Massachusetts Institute of Technology and a master's in journalism from Columbia University.

Nutt says "The Seekers" series, which explored five of the biggest unanswered questions of science, enabled her to combine her "love of philosophical questioning, descriptive writing, and all things science." To this daunting task, she brought the philosopher's willingness to tackle enduring mysteries, the reporter's zeal for puzzle-solving, and a poet's sensibilities to stir the imagination about even the most esoteric subject. She grounds each installment at the bottom of the abstraction ladder by pitting individual scientists and thinkers, each seeker vividly rendered, against the thorniest issues of human existence—from where the universe began to where it will end. With eye-opening analogies, vivid metaphors, and an authoritative tone built on six months of research and interviews, story planning, and dogged efforts to convey the complex with accessible prose, Nutt has produced a classic of explanatory journalism. "The Seekers" enables a lay readership to share the excitement and wonder of such challenging fields as neuroscience, physics, and astronomy and join the quest for answers to mysteries that, for all mankind's progress, continue to puzzle the best minds of our time.

—Christopher Scanlan

[Editor's Note: Two of Nutt's stories, "Faith's Place" and "Genesis," have not been included here because of space considerations. The full text of those stories can be read on the CD-ROM included with this edition of Best Newspaper Writing. Illustrations by Andre Malok that accompany each story also are included on the CD-ROM.]

'The seekers':
The mind's 'I'

DECEMBER 1, 2002

NEW YORK—Maps are the tools of dreamers. A map gives substance to possibility, truth to discovery. In the 16th and 17th centuries, cartographers were called "world describers." In the 21st century, it is neuroscientists who are pushing back the boundaries, attempting to describe that final *terra incognita*, the human mind.

In 1637 the mind was front and center when Descartes announced, "I think, therefore I am." Having proven his own existence, the French philosopher then asked himself the mother of all follow-up questions: "What is this 'I' that I know?"

Nearly four centuries after Descartes essentially threw in the philosophical towel, Todd Feinberg, a neurologist at Beth Israel Medical Center in New York City, and Julian Keenan, an experimental psychologist at Montclair State University, believe they are close to mapping the place in the brain where the sense of self is formed.

Feinberg, author of *Altered Egos: How the Brain Creates the Self*, treats patients who have neurological damage, studying how their injuries have robbed them of the key ingredients of their identity.

For many of his patients, stroke, disease and physical trauma—especially in the right hemisphere of their brains—have resulted in a kind of self-alienation. They are people whose brains have lost their way.

Keenan, author of the soon-to-be-released *The Face in the Mirror*, is researching those same ingredients through experiments that involve magnetic stimulation of the brains of healthy subjects, testing for the thing that he believes makes us uniquely human: self-recognition.

Among all the species on the face of the earth, human beings alone inquire about who they are. Feinberg and Keenan are among a small band of scientists reaching through the mists of memory and emotion to explain how this could be.

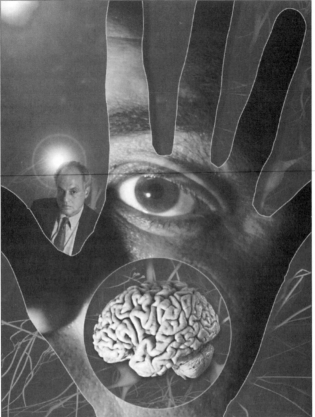

Photos by Patti Sapone. Illustration by Andre Malok.

THE ALIEN HAND

Todd Feinberg hunches in his chair as his theory of the fractured self is played out in front of him in a simple game of cards. An elderly couple sitting across from him are playing war, in which two players simultaneously pick up cards from their own halves of the deck and place the cards next to one another. Whoever has the card with the higher face value wins the round.

Sylvia is moving the game along at a clip, and it's clear why. Every time she picks up a card from her own pile with her left hand, she is compelled to pick up a card from her husband's pile with her right hand.

Feinberg, a psychiatrist as well as a neurologist, is fascinated. Quite literally, Sylvia's right hand doesn't know what the left hand is doing. Only occasionally, and seemingly unconsciously, does Sylvia (not her real name) realize that her right hand is meddling with the game, and when she does, she places the hand between her knees and squeezes it to try to keep it from misbehaving.

The 72-year-old woman, who owns an antique store in New Jersey with her husband, suffers from alien hand syndrome, a rare neurological condition. A stroke several months ago damaged Sylvia's corpus callosum, a broad band of 200 million fibers that bind together the left and right hemispheres of the brain. Signals from the left hemisphere, which would normally inhibit the actions of Sylvia's right hand, are not getting through to the other side of the brain. The result is that her right hand seems to have a life of its own.

When she speaks to her husband on the phone from her room in the Center for Head Injuries at JFK Johnson Rehabilitation Institute in Edison, she cradles the receiver with her left hand, but her right hand frequently reaches out and disconnects the call.

When she eats with her left hand, her right hand will wipe the table with an imaginary cloth.

And when she plays checkers, she moves her own piece with her left hand, and then her opponent's with her right.

Sylvia, for all intents and purposes, is a woman of two minds. Which is why, says Feinberg, she not only has a damaged brain, she has a fractured self.

"Alien hand syndrome tells us a lot about brain unity," says the 51-year-old doctor. "It tells us that there is no consciousness or mind that does not require cerebral integration. If you destroy or damage the corpus callosum, there are times at which the brain can act as though it was possessed of two minds, two consciousnesses, two independent entities."

Only in the 20th century did the brain become the primary focus in the search for the self. The ancient Egyptians thought the self, or the mind, was located in the bowels. The Sumerians and Assyrians thought it was in the liver, Aristotle the heart.

Descartes thought they were all wrong. The mind and the body, he wrote, were two separate entities. The body was a physical organ, a complex machine that walks, eats and sleeps, and the mind was a disembodied spirit, intangible and unobservable but altogether real.

In 1949, British philosopher Gilbert Ryle said Descartes' dualism was preposterous. An independent, invisible secret agent inhabiting the body? That would mean there was a "ghost in the machine." Ryle rejected the idea of two separate entities. There was, he contended, no intangible self, no "homunculus," or miniature man, directing a person's thoughts and actions from the inside. Instead, a person simply *was* his thoughts and actions, and the world was processed entirely by the gelatinous gray and white matter inside our skulls.

The mystical mind was out, the hard-wired brain was in.

SHIFTING LANDSCAPE

Mapping the brain, of course, has not been an easy task. A dense tapestry threaded by archipelagoes of nerve cells, the brain consists of billions of neurons and trillions of synapses. It is the most complex object on the planet. The heart pumps blood, the lungs ingest oxygen, the stomach absorbs nutrients, but the functions of the brain are manifold. It monitors the body's basic processes, coordinates physical movement, perceives, thinks, acts and feels. It is an executive branch of government that ceaselessly plans, reacts and interacts with the organic world around it.

It takes millions of neurons firing in sequence to create the simplest thought, and in the same way the Greek philosopher Heraclitus believed one never steps into the same river twice, we cannot have the same thought twice. Every sensation, every idea, every action creates a unique firing pattern, and each firing pattern creates a wave of neuronal activity that reacts to the one that came before it. At every moment, the landscape of the brain is being redrawn.

The idea that this puzzle of brain activity could be assembled into a single, subjective consciousness has perplexed Feinberg for most of his life. How does a 3-pound lump of matter become a "me"?

"The first thing that I remember discovering in life was that I had a brain," says Feinberg, founder and chief of the Yarmon Neurobehavior & Alzheimer's Disease Center at New York City's Beth Israel Medical Center. "I couldn't have been more than 6 years old, and one day I said to myself: 'I have thoughts and I have experiences. I have consciousness. But where are they? Where are they located? How come I can't see them? How come they can't be touched and measured and weighed?' And I just could not believe that. Ever since, I've been obsessed with the mind."

In truth, the life of any one mind is irremediably closed, colored by experiences and bounded by the uniqueness of individual perspective. "The mind is its own place," wrote Ryle, "and in his inner life each of us lives the life of a ghostly Robinson Crusoe...blind and deaf to the workings of one another's minds and inoperative upon them."

"There is no way to find out if your experience of the color red, for instance, is like my experience of the color red," says Martha Farah, director of the University of Pennsylvania's Center for Cognitive Neuroscience. "But if you define consciousness as mental content—the information contained in thoughts that is reportable by the person, and which they can reflect on and talk about—then, in that sense, consciousness is a valid subject of scientific study."

It is the content of consciousness that particularly interests Feinberg. The son of two psychologists, he was reading Freud in the second grade and by high school had steeped himself in abnormal psychology. After graduating from the University of Pennsylvania summa cum laude and receiving his medical degree from Mount Sinai School of Medicine in New York, Feinberg took on a dual residency in psychiatry and neurology, becoming an expert on both sides of the Cartesian coin—the mind and the body.

Like the best scientists, Feinberg is a tightrope walker, searching for purchase on the subtlest threads of evidence, trusting only his sense of imbalance to tell him how much farther he has to go. Every day, he tests the wire.

"When I got out of the shower this morning, I stubbed my toe and it hurt and it hurt," says Feinberg, who lives with his wife and teenage son in Tenafly. (A daughter studies psychology at Syracuse University.) "And I said to myself: 'Boy, if that isn't mysterious. Why and how am I in pain if those neurons that are telling me I'm in pain aren't themselves throbbing in pain?'

"Where is that pain? When I stubbed my toe I didn't grab my head in pain. I grabbed my toe. If I had an 'auto-cerebroscope' and I could look through it and observe my own brain, I might see neurons firing in patterns, but I'll never find that pain. I can't touch it. I can't see it. I can only experience it.

"And that, in a nutshell, is what is so mysterious about consciousness."

BILLION-PIECE PUZZLE

Subjective experience can't be seen or heard or touched. It simply is. Feinberg calls this the "transparency problem."

There is a second aspect to self-awareness that deepens the mystery, the "binding problem," which is this: How do billions of different neurons come together to form a single unified self, and if we know where the neurons are located, why can't we find the self?

It's a bit like looking for Beethoven's Fifth Symphony in the sheet music. The score includes all the notes played by the violins, the cellos, the timpani and so on. But where is the music, this thing called "Beethoven's Fifth Symphony"?

For Feinberg, solving the problem of the unity of consciousness is like building a cathedral from a billion blades of grass. "If you're a really obsessional person like I am," he says, "then you can't give up. You don't ever say it can't be understood. So you just don't stop."

Feinberg's office at Beth Israel is a testament to the neurologist's professional and personal fixation. Framed brain scans adorn his wall like family photographs. Feinberg points to each of them in turn: "This is an interesting one because it's abnormal. That's a normal one. That's an abnormal one." Ever the teacher, he asks his visitor about the picture just over his right shoulder: "Can you tell what's wrong with this one?" The entire corpus callosum is missing. "Amazing," he says, "isn't it?"

The secrets of the self, Feinberg believes, lie in the brains of his patients.

"As slicing an apple reveals its core, the neurological lesion or damage opens a door into the inner self," he writes in his book. "It provides an opportunity to examine the physical structure of the self and to see how the self changes and adapts in response to the damaged brain."

There are many ways to define consciousness, including the act of simple perception. Self-awareness and the ability to recognize that other people have self-awareness represent the highest order of consciousness.

"Everything, in the last analysis—every feeling, every thought, every memory, every state of mind—has to be represented by a brain state," says Gordon Gallup, psychologist at the State University of New York at Albany and one of the first to study self-recognition in primates. "These things aren't generated in a vacuum."

Many of Feinberg's patients are stroke victims, and many, if not most, have suffered damage to the right side of their brains. Because the right hemisphere affects the left side of the body (and vice versa), these patients have problems with their left limbs, as well as vision and general movement on the left side.

Sylvia is an unusual case. She was examined by Feinberg at the JFK Johnson Rehabilitation Institute's Center for Head Injuries in late September as a guest of Joseph Giacino, the center's associate director of neuropsychology, who is a frequent collaborator with Feinberg. Sylvia is Giacino's patient. Both doctors agree Sylvia has suffered an anterior cerebral artery stroke in the left hemisphere of her brain, which has led to damage on the left side of the corpus callosum, as well as in supplementary motor areas.

Basically, Sylvia's brain was deprived of oxygen and a small bundle of cells between the two hemispheres liquefied, then hardened into a scar the size of a half-dollar.

In many of the alien hand cases Feinberg has seen, the limbs act in violent opposition. (Unlike Sylvia's case, patients who have damage only to the corpus callosum will always have left-hand alien hand syndrome.) When one of Feinberg's patients tried to button his shirt with his right hand, his left hand unbuttoned it. When he picked up a forkful of food with his right hand, the left hand knocked it away. Another patient reported that her left hand tried to strangle her while she slept.

"The thing that grabs one's attention here," says Feinberg excitedly, "is the fact that you have two hemispheres in one person with competing and conflicting attentions, and that highlights the incredible unification in normal intact individuals....The sense of the self is the sense of a unified self, of personhood."

Some cognitive scientists believe this fact makes it impossible to localize consciousness to one area, or even several areas, of the brain.

"The frontal poles of the brain separate humans from all other living things," says neuropsychologist Mark Wheeler of Temple University. "But that is not going to be the whole story. You don't lose consciousness by losing a bit of brain tissue....There are physical correlates to everything. Questions like 'How does a brain state become a mental state?' I don't know how to answer. Neuroscience has done an incredible job in the last few years; the philosophy of mind hasn't moved much in 300."

DETACHMENT

In his filing cabinets, Feinberg has hundreds of scans of patients whose sense of personhood was shattered by stroke or disease. Atop the cabinet are scores of videos of many of those patients going back 18 years. In one, an elderly, hearing-impaired woman who knew sign language and could read lips looked at her reflection in a mirror. Feinberg asked her what she was doing, and she said she was communicating in the mirror with someone else, someone who was very much like her and attended the same grade school but was nonetheless a stranger.

Talking about this person in the mirror, the woman said: "She's not a very good lip reader. I had to talk mostly in sign language for her, to make her understand....She's not that bright. I hate to say that....

"She's a nice person. But one thing about her...I see her every day through a mirror, and that's the only place I can see her. When she sees me through the mirror, she looks a little, then she comes over and talks to me, and that's how we began becoming friends."

Feinberg's diagnosis was a delusional misidentification problem known as "Capgras syndrome for her mirror image," caused by atrophy in the right temperoparietal region of the brain. Except for misidentifying her own reflection, the woman was perfectly normal.

Some of Feinberg's patients suffer from asomatognosia,

in which they deny or misidentify a part of their own body after it has been paralyzed by stroke. In all of the cases Feinberg has seen, the damage was to the patients' right hemisphere, causing them to attribute ownership of their left arm to another person—a relative, a stranger—or even a pet.

Some patients try to throw the disowned arm out of bed. Others, trying to acclimate, create stories about the arm, give it nicknames such as "Toby" or "Silly Billy," or simply refer to it as "a canary claw," "a sack of coal" or "dead wood."

Feinberg's research has shown a peculiarly gender-specific phenomenon associated with asomatognosia. Women frequently will mistake their left arms for their husbands' arms. Men will frequently mistake their left arms for the arms of their mothers-in-law.

There is no cure for most of these patients, but over weeks and sometimes years, their symptoms often diminish and even disappear—a testament to the resourcefulness, as well as recuperative ability, of the damaged brain.

Sylvia, after just a few months, already has begun to recognize and gain more control over the actions of her right hand.

Feinberg believes that the sense of identity is probably a mixture—what he calls a "nested hierarchy"—of coordinated functions arising out of several areas of the brain, but he believes, too, that the right hemisphere is dominant as the source of the self.

Julian Keenan's belief is stronger, and more specific. The right hemisphere isn't simply dominant in the formation of self-awareness, he says, it is essential.

"I think there actually is a center" of the self, says Keenan as he leans back in a chair in his office at Montclair State University. "There are definite neural correlates of higher-order consciousness that, if you mark them out, the person is no longer conscious, no longer capable of self-awareness."

Just a tenth of an inch beneath the furrowed ridges of gray matter that cover the right front side of the brain, he contends, is a layer of tangled cell tissue that makes us uniquely human.

While acknowledging there may be other similarly

minuscule areas of the brain that contribute to consciousness, the 32-year-old experimental cognitive psychologist has come to the conclusion that the right prefrontal cortex—located just above the right eye—is the primary source of self-awareness.

A TOUCH OF PRINCESS DI

Two years ago, while conducting postdoctoral research in behavioral neurology at Harvard Medical School, Keenan created an unusual experiment to test for "self-face recognition," which he regards as the hallmark of higher consciousness.

"What we know, as far as self-face recognition is concerned, is that it's reserved for a very few species," says Keenan, who lives with his wife, Ilene, in Jersey City. "Only chimpanzees, orangutans and humans have the ability to recognize an image as their own. So what we wanted to do was see where in the brain that takes place."

Volunteering as test subjects were five people about to undergo brain surgery at Boston's Beth Israel Deaconess Medical Center for severe epilepsy. During the presurgical evaluation of each patient, the two hemispheres of the brain were anesthetized, one at a time, while the patient stayed conscious and alert. After each hemisphere was numbed, Keenan and his colleagues showed the person a photograph with a morphed image blending the patient's face with that of a famous person's—Marilyn Monroe or Princess Diana for the women, Bill Clinton or Albert Einstein for the men. After the testing, each patient was presented with two conventional photos, one of himself or herself and one of the famous person. They were asked which was the one they remembered seeing under anesthesia.

The results were startling. When the right hemisphere was anesthetized, four of the five recollected seeing only the famous person. With the left hemisphere numbed, all five patients remembered the morphed picture as a photo of themselves alone.

"We really saw that the right hemisphere was the big player in self-recognition," says Keenan, "and in particular the right prefrontal cortex." His conclusion: That is where the self resides.

For Keenan, thinking about thinking is a deeply personal preoccupation. It's easy to imagine what a scan of the young psychologist's brain would have looked like: storm clouds of electrical activity roiling through the right hemisphere, firing up neurons as if they were lights on the Rockefeller Center Christmas tree.

"It started when I was 15 when I read *Gödel, Escher, Bach* by Douglas Hofstadter," says Keenan, referring to the 1979 best seller about mathematics, art and music, "and that book has just always stayed with me—all those self-referential systems. We all think about our own thoughts. We all think about, 'Am I the only person on this planet and everyone else is just a robot?' We all have these sorts of ideas about our own thinking, about the little voice in our head....I guess I've always thought that everyone thinks like that."

Keenan is an abstract painter and a musician and likes to speak in visual terms. In considering the brain, he cites an article by John Updike about baseball Hall of Famer Ted Williams on the eve of Williams' retirement.

"Updike described Williams, who at that point was old and injured, as looking like a Calder mobile with one of its threads cut. I thought that was the most beautiful description. Everything went off balance just a little bit. And as I read that, I thought: What a great description for the brain. There are these separate sorts of units and they're all in balance, and even though they may look independent, damage to one area will affect other, far-reaching areas."

Every year Keenan asks students in his Introduction to Physiological Psychology course to create a mobile with the brain as the governing theme, and he hangs the best ones in his office. As he speaks, a mobile of a neuron, made out of multicolored pipe cleaners, dangles delicately overhead.

PEEKING AT THE DARK

While Keenan and Feinberg are traditional materialists, believing that the mind is nothing more than brain functions, others, like Daniel Dennett, a cognitive scientist at Tufts University, believe the mind is nothing at all—that mental states don't arise from neural states, they *are* neural states. Dennett once declared about consciousness: "It's like fame. It doesn't exist except in the eye of the beholder."

Colin McGinn, philosopher of mind at Rutgers University, also believes the self is elusive, but not because it is nonexistent; because it is fundamentally unknowable. "We're trapped inside ourselves, inside our own language," says McGinn. "For that reason, trying to describe the contents of our consciousness with the same tools, the same words is inadequate."

William James, the pioneering 19th-century philosopher and psychologist (and brother of novelist Henry James), said that trying to describe introspection was like "trying to turn up the gas (light) quickly enough to see how the darkness looks."

Keenan, however, believes the science of consciousness can transcend linguistic limitations.

In a new series of experiments at Montclair State, he is using a device called a transcranial magnetic stimulator to measure how active each hemisphere of the brain is in tasks involving self-recognition. When gently placed against the skull, the stimulator—which looks oddly like a thick, metal Mardi Gras mask—creates a magnetic field that painlessly deactivates a specific area of the brain for a moment as brief as a hundred-thousandth of a second. When the device is held over the area of the right prefrontal cortex—the area Keenan believes is the source of self-recognition—subjects routinely take a fraction of a second longer than normal to recognize their face on the computer screen. When the stimulator is held over the left frontal region, nothing happens.

"Again and again, what we're seeing is that the processes of self-evaluation are preferentially engaged in the right hemisphere," says Keenan. "And it is that ability to recognize one's own face that appears to be a hallmark of consciousness. To know that our own face is ours inevitably requires knowledge of the self. Without self-knowledge, it would be seemingly impossible to recognize who we are."

Farah, the Penn neuroscientist, whose primary research is in the neural correlates of cognition, believes self-recognition studies are helping to advance the scientific study of the mind. "A lot of the work on sense of self and the brain is pretty flaky," she says, "but Keenan's and Feinberg's work is credible. Keenan has found distinctive patterns of brain activity that correlate with processing one's own face compared to other people's, and Feinberg finds that certain brain lesions disrupt a person's ability to recognize their own face or arms as belonging to them. This tells us that one's sense of physical self is the result of specific brain systems."

Keenan claims to be obsessed by his work, and a sleeping bag wedged atop the bookcase in his office attests to that. "There's always so much more to know," he says. "There's always just another level of understanding. You think you have a clue, and then you find out you have no clue, and it goes on and on and on. It's never-ending. You can never know enough."

Still, Keenan believes that in the next 10 years he will know enough to have a new map of the brain with more precise coordinates of the self. Describing subjective experience may forever be elusive; describing what it is that makes us most human, he says, is not.

That's all Feinberg is looking to do, too, and he believes the search is profoundly important: "You could argue that aside from intelligence, the sense of the self is probably the greatest human achievement. Without that sense of being a being, where would we be?"

'The seekers':
Defying the years

DECEMBER 2, 2002

OAKLAND, Calif.—Time unravels us. Day by day, it peels away the layers of our lives until nothing is left but the nub of our own mortality.

Human beings are the only animals on the planet capable of contemplating their own demise. We mourn, we memorialize, we philosophize and we pray. And when it happens on that rare occasion that we "cheat" death or "escape" our fate, we believe, just for a moment, in the myth of immortality.

Today scientists are tempting fate in ways never before imagined as they demystify the secrets of longevity. Biochemist Bruce Ames believes that vitamins can repair damaged cells and make them "young" again. Molecular biologist Judith Campisi is studying how to keep cells from aging.

Both believe that while there may be no actual Fountain of Youth, no scientific Dorian Gray in a Bottle, reversal of aging and an extended life span are now on the horizon.

Bruce Ames is a chain-reaction thinker—one thought always leads to another—which may explain why the senior scientist at Children's Hospital of Oakland Research Institute is so restless. Ames, 73 and wiry, often starts a conversation sitting down but invariably finishes it standing up, practically sprinting across his office to a blackboard to illustrate something about unattached free radicals or mitochondrial decay.

Chain-reaction thinking leads to big ideas, and Ames is a big idea man. Genes. Cancer. Nutrition. Aging. He has tackled them all, publishing more than 450 articles and becoming one of the most frequently cited scientists on the planet.

"I told a colleague recently that I was doing the best work in my career," says Ames, who is also a professor of biochemistry at the University of California at Berkeley, "and he looked at me and said, 'Bruce, you've been telling me that for 30 years.' I guess that means my enthusiasm genes are undamaged."

Ames should know. Damaged genes have been his business for half a century. Ames grew up in Manhattan as the son of a high school chemistry teacher and a mother who wanted him to be a doctor. Instead he became a researcher, graduating from the Bronx High School of Science before getting his undergraduate degree at Cornell and his Ph.D. in biochemistry at the California Institute of Technology.

In the 1950s Ames was a researcher in a lab at the National Institutes of Health, investigating ways to test for genetic mutation. His petri dish protocol ultimately proved that genes damaged by certain chemical substances often gave rise to cancer. By the 1970s, the "Ames test" was the world's most widely used method for identifying potential carcinogens in everything from clothing to hair dye to pharmaceuticals.

"It's just problem-solving," says Ames about his research methods. "If you have two odd facts in your head and suddenly they fit together, you see some new way of explaining something."

That's what happened nearly a decade ago, when Ames turned his focus from cancer to aging.

How and why we age has been a mystery since humans first contemplated their own mortality. It is one of the most complex of biological processes: The human body contains more than 250 types of cells, and each type has its own peculiar aging characteristics.

There are scores of different theories about aging, but all of them can be broken down into two broad camps: theories that regard aging as the result of normal wear and tear from environmental insults and metabolic processes; and theories that regard aging as the result of a pre-programmed genetic plan, a process that begins at birth, or even at conception, and continues until our "biological clock" runs down.

As a scientist who loves studying process almost as much as its results, Ames falls in the wear-and-tear camp. His years of watching the cellular chaos created by cancer has given him perspective on the degradation of cells that comes with aging.

"In 6 million years of evolution, we've gone from a short-life creature to a long-life creature," says Ames,

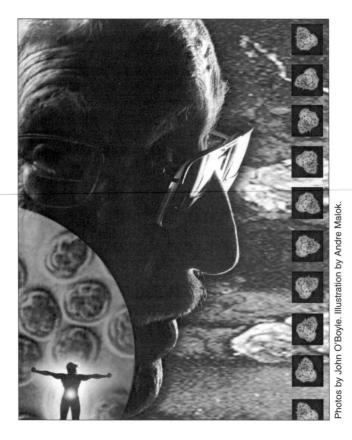

Photos by John O'Boyle. Illustration by Andre Malok.

"and age-specific cancers have gone up. Thinking about that said to me: A lot of cancer is just about getting old. And that got me interested in aging."

Two odd events kept jangling about in Ames' head: the rise in cancer and the increase in free radicals with age. Free radicals are molecular miscreants, compound substances that create havoc inside cells by stripping other molecules of their electrons. Was there a direct link between free radicals and aging? Was it possible that free radicals actually contributed to aging?

THE TINY FURNACES

Ames began by looking at mitochondria, where free radicals are produced. Mitochondria are tiny structures inside every cell that act like furnaces, manufacturing most of the energy that is used by the body. Some cells with high metabolic rates, such as those in the heart muscle, contain many thousands of mitochondria. Other types of cells may contain as few as a dozen.

As energy-producing machines go, mitochondria are spectacularly efficient. Of the oxygen consumed by an average cell, the mitochondria convert 95 percent of it to help turn food—fats and carbohydrates—into a chemical fuel known as adenosine triphosphate, or ATP. Every time we breathe, in other words, we're giving an energy boost to our cells.

During that process, mitochondria steal electrons from oxygen molecules in order to function more smoothly. But therein lies the problem. During those acts of larceny, a mitochondrion sometimes "misplaces" the electrons it is stealing. Like money flying out the back of a Brink's truck careening around a corner, these misplaced electrons—now called free radicals—scatter around the insides of cells, bonding indiscriminately with other molecules.

This mischief is called oxidation, and it allows free radicals to become chromosomal rototillers, breaking and mangling DNA at will.

Too many free radicals create a kind of cellular pollution that stiffens cell membranes and wears down enzymes. Too much damaged DNA results in cell mutations (which can cause cancer). Both are signs of aging.

If not for these free radicals, Ames realized, mitochondria could be a cellular Fountain of Youth.

In 1990 he and his colleagues at Berkeley announced the findings of their study. They'd discovered twice as much free radical damage in tissues of 2-year-old rats as in those of 2-month-old rats. Ames had found a crucial link among oxidation, DNA mutation and age: Free radical oxidation doesn't just rise with aging, it causes it. The more that mitochondria "leak" free radicals, the more those radicals end up damaging the mitochondria, which in turn leak even more free radicals.

This vicious cycle gets only worse with age. It is the ultimate biological irony: The thing we most need to live—oxygen—is the very thing killing us.

Ames estimates that the DNA in each cell of the human body experiences at least 100,000 "hits," or instances, of free radical damage per day.

"Living is like getting irradiated," says Ames. He admits it's a slight oversimplification, but free radicals created by radiation do the same thing as free radicals created by breathing. "With age, despite the mitochondria trying to keep it all in check, the level of free radicals goes up, which means the level of oxidized protein goes up, which means the level of DNA damage goes up."

Most scientists believe that mitochondrial health is only one cog in the aging wheel.

"Aging is complex and will not be explained by one gene or mechanism," says Jerry Shay, who holds the Distinguished Chair in Geriatric Research at the University of Texas Southwestern Medical Center. Shay believes Ames' research is promising but that other biological processes affecting longevity must be taken into account, since "different tissues may have fundamentally different mechanisms underlying their maintenance and repair."

To prove that mitochondrial dysfunction actually causes us to age, Ames decided to work backward. If he could find a way to restore mitochondrial health by lowering free radical damage, he could improve cellular function. In essence, he could turn back the cells' biological clocks.

WHEN IN ROME

Ames is in no hurry to turn back his own biological clock. He likes to joke that he gets his exercise by "running" experiments, "skipping" the controls and "jumping" to conclusions. His wife of 40 years, biochemist Giovanna Ferro-Luzzi, heard the joke for the 50th time recently and exacted her revenge: "She got me a personal trainer."

Ames says he has time for only about an hour a week with the trainer, but his wife insists they walk the two miles to their favorite Italian restaurant, Oliveto, for lunch at least three times a week.

It was while visiting his wife's native country in the mid-1990s—they have a house in Tuscany and an apartment in Rome—that Ames got the idea for how to improve mitochondrial health and perhaps slow, or even reverse, the aging process.

A dietary supplement known as acetyl-L-carnitine, or Alcar, was sweeping Italy. The latest nutritional fad was being marketed as a pick-me-up, and Ames understood why: Alcar is a naturally occurring biochemical involved in the transport of fatty acids into the cell's mitochondria. In other words, Alcar helps cells produce energy.

When Ames got back to his lab, he started feeding Alcar to his old rats.

And the old rats loved the stuff. Within weeks, they appeared re-energized, and their biochemistry was running more smoothly. There was a problem, however. As the Alcar improved mitochondrial health, it also appeared to increase the level of free radicals. Ames decided to add another nutritional supplement to his rats' diets, the antioxidant alpha lipoic acid. Another naturally occurring chemical, lipoic acid, he thought, should work by tuning up mitochondrial function, thereby lowering free radical oxidation.

The results were staggering. Said Ames earlier this year, after the findings of his research team were published in the Proceedings of the National Academy of Sciences:

"With these two supplements together, these old rats got up and did the Macarena....The brain looks better, they are full of energy. Everything we looked at looks more like a young animal."

Some researchers believe the hope offered by maintaining healthy cells or rejuvenating old ones is limited.

"You can achieve immortality at the cellular level, but I don't see how it would be practical in extending life span," says Robert Lanza, the medical and scientific director of Advanced Cell Technology in Worcester, Mass. "There's a wall at 120 years. We can continue to piece things together. But we're like tires; there are just so many times you can be patched up."

Ames acknowledges he has not discovered the Fountain of Youth but lays claim to a Fountain of Middle Age. The evidence, he says, lies not only in the physical rejuvenation he observed in his rats, but in their improvements on cognition and memory tests. Says Ames: "It was the equivalent of making a 75- to 80-year-old person look and act middle-aged."

Ames looks every bit the part of an elderly gent, with his white hair, bifocals and quaint bow tie. While he has a penchant for mixing plaids, his mind is relentlessly mixing and matching ideas.

"I was always sort of a B-student in school, but I loved reading enormously. Still do. I was always a pretty creative thinker. I try to be a generalist. I make my living as a big picture guy, always looking for the next big idea."

Ames put his current big idea into a pill. In 1999, he and a colleague, Tory Hagen, founded a company to sell the energy formula as a dietary supplement. The pill, available over the Internet, includes 200 milligrams of alpha lipoic acid and 500 milligrams of acetyl-L-carnitine, but Ames says the two nutrients just as easily can be purchased separately at any health food store.

While Ames and Hagen's company, Juvenon, licenses the supplement, the University of California holds the patent. Juvenon has yet to make a profit. If it does, the university will get a third. Another third will go to the university's department of molecular and cell biology, where Ames is a professor, and the remaining third will be split by Ames and Hagen, now at the Linus Pauling Institute at Oregon State University.

Clinical human trials are ongoing. Ames, for one, is satisfied enough with the animal results that he takes a dose of his own supplement twice a day. He admits he hasn't noticed any significant changes in himself just yet.

"Is it a reversal of aging or just a slowing?" he asks himself out loud. "The rats seem to do better on the IQ test as well as the treadmill test, so that looks like a reversal....

"I don't want to overhype it. If you're an old rat, it looks very good. But we still have to wait for the results from the human trials. There's every reason to think it's going to work in people. I'm very optimistic."

THE TICKING CLOCK

In her basement office in nearby Berkeley, Judith Campisi perches herself on the edge of a chair and speaks with a wide-eyed enthusiasm usually reserved for first-year graduate students. Campisi is a senior molecular biologist at Lawrence Berkeley National Laboratory. An expert in the genetics of aging and a proponent of the "biological clock" theory, the 54-year-old scientist believes that "reprogramming" human genes to extend life span may not be far off.

It is 7:30 in the evening and Campisi is in no hurry to go home. "I have no separation between my work life and the rest of my life," she admits without hesitation, and the evidence is all around her: three empty yogurt cups in the wastebasket, and on a shelf below a side table, a kind of researcher's survivor kit—a couple of cans of Progresso hearty chicken soup, a container of Cafe Vienna coffee, a makeup mirror and hand lotion.

Piles of papers rise from the floor like unsteady chimneys, forcing pedestrian traffic to take a serpentine route through the room. The stacks are layered with journals bearing such titles as *Trends in Cellular Biology* and *Experimental Gerontology*. On a nearby table, *Handbook of the Biology of Aging*, a textbook co-written by Campisi, sits atop a tower of paper nearly as tall as the 4-foot-10 biochemist.

Campisi's research focuses on the telomere, a structure containing a repeated DNA sequence that is found on both ends of every chromosome in the human body. In 1990, Calvin Harley, now the chief scientist at Genron, a California biotech company, discovered that as cells divide, the telomeres of the new cells are shorter.

A few years later, it was shown that in some cells the telomeres get shorter with age. When telomeres become too short, they send a signal to the cell to stop dividing, and a natural cellular state called senescence ensues. Campisi believes the primary function of senescence is to fight off cancer.

"Senescent cells are not dead," she says, "they're perfectly alive, they metabolize, but what they can never, ever do again is divide. And if you can't divide, you can't form a tumor....

"It's only in the last .00001 percent of human evolution that we have had the luxury of living in an environment where the food supply is good, infections are pretty much kept at bay, and there are no lions jumping out of the savanna to kill us. But for the vast majority of evolution, we evolved under very hazardous conditions. The life span was probably only 25, 30, 35 years at most. So think about what happens. If all evolution really does is devise a system to keep an organism—keep us—cancer-free for 30 years, well, then it does a pretty good job."

What it doesn't do is keep us young.

Campisi's research has shown that the longer we live, the more senescent cells our bodies accumulate, and it's those senescent cells, she says, that may play a leading role in making us look and feel old. If she can prove this hypothesis, Campisi will have identified one of the main contributors to aging: We age not because our cells die, but because they stop dividing.

"We reasoned several years ago that because the senescence response is an arrest of cell proliferation, but not cell death, after about age 50 we start to see significant numbers of these cells appearing. And we know from our culture studies that these cells don't function properly, and so we're filling up with these dysfunctional senescent cells the longer we live, and so this may be an important reason we age."

FOOT IN BOTH CAMPS

Campisi, like Ames, came to aging by way of cancer research. She came to research, however, by way of a Catholic girls high school.

"When I finally got to college," she says, "I decided I wanted to take classes with lots of guys. I was good at science and I liked it, but the best part was all those men majoring in it."

Campisi, who was born in Queens, graduated from the State University of New York at Stony Brook in 1974 and stayed on for her doctorate, which she received five years later. Along the way, she married, divorced and settled into a career in cancer research. In the mid-1980s, during a postdoctoral fellowship at Boston University, a colleague came calling with an offer.

"He was putting together a project grant on aging, which I wasn't even interested in at the time," says Campisi, "and they needed one more scientist. He said, 'Do you think we could get you interested in a problem called cell senescence?' The funny thing is, he didn't think senescence had anything to do with aging."

Campisi came to see that cancer researchers were looking at one aspect of senescence, researchers on aging were looking at a different aspect of it, and "nobody tried to get those two to come back and talk to each other."

Campisi didn't have to. She looked at both aspects herself, and like several other molecular biologists discovered a critical connection among cancer, aging and cellular senescence.

"When the telomere becomes dangerously short but not completely gone, it sends that signal to the cell to stop dividing," she says. If it didn't, the DNA tips on the end of the chromosome would become raggedy, and the chromosome would start seeking out other broken chromosomal pieces—and "that," says Campisi, "is the hallmark of cancer.

"Now, how does a healthy cell know that it doesn't have a broken piece of DNA? The telomere."

Telomeres allow cells to senesce, and if such cells stop dividing, they can't form a tumor. "The question is," says Campisi, "what happens to an organism that begins to accumulate senescent cells with age?"

Cancer, again, may hold the key.

While normal cells can divide only so many times (known as the Hayflick Limit), cancer cells are essentially immortal, and in 90 percent of them telomerase, an enzyme, can be found. Telomerase replaces the bit of telomere clipped off after each cancer cell's division.

If telomerase production can be turned on in normal cells, it seems reasonable to assume that normal cells could be immortalized.

"One thing we've learned from the mouse model," says Campisi, "is that you don't want cells to not senesce at all, because if you do that, you have cancer. What would be great would be to have some of those senescent cells die, so that they don't accumulate with age. That's what we're working on. It's not going to be easy to do that, but that's the idea, that's the long-term goal."

Campisi credits her scientific creativity to her wide-ranging education, which includes an undergraduate degree in chemistry, a Ph.D. in biophysics and postdoctoral research in the biology of cancer.

"I kind of learned at an early age not to be bound by field or science or even technique. And so I think when you have that kind of broad training, you move between fields very easily." Moving between fields allows Campisi to keep looking for the next thing she needs to know. "You have to have this fire in the belly to know the answer to something, and then you just go and find out."

Research, says Campisi, is a lot like one of her favorite pastimes, cooking. A little of this, a little of that—the best of meals are unplanned, the result of intuition and experimentation. "I consider recipes advisory only," says the microbiologist.

Likewise in her research. Campisi enjoys creating her own path to an answer, pursuing solutions not with a sprinter's speed but at an ambler's pace, taking the time to search out familiar territory for missed clues and overlooked details.

"I have this philosophy of I just start doing this random walk," says Campisi, "and eventually I wind up where I need to go."

Currently, she is walking her way through the complex problem of aging by trying to identify the molecular mechanisms responsible for cellular arrest, studying the defective genes in premature aging diseases, and determining how telomere length is regulated. The payoff from that research, she hopes, will be a postponement of aging.

Some scientists, such as Jay Olshansky, a professor of public health at the University of Illinois at Chicago, express caution when it comes to the promise of research into aging.

The co-author of *The Quest for Immortality* said last year: "When we survive into old age, just as with automobiles and race cars, things start to go wrong, and unless we can change the structure of the body itself or the rate at which aging occurs, then inevitably things will go wrong as we push out the envelope of human survival."

Lanza, of Advanced Cell Technology, believes the problem of wear and tear will soon be overcome.

"I think there's no question that in two or three decades we'll be able to replace every part of the human body," says Lanza. "Whole organs, like blood vessels and bladders, have already been grown in the lab."

Like Ames, Campisi believes the secret to longevity is about maintaining a balance in the biological processes, whether it's mitochondrial function or the stability of the DNA.

"Eventually you run out of cells, which is why immortality is not on the books," she says. "But a reversal of aging—as long as you define the aging process segmentally—is within our grasp.

"We really are talking about how to preserve the health of tissues for the maximal period of time, for a very long and healthy extended middle age."

'The seekers':
How will it end?

DECEMBER 5, 2002

PASADENA, Calif.—The unknown is a great seductress. Never is this more obvious than when we look up into the illimitable darkness of night. In its capacity to enchant, the universe has been siren and muse to poets and scientists alike.

Some 70 years after the discovery that there were galaxies beyond the Milky Way too numerous to count, the most elusive questions of cosmology are beginning to be answered.

Scientists believe they now know what happened in the first microsecond of creation, how the big bang got started and how seeds of energy gave birth to matter.

What they still don't know is how it will all end.

The answer lies within the fabric of space itself, where a titanic tug of war is being staged between gravity and a mysterious dark energy, a repulsive force that is tantalizing scientists with its tenacity.

Understanding dark energy and how it affects space could help in figuring out the future of the universe, whether it is destined to continue expanding, fall back on itself in a violent implosion, or be consumed by everlasting darkness.

Two forces. Three possible futures.

Astronomer Wendy Freedman has all but determined the speed of the universe's expansion. Physicist Paul Steinhardt is working to understand how dark energy affects that expansion.

Together, these discoveries could tell us what will become of the universe hundreds of billions of years from now.

THE ELUSIVE NUMBER

Like many scientists who have a passion for what they do, Wendy Freedman remembers the exact moment her fascination with astronomy began—on a summer night, beside a lake, under a trellis of stars ribboned by darkness.

Leaning back in a chair in her second-floor office at the Carnegie Observatories, Freedman smiles, her soft brown eyes squinting slightly as if to better focus the memory.

"I was 7 years old and we were on vacation at Lake Simcoe in Toronto," says the Canadian native. "And I remember that the sky was very, very dark and my father told me that the light from the stars we were looking at had left a long time ago, maybe so long ago that those stars weren't even there anymore. And that just knocked my breath out."

Freedman, 47, is a soft-spoken anomaly in a field historically dominated by testosterone and braggadocio. But she is a no-nonsense astronomer who has spent 25 years reeling in galaxies with a telescope and transforming their starlight to data.

Templing her fingertips together, she talks about her decade-long search for the Hubble constant, a number that would tell her how fast the universe is moving. That simple, two-digit number had been the quarry of some of the 20th century's greatest astronomers—until Freedman bagged it in 1999.

"It took many, many years and there were lots of low points," she says. "You keep measuring and remeasuring, and problems come up with calibrations, and things go wrong with the telescope, and it seems like you're never, ever going to finish and find the answer."

Many before Freedman certainly had tried, beginning with Edwin Hubble himself, the American astronomer who first demonstrated the existence of galaxies outside the Milky Way (and for whom the Hubble Space Telescope is named). It was Hubble who, in 1929, was the first to observe galaxies rocketing away from each other. His conclusion, that the universe was expanding, was viewed by many as a second Copernican Revolution, further displacing the notion that the Earth was the cozy, static center of a one-galaxy universe.

The question that plagued Hubble and other astronomers for years afterward was how to measure the speed of that expansion. The answer looked simple. Find distant stars and then measure two things, the speed at which they are receding from Earth, and their distance.

Photos by Patti Sapone and John O'Boyle. Illustration by Andre Malok.

Easier said than done. A star's outward speed, known as redshift velocity, can be calculated by observing the wavelength of the star's light (the longer and redder the wavelength, the faster the star is speeding away), but distance is another matter altogether.

In 1838, the distances to the stars nearest Earth were measured for the first time using a simple geometric principle known as triangulation, or parallax.

To understand how parallax works, hold your index finger in front of your face at arm's length and look at it while quickly covering one eye and then the other. Your finger appears to jump back and forth because you are looking at it from two angles. Now hold your finger directly in front of your nose and do the same thing. Your finger seems to jump more dramatically. The same thing happens when looking at stars from two different sides of the globe. The closer the star or planet is to the Earth, the larger the parallax.

For an object far beyond the boundaries of the Milky Way, however, parallax is almost impossible to detect. To measure the distance to extragalactic objects, a different tool is needed: a type of highly luminous star called a standard candle.

Among the best standard candles are a class of stars known as Cepheid variables. Cepheids blink in predictable patterns and with predictable intensity, which allows astronomers to know exactly how bright—and therefore how distant—they truly are. Combined with stellar velocity, the distance calculation produces a kind of cosmic speedometer for the expansion of the universe.

Freedman has been studying Cepheids for two decades, and her brain is brimming with facts and figures about the stars. When she talks, she wields those statistics like a mathematical seamstress, using numbers to buckle her sentences together and snap thoughts into place:

"Cepheids had been studied really well for seven decades. Our project was to…look at those Cepheids and also to find more of them at larger distances. We looked at 800 in 24 different galaxies. A typical galaxy has between 50,000 and 100,000 stars, and we took 32 different images of each galaxy.…

"The breakthrough that the Hubble telescope provided was by getting up above the Earth's atmosphere, where we didn't have the blurring that takes place and where we could survey galaxies that were at a distance 10 times as great as we normally could see from the ground."

With the Hubble Space Telescope, launched in 1990, Freedman knew if she could find Cepheid variables far enough away, she'd have a set of candles by which she could measure how fast the universe was expanding.

THE GANTLET

The daughter of a medical doctor and a concert pianist, Freedman always had an affinity for research. When she arrived at the University of Toronto as an undergraduate, her intention was to study biophysics, but a freshman astronomy course reminded her of those summer nights on the lake with her father—and her fascination with the stars.

"I wrote term papers first on the solar system and then star formation and later did a senior thesis on galaxy evolution," says Freedman. "I even had a teacher tell me he was sorry I left the solar system. So I guess I've been moving farther and farther out as I've gone along."

Freedman continued on at Toronto for her Ph.D. in astronomy, eventually married her graduate adviser, Barry Madore, and then began a postdoctoral fellowship at Carnegie Observatories. Within three years she had become the first woman staff member in the institution's nearly 100-year history.

Founded in 1903 by George Hale, one of the leaders of modern astrophysics, the Carnegie Observatories is a small two-story building nestled among suburban homes on a tree-lined Pasadena street. The wood-paneled hallways are populated less with the living—all of them appear to be behind closed office doors—than the dead. Newton, Einstein, Hubble—the brightest lights of science—form a kind of gantlet as they peer down from paintings and photos that line the Observatories' corridors.

As soon as Freedman got to Carnegie, she drew up plans for a project involving the Hubble Space Telescope: to determine the speed of the universe by finding the most distant variable stars ever observed. The pitch worked. Freedman's Extra-Galactic Distance Scale project was named the key, or primary, project of Hubble before its launch.

Freedman's euphoria was fleeting. Hubble's first observations brought bad news: Instead of new vistas, there was a cosmic blur. The telescope had a flawed lens, and it would be three years before shuttle astronauts could fix the problem. When they did, Freedman had new hope for the success of her hunt for the Hubble constant.

Her best chance was to find a Cepheid variable in the Virgo cluster, the nearest big cluster of galaxies to the Milky Way. If she could find a variable star in Virgo, Freedman thought, it would be more than twice as far as the most distant Cepheids then known and would make an ideal standard candle for measuring the Hubble constant.

The telescope was trained on the edge of the Virgo cluster at a spectacular spiral galaxy known as M100. With more than 100 billion stars, M100 can be viewed face-on through a telescope, its majestic swirling arms filled with bright blue clusters of hot, newborn stars and winding avenues of dust and gas.

The 30 members of the key project team honed in even closer on M100—on one of its outer arms laced with young massive stars. They pored over nearly three dozen exposures taken over a two-month period, searching for flickering Cepheids as if they were diamonds in a sunlit sea. It took the computers a month just to crunch the data and another month for the key project team to read through it all.

Most of the time Freedman woke at 3 a.m., and though she, her husband and their two young children lived just a mile and a half from Carnegie, she would boot up her computer at home, impatient to study new data.

On May 9, 1994—her daughter Rachel's birthday—Freedman saw stars that seemed to have that certain brightness.

"I remember sitting there and looking at my computer, and it was amazing. Not only were they there, they were beautiful. They were really high-accuracy, low-scatter, unmistakable Cepheid variables."

Like a nearsighted person finally putting on eyeglasses, Freedman had found what she was looking for, and by the time she and the team finished studying all the images from the Virgo cluster, they had 20 Cepheid variables—20 different standard candles that would help them nail down the Hubble constant.

"It's like when you're hiking and you're looking at some distant sight, or you're climbing and it just looks like you're never going to get there and you slog on, and you have nice times but you have hard times, too, and then suddenly you're at the top and you did it and it's exhilarating."

THE CONTRADICTION

By the summer of 1999, Freedman and her team had the answer that had eluded astronomers for 70 years. After more than 400 hours of observation time on the Hubble Space Telescope, after the sampling of 800 known and newly discovered Cepheids in two dozen galaxies over a swath of sky millions of light-years across, the Hubble constant was no longer a mystery. They had a number, and it was 72.

The universe, the team concluded, was expanding at a rate of 72 kilometers per second per megaparsec (3.26 million light-years) of distance. This means that two galaxies 3.26 million light-years apart are moving away from each other at an average of 160,000 miles per hour, and galaxies twice as far apart are moving away from each other at twice that speed.

Hubble constant in hand, Freedman's team was able to rewind the film of creation back nearly to the beginning of time. But when they did, they had a problem. The age of the universe appeared to be only 8 to 10 billion years old—younger than the generally accepted age of 14 billion years, younger even than some of the stars in our own galaxy.

Other astronomers, notably a team led by Allen Sandage, who works just down the hall from Freedman at Carnegie Observatories, had been making different kinds of measurements that fit with an appropriately older universe. But Freedman's team seemed to have the more commanding data—different methods of measurement, over a wider and more distant range of objects. So where was the error?

In the fall of 2001, two independent teams of astronomers, one led by Saul Perlmutter from the Lawrence Berkeley National Laboratory in Northern California, and another led by Brian Schmidt of Australia's Mount Stromlo Observatory, found an explanation.

There wasn't a miscalculation of the Hubble constant, the two astronomers concluded. Freedman's team simply didn't know that another, completely unexpected factor was affecting the expansion of the universe—something they simply called "dark energy," an inexplicable force continually working against gravity.

The universe wasn't just expanding, it was expanding at an accelerated rate, not slowing down as was previously thought.

The discovery astonished astronomers, but it helped clarify the age problem that arose with the Hubble constant. The new calculations showed that today's accelerating universe had taken a lot longer than 8 to 10 billion years to expand to its present size—14 billion years was back on the map.

There is some bad news, however. If dark energy continues to cause the hyperexpansion of space at its present rate, the fate of the universe appears horrifyingly grim.

Long after the sun has expended all its hydrogen, becoming bigger and hotter and turning the Earth into a cinder, stars and galaxies will speed away from each other. Eventually, vast stretches of black space will push the clusters so far apart that, for all intents and purposes, there will be no more starlit nights.

Galaxies will die, no new stars will be born and, right before the end, only black holes will fill the infinite darkness until even they are consumed, leaving, at the very end of time, pretty much nothing at all.

Said Michael Turner, a world-renowned cosmologist at the University of Chicago, last year: "We live in a preposterous universe....Dark energy. Who ordered that?"

The presence of dark energy wasn't a complete surprise. Ninety-five percent of the universe is a mystery. Only 5 percent of space is filled with known matter—stars, planets and interstellar gas and dust. Astronomers believe an additional 30 percent of the universe contains "dark," or unknown, matter—perhaps subatomic particles that have yet to be detected. The rest, a whopping 65 percent, is this dark, repulsive energy that works in opposition to gravity and is seemingly accelerating the universe into extinction.

THE INFLATION CHALLENGER

The discovery of dark energy had opened a window onto the future, and the view was staggeringly bleak. But could there be a different theory, a way of understanding the universe that told a different story?

It's exactly the kind of question Paul Steinhardt had been waiting his whole life to answer.

The path to the end of the universe, however, started with a question about the beginning.

The 49-year-old Princeton University physicist was an early contributor to inflation theory. First set forth in 1979 by Alan Guth, inflation says that the big bang was set in motion by a fluctuation in an energy field that suddenly and exponentially stretched the size of the universe in the first microsecond of creation.

Steinhardt provided some crucial refinements to inflation theory, for which he shared the prestigious Paul Dirac Medal in physics with Guth of the Massachusetts Institute of Technology and Andrei Linde of Stanford University earlier this year.

Ironically, Steinhardt is now taking dead aim at inflation. He is a rambunctious scientist, a muscular thinker who prefers the discomfort of nagging questions to the boredom of accepted theory.

"There was always a question in my mind that maybe we just haven't been imaginative enough to think of an alternative to inflation," says Steinhardt. "Probably because I was looking at inflation at close range, I also could see its flaws, incompleteness, and so I've always had my eye out for alternatives. I think that's the way as a theorist that you test an idea, to see how difficult it is to come up with an alternative."

Finding an alternative to inflation was no quick fix. It meant coming up with an entirely new, even revolutionary, model for the universe.

Eight months ago he and Neil Turok of Cambridge University, England, presented their new theory, dubbed the cyclic model, to the public. For Steinhardt in particular, the alternative had a significant advantage over inflation: It made dark energy the "good guy"—an infinite but ever-changing force that would endlessly expand and contract the universe. There would be no cosmic armageddon. The universe—or a series of different universes—would go on forever.

"Cosmology has this problem that we can't go back in time and actually see how things were. Our information is through a kind of fossil evidence, so it's always an issue whether you're interpreting that fossil evidence correctly. So you develop a good story—the big-bang inflation is a good story, and everything seems to fit in it. But how do you know it's the only story?"

Steinhardt began his search for a different story in 1998. First he looked at "brane theory," the branch of physics that suggests there are multiple universes, or membranes, existing in multiple dimensions. What if the big bang was simply a collision between two branes? And out there pushing them together was dark energy?

In cyclic theory, instead of inflation and big-bang expansion, universes undergo an endless sequence of cosmic epochs—bangs and crunches—that begin when two membranes collide like two weather systems slamming into one another to create two new ones.

"This assumes that time has no beginning," says Steinhardt, "or at least that the big bang is not the beginning; rather that the universe has gone through many stages of expansion and contraction."

The cosmological community is intrigued by the cyclic model but not altogether convinced. "It has a certain aesthetic attraction," says Arthur Kosowsky, a theoretical cosmologist at Rutgers, "in that you don't have to worry about what caused the big bang, which in the inflationary model is likely a question for metaphysics rather than science. Right now the cyclic model is very new. It seems likely that variants and subtleties will continue to be uncovered for a while."

Juan Maldacena, a theoretical physicist at the Institute for Advanced Study in Princeton, is more skeptical. "It's interesting, but it involves some assumptions that are less well motivated than the assumptions of inflationary theory. It is nice to have an alternative, but I would still bet my money on inflation."

WHERE EINSTEIN HESITATED

For Steinhardt, the cyclic model serves a dual purpose—it eliminates the question of what existed before the big bang, and it makes dark energy the force that causes branes to collide. "Expanding and contracting, heating and cooling, being highly dense to being highly under-dense: The best way to produce these features in the cyclic model is by using the physics of dark energy," says Steinhardt.

Dark energy made its first appearance as a hypothetical early in the 20th century. When Einstein was refining his general theory of relativity, he was forced to assume the existence of a mysterious force (which would later be called "dark energy") in order to keep gravity from causing the universe to contract. At the time, Einstein and nearly everyone else believed the universe to be static and essentially unmoving, so the father of relativity factored in what he called a "cosmological constant," represented by the Greek letter lambda, to balance gravity and keep the universe essentially unmoving.

Einstein, however, was never comfortable with his "fudge factor" and later, when Hubble discovered that in fact the universe was expanding, Einstein called the cosmological constant his biggest blunder.

But maybe it wasn't. Perlmutter and Schmidt brought Einstein's fudge factor back into the picture. How else to explain this repulsive, antigravitational force, this acceleration, that is trying to tear the universe apart?

There are two fundamentally different ways of viewing dark energy. Either it is like Einstein's cosmological constant and is woven into the fabric of space, or it is something that inhabits space and is more unpredictable.

Steinhardt believes the latter—that dark energy is actually an energy field that interacts with matter and can change in intensity. He calls this dark energy "quintessence."

Steinhardt considered different names for his particular explanation of dark energy—other scientists were independently calling it the "x-factor" and "funny energy." Finally he let his children select "quintessence" from among several of his own suggestions. Coined by Aristotle, quintessence means "fifth element." The ancient Greek philosopher believed that the universe was composed of four elements (earth, air, fire and water) and a fifth, ephemeral substance, called quintessence, which held the planets and stars in place.

The advantage of quintessence in scientists' calculations is that its energy varies. Early in the universe, when matter dominated, quintessence might have been weak, but with expansion it is now exerting a stronger force.

An energy that varies means the density of the universe is not fixed, nor is its fate. A universe propelled by quintessence is constantly changing, endlessly cycling through periods of expansion and contraction.

Most cosmologists feel forced to choose among three very different futures for the universe:

■ A future where the universe speeds off into nothingness because it is too light—that is, there is not enough matter exerting a gravitational pull to hold it together.

■ A future where the universe collapses back onto itself in a big crunch because there is too much matter exerting a gravitational pull.

■ A future where the universe expands infinitely but

ever more slowly, because its weight is perfectly balanced against expansion.

In Steinhardt's cyclic theory, all three scenarios play a part.

The weight of his "multiverse" is always changing, as universes bang, crunch and then bang again.

"I think the quintessence model is economical," says Marcelo Gleiser, an astrophysicist at Dartmouth College. "It gives us a way to show how dark energy can evolve and change....Of course, we still need to find the facts that justify it. But so goes theoretical physics. Often ideas precede observations."

THE LURE OF DISCOVERING

The fact that Steinhardt is proposing an entirely new way of viewing the universe—when no one else is really looking for one—is just part of his nature, he says. Big questions need big answers, and he wants to be in the middle of the battle to find them.

The son of an Army lawyer who died when Steinhardt was only 9, he spent the first few years of his life on the move. After settling in Miami with his mother and siblings, Steinhardt quickly took up math and science.

"I remember my father used to tell me these very dramatic stories of people like Madame Curie and all that and about moments of discovery," says Steinhardt as he sits drinking yet another cup of coffee in his office at Jadwin Hall at Princeton. "And ever since then, I thought that was just a wonderful thing, to be the first person to know something, which is the greatest fun in doing science—that moment when you think you know something important that no one else knows."

Steinhardt studied particle physics as an undergraduate at the California Institute of Technology and as a graduate student at Harvard University. It was at Harvard that Steinhardt, as a physics post-doc, happened to attend a weekly visitor's lecture in which Guth was the guest speaker, talking about inflation.

"That's really how I got into cosmology," says Steinhardt. "And I always thought that his talk was the most exciting and the most depressing talk I ever went to. Ninety percent of it was about how inflation solved so many questions about the universe, and then the last 10 percent was how, unfortunately, once inflation takes hold it never ends."

Laughing, Steinhardt says: "I thought, well, I'll spend a few weeks and try to see if I can find a way around this problem."

It was more like a year and a half, and when he did find a solution, he was hooked on cosmology. What better place than the universe to seek out new discoveries and find answers to age-old questions?

"Cyclic theory is an attempt at a better theory....My goal is to explain as much data, with as powerful a theory, as possible....That's what drives me."

The attraction of quintessence for the nonscientist is its hopefulness. If dark energy is a cosmological constant, then it will never change and the universe will expand forever until all that is left is a vacuum. But if dark energy is quintessence or something like it, then the universe could one day decelerate or contract and be spared its gloomy fate.

"Quintessence is just a much more exciting and appealing interpretation of what the dark energy is," Steinhardt says. "It's something really, really important. It's not just important for the future, it's important for the whole story."

Steinhardt doesn't know yet how to measure quintessence.

More than most, however, he understands that science is a cerebral ballet of leaps between the known and unknown, between truth and possibility, and that it is the capacity for wonder that inspires the dance.

"Thought is a flash between two long nights," wrote 19th-century mathematician Henri Poincaré, "but this flash is everything."

For Steinhardt, it is thought that creates the story of the universe, a story that astronomer Wendy Freedman continues to read in the stars. The numbers at the heart of the story are almost within reach.

Like all scientists, Steinhardt and Freedman are seekers. Curiosity is stitched into their genes, and the search for ultimate answers is fueled by their uncertainty.

"The goal is to get these secrets out of nature," says Steinhardt. "Whatever it takes."

A conversation with
Amy Ellis Nutt

CHRISTOPHER SCANLAN: Where did the idea for "The Seekers" come from?

AMY ELLIS NUTT: Somewhere on Route 95 south between Wilmington, Del., and Baltimore, Md. I was working on a story about a 180-year-old mystery that involved buried treasure and numerical ciphers that people have been trying to solve for nearly two centuries. I was interviewing everyone from a professional cryptographer to a treasure dowser, and there was one thing common to all of these people: tremendous passion for solving a mystery. I was also listening to an NPR story about people looking for the ivory-billed woodpecker, thought to be extinct, that some people believe has been heard in the last few years deep in the Louisiana swamp. The idea that it might still be around has compelled these people to spend enormous amounts of time in these horrendous swamps. The idea of the search crystallized at that moment, a series about seekers: people who have a passion to find an answer. The series evolved from there.

At first I was considering people doing everything from searching for a nearly extinct bird to the detective who has been searching for the missing person for the last 30 years. Through conversations with editors, it developed into more mainstream kinds of searches. That was when my philosophical background kicked in. I did a little more digging and reading and realized that some of the big questions that I had studied in philosophy are now being tackled by scientists. I thought it would be a perfect combination of deep thinking and great science and the people who are looking for answers to things that previously were considered unaskable.

Can you talk a bit about these conversations?

I have terrific editors here who are used to me coming up to them saying, "I have this fabulous idea." They're very patient with me. They listen and don't dismiss when I have trouble formulating an idea, because it takes some time. They encouraged me to write up more specifically what kind of people I would like to write about, and I did that. Fran Dauth, the managing editor, suggested that a story about people who have this tremendous passion would be better served if I found people who were less on the fringes of life and more serious about their pursuit. I went with that. I've always had an interest in popular science and, in particular, physics. Questions about philosophy often cross over into questions about physics and the nature of the universe.

It sounds like you and your editors are collaborators.

Yes, very much so. I have great respect for them and I know they do for me, and they give me a lot of latitude. I get to write for virtually any section of the newspaper, which is pretty damn cool. The head of the newspaper, Jim Willse, was a fan of this from the beginning. He was just really intrigued with this idea, and he thought, "Hmm, something explanatory. Well, why not explain everything?" With that kind of enthusiasm I felt very positive. They basically left me alone to develop it after we nailed down the topics and the approach.

I realized early on that this stuff was so cerebral that I really needed to wed the ideas to the people in the story. That's why it's called "The Seekers," not "The Questions" or even "The Answers." Because to me it's about the people who have this passion, who are looking for these answers, as much as it is about the questions they're trying to answer. And I knew that was what people would relate to.

Everyone has, if you're lucky, something in your life that you have a passion for, and it doesn't matter if you're a Little League manager or an astrophysicist. I knew that the way to tell the stories of these rather abstract fields was to tell it through the voices of these people, and to bring in their whole lives. I very much wanted to know why these people became seekers and how they were formed and how their current pursuits were formed by their past experiences.

Often with projects, reporters have an idea and they

go off and start digging and they collect a mound of stuff, and then they have to fight their way through it. It sounds like you and your editors really did a lot of focusing up front. Is that a correct observation?

Yes, I think so. I do enormous amounts of research. I just love that aspect of reporting. I love to make myself a mini-expert, and I knew I obviously needed to do that for this project. I knew I had to really nail down what questions I was going to look at and specifically how each of these people was approaching these questions. I concentrated on the kind of work that each of these people was involved in. And I wanted each story to have two people. I wanted to have one who was more of a theoretician and one who was more of an experimental person, or at least to have two people taking two different approaches. That was all very specific and was very planned out ahead of time. Once all that was nailed down—I did a tremendous amount of reading and research before each interview and then did the interview.

The writing actually was the easiest part of the whole thing. I spent exactly two weeks writing each of the articles and gave myself that much time and finished it on time, which I think surprised everyone.

If I had to identify one hallmark of these stories, it is authority. Where does that authority come from?

I think that my lack of intimidation about taking on the universe probably has to do with my background in philosophy. I have a graduate degree in it, and it's one of my first loves. I remember specifically walking up the steps out of the basement cafeteria at St. Bernard's Grammar School in Plainfield, N.J. I was in the fifth grade and I was thinking to myself, "What would there be if there were nothing?" I was already deeply attracted to the paradoxical and, I suppose, the cosmic at a very early age. And poetry has been always my first love. It was what I wrote as a child, then as an adolescent and in college. When I realized I probably was not going to become a famous American poet, I became an academic. But I have a deep and abiding love of poetry, both the reading and the writing of it. I didn't realize until actually working on the series how much that would come to bear in the ability to describe and to use imagery to convey a thought.

I give tremendous credit to Jim Willse, who said one thing that guided me through all this. Before I'd written a line and even done any interviews, he said, "This series will rise or fall on your ability to make analogies." And I said, "Yeah. I can't wait." And that's really what poetry is: It's about analogies, it's about metaphor, it's about making the abstract graspable.

I think all of those things served me well—my love of poetry and the use of imagery in description in trying to convey thoughts, and the love of philosophy and big ideas and trying to get to the bottom of something.

How did you become enough of an expert—not only to be able to understand the material, but to be able to make it clear to people who don't know a red shift from a Red Bull?

I had taken one astronomy course in college. I've been reading this stuff actually on my own for so long, and I'm a great fan of everyone from Oliver Sacks to Alan Guth. I've always been addicted to *Scientific American* and *Discover* magazines.

Background reading lists accompany each story. Is that what you read to get up to speed?

Actually, they list just a fraction of what I read. I started subscribing to *Astronomy* magazine and *Science News* and literally raided bookstores and libraries for every book they had on the beginning of the universe. I read academic papers online. I asked everyone I interviewed where I should go from there, what things I should read of theirs, as well as what other things I should read. That was a great help.

How did you identify the people you wrote about?

It's one of those things that I could never have done before the advent of the computer and the Internet. I would spend hours online going from one site to another and one reference would take me to another link, to another link trying to find out who were the people who were mentioned and who were more prominent. I didn't want to interview Stephen Hawking. I wanted to interview the people who were seminal but whom others had really not heard of—people who are quietly working, quietly seeking answers. Of course, as a reporter for a New Jersey newspaper, I was looking to see if I could find some New Jersey people.

I was enormously lucky. I spent probably two months just finding the people to interview—people who are on the cutting edge and who are doing really great science, but people who I could sense seemed to be particularly passionate about one thing and who had stuck with it for a long time. For example, Wendy Freedman. Despite all the problems with the Hubble telescope, she's worked on finding this Hubble constant for years.

You can tell a little bit on the phone, but not until you really meet them and look at them, do you know if they're the kind of people you've been looking for. I lucked out in every single case. They were all wonderfully gracious in giving me so much of their time, but it was a little bit of magic that all of these people were just the right people to tell the stories and that they had such interesting beginnings.

Did you go in with a lot of questions prepared?

Yes and no. In my head, I knew everything I wanted to ask and I had a few notes and often I had material with me that I wanted to ask them about, but I didn't usually have to open it up. It's funny. You get to a point at which you've read so much and you think you know this person sort of inside out. I didn't really need to write anything down. I knew just what I wanted to ask them.

Was it hard to get the scientists to talk about the beginning of their passion?

It sometimes took a little coaxing. Wendy Freedman was very shy, but she had some great moments and she really does have sort of a sparkle in her eye. All of them had great stories. It's amazing. When I asked each one of them, "Was there a moment, a time in your life, when it sort of all came together for you, when you realized what you wanted to do?" almost all of them had a moment. Wendy Freedman said it was out on the lake looking at the stars with her father. Almost all of them had that, and it was beautiful.

So is there a moment when that passion began for you?

I think I have those moments all the time. You have that interview with someone that's, "Wow! That was so good!" And this person just blows you away for one reason or another. I think the first time I had it was when I was in journalism school. We had to do an art story in our neighborhood. I went to an outdoor sculpture park and spent the day out there, and the first person I ran into was just an ordinary, blue-collar guy walking through the sculpture park. In talking to him I realized that here was a pretty ordinary guy who had a deeply artistic soul, and he probably didn't even know it, but something drew him to that spot.

And that was the moment that I realized, "Forget fiction. Life! Real life has the most wonderful stories!" Life unfolds like a novel in so many ways. Everybody has a story. You don't need to make it up. You just need to look for them and ask questions.

How did you organize your material?

I kept an 8-by-10 notebook in which I had sections. I had one where I wanted quotes and references to the topics in general, anything I found that was related to people who are seeking things. And then I had sections for each of the topics that were devoted to books I should be reading.

When I was writing each topic, I went back and looked at particular quotes and things I thought exemplified it. Or if I had an idea of an image, I would write it down so I could keep track as I was going. That one notebook was huge. That was sort of my outline, my guide.

When did you know you were ready to write?

I had a teacher once at J-school who said that you should

never leave an interview unless you know what your
lead is going to be, and I kind of extend that. I usually
don't leave an interview until I know what my lead and
my kicker are going to be. As I was listening to these interviews, I knew certain things were going to be crucial
images. I was already thinking in images and similes and
analogies as they were talking. So for instance, in "Genesis," [included on the CD-ROM] when Chuck Bennett
talked about the fingerprint, I thought, "That's going to be
huge." I would listen for words or phrases or smaller concepts in the interviews that would enable me to tell the
bigger story. I knew those were the things that I would
have to use early on. And I'm pretty sure that I didn't
leave any of those interviews until I knew where I would
begin their stories, and I think I knew my initial leads.

**Each lead takes an almost cosmic view of the subject.
Why did you choose to open each story that way?**

Anecdotal leads weren't the way to begin. These were
such big ideas that I had to begin with leads that presented
the idea. These stories had such huge scope that I felt I
needed to tell the reader right up front, "This is really
big." But I also needed to tell readers why they were going to care about it. So that's why, for instance, in talking
about the universe in "Genesis," I made the connection to
the fact that every element, every part of who we are and
everything around us, essentially our chemical structure,
comes from the birth of the universe. So in case they were
thinking, "Why do I care?" I was trying to tell them they
should care because we're all really deeply and intimate-
ly connected with the universe.

**Were you conscious of the ever-present threat of los-
ing a reader?**

That was where I had great advice from my editors, like
"I think you should cut to the chase here faster and do
less on this." I took their advice every single time because I knew that it was going to be easy to lose people.
And that was also why it was important to me to have
personal aspects of these people's lives in there because
it also lightened the heaviness of the story.

Analogies pepper these stories. Why did you use them and what's your process for writing them?

I was following the mantra of Jim Willse when he said that success would ride on my ability to make analogies. I try to visualize. When I was reading about how free radicals just kind of trail away and get lost, I visualized that in my head and I saw things kind of flying out. I thought of something moving fast and something being lost, and the image of money flying out the back of a Brink's truck popped into my head.

That's what you do in poetry. It's an abstract idea, but you have to visualize it. You have to describe it. You look for iconic imagery. I sometimes tell this to writers. When you feel kind of dried up, sometimes just reading poetry frees your mind to think of forming images. I think it's great to read books about writing and it's great to read novels and it's great to read great nonfiction writing, but poets are unique in their ability to use a modicum in terms of language and yet have acuity of description.

Is that something that happened as you were drafting the story?

Most often it was while I was writing. Sometimes I'd have to stop and think, "How do I visualize that? How do I say that?" But I often thought of analogies while I was driving to work. I have notebooks under the visor, in the side pocket, and in the glove compartment.

Parallelisms seem to be another hallmark of your writing. For instance, in "Defying the Years" [included on the CD-ROM] you write, "Three days a week, he takes pictures of kidneys, lungs and hearts, looking for signs of disease. Two days a week, when he has willing subjects, he takes pictures of the brains of deeply religious people, looking for signs of God."
Are you conscious of using parallel structure?

That's just ingrained in me. It was also something editors Susan Olds and Rosemary Parrillo reminded me to do, which is to make it as easy on the reader as possible. The concepts we were dealing with were going to be hard enough, so make it easier on the ear and the eye to follow. And it's easier to follow if you show a tighter connection, if you write in parallel, write in analogies, because you have to with this kind of a story. You're not making it *simple-minded*, you're just making it simple and digestible.

How many revisions did the stories go through?

There were minor things in each where they wanted me to clarify something or add something, but there wasn't a whole lot of tinkering with the first three. Most of the major tinkering was with the final two.

Do you read your work aloud?

I think that's just absolutely critical. I was taught that very early on, and I try to do it with everything. It's hard to do sometimes on deadline or you're in the newsroom when you're saying something out loud. It's especially important, I think, with a lead. It's music. You have to hit the right notes to get the person to listen.

Each part of this series was accompanied by arresting graphics and photos. What you were trying to achieve with these elements?

I'm one of those firm believers that when people are looking at a newspaper, they look at the art and the photos first. If they find them interesting, they're going to read the article.

How did you collaborate with the project's visual journalists?

Andre Malok was the designer of the art that appears on the cover of each one. I gave him the leads to all of my stories and I would tell him a little bit about the people. He wanted to know some key ideas or phrases, and I would give him a little bit of background about the people and the images they used when they talked to me. So I was kind of thinking in visual terms, too. For instance, Charles Bennett spoke about how he was looking for the fingerprint of the universe, and so I knew that was something I should tell Andre. Then he used that analogy. I gave him the Hubble constant equation as something he might want to work into his art, and we collaborated on the glossaries that appear with the stories.

Did this work help your stories?

First of all, I think it helped the reader because I think it grabbed the reader. Andre's illustrations were beautiful representations of the things I was going to hit on in each of those stories, and he was visualizing the metaphors. Chuck Bennett was looking for the finger-print of the universe in the temperature, in the cosmic background radiation, and that's what I get from look-ing at Andre's illustrations. I think for me—and I think maybe for the reader, too—it's the way he captures the cosmic quality of all these questions.

What is it about the *The Star-Ledger* that made this series possible?

I credit Jim Willse. He's a guy who likes to push the en-velope, and he really brings that to the newspaper. He has made this a very special place to work by allowing writers the freedom to do the kinds of things we do.

Do you think newspapers should do more of this?

Absolutely. I believe that most people are fundamentally curious about themselves and about the universe and about what it all means, and basically that's what the series was. It was, "What does it all mean?" And as heady a question as that is, I think it's something that we all think about, and I think there's a hunger for that.

What are the kinds of things you think newspapers could tackle?

I think a newspaper could tackle anything. Why does *Discover* magazine have to write about evolution? I have an idea about writing about evolution from the as-pect of a butterfly and the patterns on a butterfly's wings. If you can tell the story in the right way, I think someone is going to relate to it. I don't think there should be any limits. I think you can tell stories that now only appear in science magazines or philosophy journals. And I think the response from some of the readers we had to the series was very much proof of that. I heard from a number of teachers and academics and people like that, but I also heard from retired Newark cops. My brother, who works at Merrill Lynch, passed a security guard one day who had one day of the series open and he was highlighting it. That kind of thing was the most satisfying aspect of this.

You write that these fields of science are "historically dominated by testosterone." Did you make a conscious decision to be diverse?

Yeah, I definitely did.

How successful were you?

I think I was pretty successful. It would have been nice to have someone of color and maybe at least one other woman. I think you're always conscious of that. I think no matter what your topic, a journalist is always conscious of trying to get diversity because I think readers look for that. I didn't ever set out to find a woman physicist. But when things would lead me to someone who was a woman, I would pay particular attention. And as it happened, I think I lucked out in the couple of women I did find.

What was the biggest challenge of doing the series?

The hardest part was with the last two, with talking about concepts that even scientists will admit are fundamentally incomprehensible. It's tough to get your head around those kinds of concepts, and so the biggest challenge was trying to make very foreign ideas, such as a universe that's flat and infinite, acceptable to a reader and understandable to a reader, and those were definitely the hardest parts of the series.

And how did you overcome them?

Jim was a great help on those last two because he would say, "I just don't quite get infinity here and the way you use it. Can you describe it in another way?" And I would go over it different ways and think of different analogies, and we would just go back and forth on that until he said, "Okay, I understand it." He was the primary sounding board on those last two for the concepts that were the most difficult, about the shape of the universe and the fate of the universe.

What advice would you give other writers trying to write about a complicated subject so people can understand it?

The most obvious, do your homework. I mean just read everything you can and take good notes and use multi-colored Post-it Notes and pens. They really helped me. I had a key above me at all times—what color was which topic just in case I kept forgetting. Purple was the end of the universe; green was immortality; pink was the search for the self. Each topic had a color Post-it Note and pen color, so anything I underlined or highlighted or posted I knew what it meant and knew where to go to find it.

The other thing I would say is, if you're going to write about a complicated subject and spend a lot of time on it, first of all be sure that it's something that you're really interested in and you're really curious about, because that's the best way to approach something. And get to know the people who are working on those things because they'll give you the best insight, and they're the ones who can tell the story best. You're sort of telling their story secondhand.

And keep it simple and try to visualize things for the reader. Try to think of those visual analogies because you're trying to make it as easy as you can for the reader to understand without making it simple-minded.

How did this experience of reporting and writing this series change you? Or affect you?

I have to say it was so enjoyable to do that I was often up in the middle of night. I would often get out of bed at 5,

5:30 because I just wanted to start reading or writing. Sometimes I was at the newsroom at 6, 6:30. I just loved coming to it every day. I don't think I needed to be infused again with the idea of what joy there is in journalism and in just seeking to know things, but it was absolutely re-affirmed in this because, to me, there's nothing more pleasurable than learning about something. You go and talk to someone and you see the passion in their life and it just reinforces the passion you have in yours. Talking to these people was just so inspiring because I felt a kinship with what they were doing, and I felt a great privilege in being able to write about what they do and to write about their particular passions. But it was also a great pleasure because I identified with all of it. And it just reinforced in me this feeling that there is just so much in the world to write about.

I always used to think that the most fanciful stories were in fiction, but they're not. They're in real life. Everybody has a story to tell. Everybody does. And sometimes it's an unexpected story and sometimes it's a story you don't think is going to move you. But I think and I hope that the stories of these people on the questions that they were working on moved people. They moved me. As someone who likes to tackle the big ideas, these are people who are spending their professional lives tackling big ideas and not letting go; and there's something to be learned about the human spirit, whether it's in someone recovering from an illness or someone who is looking to figure out how the universe is going to end. They both reflect universal themes about the human condition. It just reinforces in me that I have the best job in the world, and I can't imagine anyone wanting to do anything else other than be a reporter.

Writers' Workshop

1) To make the complex scientific subjects of "The Seekers" accessible to readers, Amy Ellis Nutt repeatedly relied on the analogy, a rhetorical device that explains the unfamiliar by comparing it to something familiar.

For instance, to describe the result when cell structures known as mitochondria steal electrons from oxygen molecules in order to function more smoothly, Nutt wrote, "Like money flying out the back of a Brink's truck careening around a corner, these misplaced electrons—now called free radicals—scatter around the insides of cells, bonding indiscriminately with other molecules."

Find other examples of analogies in the series and then discuss how analogies aid the reader. What are the pitfalls of using such a device?

2) In *Language in Thought and Action*, a classic linguistics text, S.I. Hayakawa described an "abstraction ladder" that grouped general statements on the top rungs and descriptive ones on the bottom. Some teachers argue that the best writing travels up and down this ladder, alternating abstractions with concrete examples to effectively convey information, "showing" as well as "telling." Consider how "The Seekers" explains complicated material about philosophical and scientific mysteries by using the detailed stories of scientists who are trying to solve them. How and why does it make this challenging material easier to grasp?

3) In "Defying the Years," Nutt describes a dietary supplement developed and marketed by scientist Bruce Ames. The formula had a stunning effect on laboratory animals; in his words, "These old rats got up and did the Macarena." One *Star-Ledger* editor questioned the ethics of including information about the supplement in the story, in effect providing free advertising. Nutt felt leaving it out would omit important information especially because she also reported Ames's financial stake and that "the two nutrients just as easily can be purchased separately at any health food store." Argue the ethics of including information about the supplement in the story. Identify the stakeholders, those who would be affected by the decision to publish or not.

4) Nutt argues that newspapers can—and should—tackle lofty subjects such as those explored in "The Seekers." "Why does *Discover* magazine have to write about evolution?...I think you can tell stories that now only appear in science magazines or philosophy journals." What do you think? With your colleagues or classmates, brainstorm a list of stories that would address other mysteries of life.

Assignment Desk

1) To get approval for "The Seekers," Nutt had to write and rewrite a "pitch" to her editors, a detailed proposal that described her reporting and writing plan. For each story, Nutt identified the question she sought to answer along with the individuals she planned to profile and sketched the shape of the story, including the leads she planned to use. The advance work was so detailed, Nutt says she didn't even use an outline for any of these stories.

Report and write a one- to two-page pitch for an ambitious story you'd like to undertake. Do enough research so you can write a prospective lead and nut graph that sums up the story's theme and outline the reporting that will be required.

2) Nutt's editor, James Willse, told her that "The Seekers'" success would ride on the ability to make analogies. Look for opportunities to employ analogies in your work. Find a complicated process on your beat and draw an analogy that makes the unfamiliar familiar to a reader.

3) To understand the value of Hayakawa's "abstraction ladder," group the concepts of each story in "The Seekers" at the top of the abstraction ladder and the concrete examples that Nutt employs to help the reader understand them. Do the same for one of your stories. Where on Hayakawa's ladder would you place the information in your stories? Do your stories travel up and down the ladder or clump at the top or bottom? For instance, does a story about a rash of burglaries in a neighborhood report statistics but also include the experiences of crime victims—the theft of a family heirloom or a big-screen TV that was a birthday gift?

4) Nutt included a list of books and websites, drawn from the voluminous research she did for "The Seekers." The next time you produce a story that requires extensive reading and research, give your readers the benefit of a selected bibliography.

The Dallas Morning News

Barry Horn

Finalist, Non-Deadline Writing

Barry Horn writes sports for *The Dallas Morning News.* He is a New York native with a bachelor's degree from New York University and a master's degree in journalism from Northwestern.

Horn, 48, is in his second stint at the *Morning News.* He started his sportswriting career at *The Miami Herald* in 1978, then moved to Dallas in 1981, working at the *Morning News* for five years. He then spent three years at the Fort Worth *Star-Telegram* before returning to Dallas in 1989.

Since 1979, his feature and enterprise stories have won numerous national and regional awards from the Associated Press Sports Editors, the Associated Press Managing Editors of Texas, the Texas Daily Newspaper Association, and the Press Club of Dallas.

Horn and his wife, Sharon, have three children: Zachary, 17, Alex, 14, and Grace, 8.

In "A Father Who Pushed Too Far," Horn treads the tender ground of explaining a family story that seemed destined for a bad ending. His use of scenes, anecdotes, and telling details delivers for readers the evidence to back up the story's premise that nothing could be less surprising than the way this family's march to tragedy would culminate.

A father who pushed too far

SEPTEMBER 15, 2002

NORTH RICHLAND HILLS—It was a throwaway line at the end of a chance meeting in a faraway place involving a college football coach, a father and his 13-year-old son.

Just something nice to say to the father of just another kid whom the coach vaguely remembered from a Texas Christian University summer camp five months earlier.

Had the boy not worn a Horned Frogs football cap to lunch that day, the coach would not have struck up the conversation over Christmas vacation in 1991.

"If your boy keeps his head on straight, he's going to have a great future," the coach told the father in parting.

Some fathers might have taken the line as simple positive reinforcement for a skinny eighth-grader before returning to the business of the meal.

Others might have been content to thump their chests for a day or two before returning to reality.

And then there was Bill Butterfield, for whom the coach's words were an epiphany, a Rocky Mountain revelation right there in Brown's Country Store in the tiny Colorado resort town of South Fork.

This father saw it as the first step on his return to athletic glory.

All along, Mr. Butterfield had focused his energies on making a baseball player out of his oldest son, Billy, while ignoring his younger boy. But as hard as Mr. Butterfield tried, that plan hadn't worked.

AN EPIPHANY

Now, an alternative stood before him—young Lance.

Lance was fast. He had sure hands. He was tough. He loved to play all sports.

Unlike Billy, he always enjoyed working out.

And Lance, 10 years younger than his brother, was still devoutly obedient.

Maybe it had been prescient for Mr. Butterfield's wife to have named their second son for her favorite football player, Lance Alworth, a Hall of Fame wide receiver.

"Bill had always been very serious with the boys when it came to sports," says Kathy Butterfield, Lance's mother.

"But that meeting, that conversation, triggered something even more in him."

Family friend Wade Parkey, who also witnessed the vacation conversation with the coach, says he tried for hours to convince his best friend that the TCU assistant was simply being polite.

But Mr. Butterfield already had heard all he wanted to hear.

"And after that," Mr. Parkey says, "nothing in Lance's life would ever be the same."

In the remaining 4-1/2 years of his life, Bill Butterfield, whose own football playing days ended in high school, did everything in his power to transform Lance into a football star.

He was so obsessed with realizing his dream that he made Earl Woods, Richard Williams and Marv Marinovich, America's poster parents for building children Tiger, Venus, Serena and Todd into athletic superstars, seem like disinterested observers.

Eventually, his obsession cost him his life.

"True, our kids need us to teach them basic skills, determination and how to compete," says Dr. Michael Arambula, a forensic psychiatrist at the University of Texas Health Science Center in San Antonio who would come to know the Butterfield family.

"But they don't need us to fulfill some unfulfilled need of the parent. Bill went ahead and provided the structure and discipline for Lance to excel, but he way overdid it. So many parents overdo it.

"Fortunately, very few go as far as Bill did."

THE REGIMEN BEGINS

Almost immediately upon the family's return from Colorado, Mr. Butterfield imposed his own strict training regimen on Lance.

He prescribed the boy's diet.

Mornings, he would provide a fistful of vitamins and supplements for the boy to shovel into his mouth.

Evenings, he insisted the boy pour weight-gaining shakes down his throat.

Eventually, Mr. Butterfield began checking the boy's bowel movements to determine whether Lance had eaten any foods he had banned from the boy's diet.

And father fed his son steroids.

Mr. Butterfield concocted his own remedies for injuries without regard to what professional trainers and doctors had to say.

Father isolated his son from friends.

Girls, father decided, were nothing more than distractions.

To ensure that nothing escaped his watchful eyes, father attended every one of his son's high school football practices. To keep up with Lance's schedule, Mr. Butterfield simply stopped going to work at the family-owned mattress business.

After games, when teammates celebrated victories or lamented defeats together, Mr. Butterfield insisted Lance spend hours reviewing his play on homemade videotapes.

To keep close tabs on whatever social life Lance managed to piece together, his father simply got into his red GMC pickup truck or rented a car to shadow him.

"To say that Bill became obsessed with every aspect of Lance's life would be an understatement," Mrs. Butterfield says wearily, after rattling off the laundry list of examples.

"He was intent on living it for Lance."

'THE PERFECT BOY'

The skinny kid did indeed grow into an outstanding defensive back at Richland High School. Lance blossomed into a 6-foot-2, 180-pound free safety who also played second base on the baseball team and ran the 400 meters in track.

The boy also brought home A's on his report card, was a "yes sir, no sir" member of a Christian youth group, and was selected to the homecoming court.

Whereas Mr. Butterfield's high school peers in the late 1960s had nicknamed him "Butt" for his hardheaded ways, Lance's friends called their more gentle buddy "Butter."

"Lance was the perfect boy, the kind parents dream of having," Mr. Parkey says.

But it wasn't good enough.

Colleges showed no scholarship interest in Mr. Butterfield's boy.

Maybe that's why soon after Lance's senior football season for the Richland Rebels in 1995, Mr. Butterfield asked his oldest son to cut him a piece of wood to use as a paddle. Billy ignored the request.

"Again, it was one of those things I blew off. I'm sorry I wasn't curious to ask the reasoning behind it," Billy said.

FREQUENT BEATINGS

Undaunted, Mr. Butterfield bought a pair of paddleball rackets and wrapped them tightly with heavy black duct tape.

Every day after school, father would wale away at Lance's buttocks.

"This is because you didn't get the…[expletive] beat out of you enough when you were younger," was Mr. Butterfield's mantra between blows. "You gonna be a mama's boy and cry?"

Lance never shed a tear. Instead, he promised himself he would try harder to please his father.

When Mrs. Butterfield tried to say something or interfere, she was treated to a profanity-laced tirade that often was complemented by a shove or a forearm.

The beatings went on for about a month.

On Dec. 27, 1995, Lance went on yet another morning run mandated by his father.

Not that he wanted to go. He told his father he wasn't feeling well. But his father insisted.

And so the ever-dutiful Lance ran.

Along the way, he stopped and invited a former girlfriend to join him.

The two had broken up on Mr. Butterfield's orders. The relationship, the father was convinced, had hurt Lance's performance on the football field early in his senior season.

Still, ex-boyfriend and ex-girlfriend ran together for about a mile before she peeled off to return home.

As he rounded the corner, heading home for the final

few hundred yards, Lance spotted Mr. Butterfield sitting in the red pickup in the driveway. Lance guessed his father had either already followed him or was about to set out to find his wayward son.

"Seeing him sitting in the driveway triggered so many memories," Lance says.

"I wasn't thinking of sports. I saw my mom being pushed around....I saw my older brother and his family who lived a block away avoiding our house....I saw my family wasn't a family anymore....I saw misery."

Back in the house, Mr. Butterfield told Lance he was going to shower.

While his father headed down the hall to the bathroom, Lance headed in the opposite direction to the kitchen.

As the water began streaming, Lance pulled out of a drawer a .38-caliber revolver the family kept and retreated to the closet in his bedroom.

For a few moments the son just sat there pondering his fate. Lance prayed that his father would not come looking for him armed with another rant before sending him off to another day's work at the family's mattress company.

"I just didn't want to talk to him," Lance says.

But Mr. Butterfield, wrapped only in a towel, walked into Lance's room—an all-too-recognizable mask crossing his face. The eyes were bulging. The familiar frontal vein protruded from his forehead.

As usual, the father had questions. Lance braced himself for another cross-examination.

Why, father wanted to know, was the boy still home and not yet on his way to work?

And what was that the boy appeared to be hiding behind his back?

The son explained he was just waiting to use the shower himself. As for what was behind his back, "nothing," Lance said.

A LIFE FOREVER CHANGED

As the father turned to leave the boy's bedroom, the son brought the .38 around, closed his eyes and pulled the trigger.

The bullet struck the father in the back.

"I'm sorry, Dad," Lance said.

As Mr. Butterfield turned to plead for help, the son closed his eyes once more and fired again.

The second bullet lodged in the father's forehead, forever ending the abuse and replacing one agony with another.

Lance, who never had been in trouble with the law, was thrust into a different hell. Filled with remorse, he plodded through the Texas criminal justice system.

At first, Lance told police there had been an intruder. But it wasn't long before he admitted shooting his father.

Eventually, he would be charged with murder, convicted of manslaughter and sentenced to prison.

"I don't want people to think what happened is right," Lance says 6-1/2 years later, momentarily staring into space while sitting at the kitchen table in his family home, 50 feet from where the gun exploded.

That's how discussions with Lance seem to go when the subject turns to his father. He relives scenes.

The tape in his head starts and stops. He dissects every frame.

"Always," he says, "there are a lot of what-ifs."

ATHLETIC ADDICTION

Lance's life might have been hell had he never touched a football or lifted a bat or taken a jump shot. His father might have become consumed with some other aspect of his son's life.

"Lance was a kid taught to follow the rules," says Paul Mones, a Portland, Ore., attorney who specializes in parricide cases and was part of Lance's defense team. "He was a good kid who fulfilled his father's wishes to a T."

Mr. Butterfield's older sister, Dianna Forsythe, says her brother had been a "control freak" since his high school days.

Sports, however, was the natural umbilical cord between father and son.

"Bill had an addiction to making his son a superstar because in his mind he got screwed out of being one himself," says Mr. Parkey, the best friend who had been Bill's classmate since junior high and friend since high school.

Mr. Butterfield had been a standout running back at

Carter-Riverside High. When he was banned from playing his senior season, it made headlines in Fort Worth.

Kathy Adams, his cheerleader girlfriend since their sophomore year, was pregnant.

Bill and Kathy did what most kids did under those circumstances in 1967. They got married.

But the rule at Carter-Riverside was unforgiving: Married students could not play varsity sports.

And so Mr. and Mrs. Butterfield transferred to Fort Worth Christian for their senior year. Bill's football career ended at year's end.

After graduation, the new father stayed at the school to help coach football.

College was out of the question.

To support his family, Mr. Butterfield reluctantly went into his father's disposable rag business.

"I don't know what Bill resented more, having to marry his pregnant girlfriend or having to work for his father," Mrs. Butterfield says.

AN OBSESSION

In the ensuing years, Mr. Butterfield seemed to derive his greatest joy from teaching Billy how to play sports.

Father taught son baseball, football and basketball and was involved in coaching all of his teams.

When Billy started to play Little League baseball during second grade, his father devised a rigorous daily workout routine around a new swing set.

Then it was on to a nearby park. Father pitched. Son swung. Mother and sister Sandy, who came along three years after Billy, scrambled to collect the balls.

When Billy did something his father didn't like, Mr. Butterfield wouldn't hesitate to throw a ball at his head.

If Billy's team played two games a week, Mr. Butterfield would reserve a field for practice on a third day.

"Baseball," Mrs. Butterfield says, "was our life."

It was about the time that Billy finished elementary school that Mr. Butterfield built a batting cage in the back yard.

Billy was supposed to go to junior high school in Haltom City, but Mr. Butterfield didn't like the coaching situation there, so he transferred him to a school in

North Richland Hills.

Billy grew into an all-district second baseman at Richland High School. He went on to play junior college baseball in Colorado. But that was the end of the line.

When Billy told his father he was placing marriage above baseball, Mr. Butterfield went into a funk.

Billy didn't care. He had been ignoring his father's demands for years.

"My problem is when I was growing up, I put a wall around me and blocked everything out," Billy says. "Consequently, I don't remember a lot of things."

While Billy was ignoring his father, Mr. Butterfield was virtually ignoring Lance, 10 years younger than his brother. He coached him for only one season of baseball. Family stories of Mr. Butterfield's forgetting to pick Lance up at school or leaving him behind were legendary.

"Lance was kind of the odd man out," says Mr. Parkey, the family friend. "Lance didn't get his father's attention until Bill realized that he had lost Billy."

THE YOUNGER SON

Mr. Butterfield was still in a fog when the Butterfields and Parkeys went on their annual Christmas trip to Colorado in 1991. He was still feeling that way when they walked into Brown's Country Store.

Yes, they knew the owner's son coached college football back in Fort Worth. But they had never laid eyes on TCU defensive line coach Scott Brown until that day.

"Bill came alive after meeting the coach," Mr. Parkey says. "He realized he had another chance, his last chance. And he wasn't going to miss out again."

Reinvigorated, Mr. Butterfield converted the garage into a state-of-the-art weight room. He installed floodlights in the yard so darkness could not interfere with his boy's training.

Mr. Butterfield had been taping Billy's and Lance's games for years. Or rather, he had his wife tape the games.

After Colorado, Mr. Butterfield began critiquing Lance's play. When Lance's eighth-grade basketball coaches noticed Mrs. Butterfield taping games, they asked Lance to bring the tapes to school for the team to watch.

One problem: Mr. Butterfield always sat next to his wife. His was the omnipresent voice on the tapes.

"Dad would offer continuous verbal onslaught about me making stupid plays and calling the coach an idiot," Lance recalls. "We'd have to tape over lots of portions. We'd be watching in the locker room and the screen would go blank. I always blamed my mother for being so bad with the video camera. It was all I could think to explain it."

At Lance's football games, Bill and Kathy Butterfield took to sitting by themselves so no one would hear the father's tirades as his silent wife dutifully taped away.

At baseball games, Mr. Butterfield would sit in his truck and watch the game from afar until it was Lance's turn to bat. Then he'd make his way to a spot behind the backstop and scream at his son between pitches.

"Keep your head down!"

"Watch the ball!"

"Keep your shoulders in! Put your weight back!"

After Lance's at-bat, Mr. Butterfield would retreat to the solitude of his truck.

He told his wife he was too nervous to sit with the other parents. He began taking Xanax, prescribed to combat anxiety. Those complemented the painkiller Vicodin that Mr. Butterfield had begun taking for kidney stones and kept popping after the stones passed, he told his wife, for other frequent aches and pains.

When friends invited Lance out, he was allowed to go after hitting a prescribed number of pitches in the backyard batting cage. Mr. Butterfield had invested in two machines: one to throw fastballs and one for curves.

"I never said I didn't want to hit," Lance says, that faraway look returning. "I didn't want to make him angry. I learned early what would make him mad, and I tried not to cross that line."

Often, when Lance made a mistake or angered Mr. Butterfield, father simply aimed the fastball machine at his head.

Lance learned to quickly get out of the way.

HIGH SCHOOL PRESSURE

It was in ninth grade that Mr. Butterfield began attending all of Lance's practices.

At home, father recounted in detail every mistake he thought the son had made and suggested how he might improve.

Lance's parents raced home after every football game to get the tape in the VCR before their son arrived. Father and son would often study the tape—start, stop, rewind, start, stop, rewind—until 2 a.m.

In his junior year, Lance hurt his rotator cuff trying to make a tackle during Richland's playoff game against Lewisville. He was afraid to tell his father, who mistrusted trainers and doctors, preferring his own home remedies.

Once Mr. Butterfield took Lance to Dr. Don Johnston, an orthopedist in Euless, to examine a broken bone in the boy's foot.

"The father came in and gave me a 20-minute monologue on Lance's exercise regimen and what he thought I should do," Dr. Johnston says.

"I told him I really don't know why he brought Lance in other than to enlighten me."

When Lance's summer league baseball coach moved him from the infield to the outfield before the 12th grade, Mr. Butterfield, incensed by the perceived demotion, stopped attending games. But the father instructed his wife to continue taping and Lance to continue with the latest decree: switch-hitting.

But Lance could not hit nearly as well left-handed. When his coaches ordered him to bat from the right side against a right-handed pitcher, Lance knew there would be trouble at home.

When Mr. Butterfield watched the tape later that night, he exploded. He threw the coffee table across the living room. He forbade Lance to ever play for the team again.

It would be Lance's final game of competitive baseball.

"After he chunked that table and told me I couldn't play baseball anymore, I stopped trying to communicate with him," Lance says.

"I loved baseball like I loved all sports. Those hours I was on the field, I was free. He wasn't telling me what to do. He wasn't criticizing me. I could tune him out.

"And here he was taking that away from me."

'HE WAS SCARY'

Mr. Parkey, owner of an insurance agency in Fort Worth, says he is reluctant to talk about the Butterfields because the first question he hears is always the same.

"Why didn't I do anything?" he says in anticipation.

"As close as I was to the family, I didn't know everything that was going on behind closed doors," he says.

Mr. Parkey knew Mr. Butterfield had a volatile temper. Mr. Parkey and his wife, Arvettia, frequently heard him curse at his wife, his children and his fate. But Mr. Parkey says he never knew there was physical abuse.

"Bill really started going downhill in the last four years of his life," Mr. Parkey says. "In the last year, he was scary."

Mr. Parkey says he will go to the grave believing his friend had a mental illness that went undiagnosed.

"I can't tell you how many times I suggested he get help," Mr. Parkey says. "But he insisted that everybody else was crazy.

"But as bad as Bill got, he was my friend. We were very close. Over the years he drifted from a guy I always kiddingly said was crazy to a guy who *was* crazy."

Mrs. Butterfield called to ask her husband's only friend to talk to him two weeks before Christmas in 1995.

"We sat in an El Chico and I talked to a stranger for four hours," Mr. Parkey says of his buddy, who had taken to eating only Rice Krispies and drinking salad oil for long periods the year before his death to regulate his weight.

"I know I should have done something," Mr. Parkey says. "But what?"

Mrs. Butterfield says she learned early in their marriage who was boss. She says she tried to leave her husband before Lance was born. She left a note and went home to her parents.

"He came, threatened my father and told me he was not going to let me have the kids. We were his possessions. They were his kids.

"I went back and started the facade that everything was

great," she says. "I tried to cover up everything. If there was one thing I was ever good at, it was covering up."

Until her son was charged with murder.

CRIMINAL OR VICTIM?

The trial of Lance Butterfield took place in the 213th District Court on the fifth floor of the Tarrant County Criminal Justice Center in late August 1997.

Lance, who had been free on bond since shortly after the shooting, pleaded guilty to murder.

It was left to a jury of eight women and four men to decide his sentence.

Prosecutor Mitch Poe portrayed Lance as a vicious killer who had coldly planned and carried out his father's execution because Mr. Butterfield objected to his relationship with his girlfriend. He pushed for life in prison.

"His father begged him to call 911 for help," Mr. Poe argued at the time and reiterates now, based on information Lance told police, "and then Lance pulled the trigger again."

How threatening could an unarmed man in a towel be?

The defense portrayed Lance as the victim of abuse who could no longer stand the pain.

It sought probation.

Paul Mones, the defense attorney from Portland and author of the book *When a Child Kills: Abused Children Who Kill Their Parents*, says Mr. Butterfield's actions were "an acid drip on Lance's personality—one minute, one hour, one year at a time until he couldn't take it anymore."

It was Mr. Butterfield's sister, Ms. Forsythe, who sought out Mr. Mones and persuaded him to help with the defense.

Aware of her brother's descent over the years, she also contributed heavily to cover the lawyers' fees.

Unlike Mr. Parkey, she had witnessed her brother many times mete out verbal and physical abuse.

"Lance defended himself," she says. "He defended his family. I honestly believe he saved his mother's, brother's and sister's lives as well as his own. Eventually, Bill would have killed them all."

Before Lance's trial, Mrs. Butterfield discovered that her husband had been keeping a journal, which she found in the garage. She trembled as she read the final entry, which was directed at her: "I have to be able to express my hurt—my pain—my animosity toward you or I will die or worse hurt my kids more than I already have or us."

'BUTTER WE LOVE YOU'

Day after day, the courtroom was packed with Lance's supporters. Mr. Poe recalls being routinely booed as he walked the hallway.

"When I go into court to prosecute a heinous crime, it's usually 'hip-hip-hooray for me,'" Mr. Poe says. "But not in this case."

"Butter we love you" was painted on the windshield of cars parked outside the courthouse.

"There was not enough room in the courtroom for all the people that wanted to testify for Lance," says Fort Worth attorney Jeff Kearney, who led the defense. "We had his father's best friend, coaches, teachers, Lance's friends, their parents, neighbors, family doctors. We had everybody."

Arthur Butterfield, Bill's father, offered a signed affidavit requesting that his grandson not be prosecuted.

The prosecution, which argued the cold, hard facts of Dec. 27, 1995, didn't produce a single witness to discredit the hours of testimony about the lifetime of abuse. There wasn't a single witness to speak well of the dead.

"People who knew Bill didn't like him," Mr. Poe says. "He was a jerk. But he didn't deserve to be killed."

TOUGH DECISIONS

In the end, the jury could not agree on a sentence. News reports at the time indicated six jurors initially favored probation, five supported a light sentence and one held out for at least 15 years.

The judge declared a mistrial.

Three months later, on the eve of a second trial, a plea bargain was struck. Lance pleaded guilty to manslaughter in exchange for a three-year sentence. He would be eligible for parole after 24 months.

Lance spent two frightening weeks at a transfer facility in Huntsville before being dispatched to the Gist Unit in Beaumont to serve out his term.

There he spent most of his time digging ditches, chopping trees and hoeing. His athletic activities were limited to jumping rope and pull-ups. He was a "yes sir, no sir" model prisoner.

On Feb. 11, 1999, 15 months after he was sentenced, parole board members agreed to release Lance on Nov. 8, four days shy of the second anniversary of his sentencing.

Lance's parole expired one year later.

Dr. Arambula, the forensic psychiatrist who testified on Lance's behalf at sentencing, says Lance's killing again "would be an uncommon event."

Says Mr. Mones, the attorney and author: "I've known children who committed parricide in cases similar to Lance going on to become doctors, lawyers, salesmen and even assistant prison wardens.

"Lance isn't the slightest threat to anyone anymore."

LIFE GOES ON

Lance Butterfield finally made it to TCU. Now 24, he is a little more than a semester away from graduating with degrees in accounting and finance. The closest he gets to the football team is Saturday afternoons when he cheers for the Horned Frogs from the stands.

Scott Brown, the former TCU defensive line coach, has moved on. He now coaches at Duke University in North Carolina.

He rarely gets calls about his decade as an assistant to Jim Wacker in Fort Worth, which ended in 1992.

The name Lance Butterfield, Mr. Brown says, replying to an early-summer inquiry, does not ring a bell. Nor can he remember any specific meeting at his father's restaurant in Colorado.

Sure, he says, he may have met Lance and his father over that Christmas break, but given Texans' propensity for vacationing in Colorado, there were many such meetings.

So many parents. So many young football players.

"I have a tendency to be a positive person," Mr. Brown says. "I may have said the boy was a good player with a fine future, but I probably have said that to dozens of parents and kids under similar circumstances."

When he hears about Lance's life since that meeting, he requests a photo of Lance that might jog his memory.

It doesn't help.

"Please tell Lance that I am very, very sorry for any hurt I may have caused," the coach says. "Please..."

Meanwhile at the house on Tabor Street, the Butterfield family home since Lance was in seventh grade, his girlfriend flits in and out at will.

In the back yard, the pitching machines are long gone. Six metal poles are all that remain from the disassembled batting cages.

Kathy Butterfield works in customer relations for American Airlines.

Billy, 34, has a job transporting industrial equipment. He visits Lance frequently with his wife and their two sons.

On weekends, Lance sometimes watches his 10-year-old nephew, Quaid, Billy's boy, play baseball.

Because Billy helps coach his son, Lance spends most games talking to his sister-in-law and other parents in the stands. He never moves toward the backstop or questions an umpire's call. He sometimes flinches when parents get too close to the backstop or shout at their boys.

"I cheer for Quaid and his teammates," he says. "That's all."

Asked whether he is happy with the way life has turned out, Lance leans back from the kitchen table and thinks for several seconds.

"I'm just glad I don't have to come home anymore to the hell that life was," he says.

"But I wish my father was here to experience this family...what might have been if only he had gotten help."

A single tear running down his cheek punctuates the thought.

Lessons Learned

BY BARRY HORN

As a sportswriter, it is important to remember that the best feature stories can almost always be found away from the Super Bowls and World Series and million-dollar paydays.

In fact, the seeds for stories I most like to explore are usually found in my own sports section's agate. It might be in a note announcing a retirement or a trade or an indictment or a death. It shouldn't take more than one or two sentences to whet the appetite.

My interest in the Butterfield family saga was born in a similar fashion back in 1997. It was in the 17th paragraph of a 23-paragraph news story that reported on the sentencing phase in a relatively low-profile murder case in which the son had admitted to shooting his father.

The paragraph: "At the end of the day, jurors began hearing testimony that painted Bill Butterfield, 45, as a mean, selfish man who blamed his family for his shortcomings and tried to relive his life through his children, particularly in the area of athletics."

Soon after, I remember telling my editor that there might be "a good sports story" here. He agreed. We got around to it almost five years later after deciding to explore the possibility of a series on youth sports.

I thought the story of an obsessed parent would be a good kickoff to the series.

The first thing I did was call the reporter who had written about a half-dozen stories on the case at the time of the trial. Selwyn Crawford assured me there was a great story there, one that went far beyond the daily trial coverage. He supplied details that had not made it into the paper and home telephone numbers of the key players.

Then came what is usually the toughest part of doing such a story—making the initial phone call. I think about how I might react if some detached voice on the telephone told me it was interested in dissecting my life for a million or so readers. I am always surprised when the person on the other end doesn't hang up.

Kathy Butterfield, the mother of the murderer and the wife of the dead man, was the first person I called. I was relieved to get her answering machine. Answering machines don't hang up.

I left a message. Of course, I knew she wouldn't call back. They never do.

Would you?

But at least I had planted the idea. I called back and spoke to her answering machine several times. When we finally connected, she at least recognized my voice and agreed to go to lunch.

It was at our second meeting that I finally took out my notebook and began taking notes. It was Kathy, the mother, who convinced her son to tell his version of events that led up to the murder.

What always amazes me in working on a story like this is how a reporter can ask intimate questions that he would never think of asking a friend or neighbor.

I know I am getting somewhere when I start learning details from one person that no one else involved in the story knew. Once a reporter begins sharing the details with other key figures, the floodgates usually open.

I will never forget the anguish in the voice of the football coach whose well-intentioned remark at a chance meeting helped ignite a series of events that cost Bill Butterfield his life. The coach didn't remember his words. Nor did he remember the Butterfield father who had taken the words as gospel.

The hardest part of reporting the story was finding someone to say something nice about the dead man. I spent weeks searching. I found no one. Not even his best friend or other family members could relate to him.

Still, I wanted people reading the story to see a piece of themselves in "A Father Who Pushed Too Far."

How many parents push their kids—"trophy children"?—in athletics to fulfill some void in their own lives? They might not push their kids over cliffs, but even gentle shoves may be out of line.

If the story gave even one reader pause the next time he or she talked to their kids about participation in sports, my intrusion into the Butterfields' lives will have been worth it.

The Charlotte Observer

Elizabeth Leland

Finalist, Non-Deadline Writing

Elizabeth Leland is an 18-year veteran reporter at *The Charlotte Observer.* Her passion is giving voice to everyday people confronting everyday problems.

It may be a Vietnamese immigrant struggling to bring his wife to the United States, or a Hispanic furniture worker confronting racism, or a teenager elected student council president even after he went to prison for robbing a restaurant. Leland seeks out stories of family, love, and conflict in the changing South.

She understands the region because she is so much a creation of these places. She was born in 1954 in Charleston, S.C., to a family of Lowcountry storytellers, was educated at the University of North Carolina-Chapel Hill, and is a veteran of the Associated Press and *The News & Observer* in Raleigh, N.C.

She is the author of two books, *The Vanishing Coast* and *A Place for Joe*, and has won many awards, including the Ernie Pyle Award and a Sigma Delta Chi national feature writing award. She also was a Nieman Fellow.

Leland and her husband, Charlotte lawyer Luke Largess, have two children, Jack, 9, and Abbie, 7. As a part-time reporter, she is just as likely to find a story on the playground as in the courthouse. Over dinner one day her husband told her about a young woman dying of Lou Gehrig's disease, and out of that conversation came "Mark Loves Heather."

Leland used the only means of communication left to Heather Yount, the movement of Heather's right thumb, as the narrative vehicle for telling a story of a couple's struggle against Lou Gehrig's disease and the marital bond their fight reveals.

Mark loves Heather

MARCH 24, 2002

BELMONT—Mark Yount kisses Heather on the lips and caresses her hand.

"Is everything OK, babe?"

A tear slides down his wife's cheek. Mark dabs it dry with a tissue.

He is reminiscing about their first year together, 1998, those intoxicating days of new love when their future seemed forever, before the breathing tube and the feeding tube, before every muscle in Heather's body quit working except in her right thumb and her hazel eyes.

Mark remembers sharing dinner at Angie's Spaghetti House in Gastonia. Hiking up Stone Mountain. Skiing in West Virginia.

"Is there anything else, babe?"

Heather moves her thumb. Yes.

She can no longer breathe on her own or eat or talk. She slides her thumb left to right to communicate. Once for yes, twice for no. She spells words with Mark's help, a letter at a time. He recites the alphabet and Heather signals when he hits the correct letter.

A?

B?

C? Her thumb moves.

Three more times through the alphabet. C-O-N-C.

"Concert?"

Her thumb says yes.

"The Elton John concert?"

Yes.

Heather and Mark sang along with Elton John at the Charlotte Coliseum on Oct. 10, 1998, belting out "Your Song" and other favorite tunes, arm in arm, dancing in the aisle. Mark thought Heather looked gorgeous, vivacious as always, her face filled with her beautiful smile.

They talked about children and family, and Mark remembers saying: Well, we should get married.

Well, I will marry you, Heather told him.

A year later, just four weeks before the wedding, but

after months of fatigue and weight loss and slurred speech, after different diagnoses from different doctors, Heather was admitted to Presbyterian Hospital with pneumonia. Twice, she quit breathing. Doctors performed a tracheotomy and inserted a breathing tube down her lungs. Mark postponed the wedding.

Heather had amyotrophic lateral sclerosis, or ALS, a nerve disease that killed Lou Gehrig in 1941 at age 37 and killed Heather's mother in 1984, also at 37. Heather is 28. She was 11 when her mother died.

MARK PROPOSES

Beeeeeeeeeeeeeep. An alarm sounds. Heather's airways are filling up.

Mark, 39, unhooks the air hose attached to her throat and slips a plastic tube down her trachea to suction out mucous and saliva.

"Is your nose OK?"

Her thumb jerks twice. No.

Mark suctions her nostrils.

"OK?" Mark's voice is soft, hushed. He looks into Heather's eyes when he talks, at her thumb when she answers. Staring into her eyes, he sees the woman he fell in love with—confident, kind, gentle. She taught first grade at Lingerfelt Elementary and whenever she ran into students around town, Heather hugged them. She was 5-foot-8, model-thin and looked like photographs of her mother. Mark fell in love with Heather long before they decided to date. He was in his mid-30s. She was in her mid-20s. He sang bass in the choir at Holy Comforter Lutheran Church. She was a soprano. They went to dinner and movies with friends from the church and, always, Mark and Heather gravitated to each other.

Seven months after the Elton John concert, Mark bought a sapphire-and-diamond engagement ring.

He invited Heather to eat grilled chicken at his house on Tuesday night, May 25, 1999. He told her it was to celebrate the last day of classes at her school. They'd go for a walk after dinner. But when Mark asked if she was ready to walk, Heather slouched down on the couch.

You go ahead, she told him. I'm too tired.

Mark went to his bedroom on the pretext of changing

clothes. He got the ring and walked back to Heather.

I've got a better idea, he said.

He dropped to his knees and opened the ring box.

Will you marry me?

HEATHER'S EYES

Mark dips a cotton swab into a solution of sterile water and hydrogen peroxide. He dabs it around the tracheotomy opening on Heather's neck, where the ventilator tube goes into her airways.

"Is that OK, babe?"

Heather's stepmother, Beverly Mauney, injects 8 ounces of a nutritional drink into Heather's feeding tube. When she finishes, Mark dabs around the opening in Heather's stomach, disinfecting where the feeding tube connects. Reci, a Yorkshire terrier, nuzzles Heather's feet. A *Seinfeld* episode is on TV, and Mark and Beverly glance up when Elaine says something funny. Heather strains her eyes to see past her sister, Ginger, standing at the end of the bed.

Mark finishes cleaning, and kisses Heather.

"I love you, babe."

Heather feels Mark's lips on hers, but she can't move her lips to kiss his. It's obvious, though, that Heather loves Mark. It shows in her eyes when she looks up at him. They grow big and round and sparkle. Mark sees love in Heather's eyes. Sometimes, he sees sadness. Occasionally, anger. Other times, just a longing for something as simple as a touch of his hands. He can tell Heather wants something. He just has to figure out what.

A? B?…H?

"Your head?"

Heather moves her thumb.

"You need a scratch?"

Mark scratches Heather's head, top, sides, back, top again.

He sits down. Every two or three minutes, he looks up from the TV.

"Are you OK, babe?"

It is not the life they envisioned at the Elton John concert, living together in Mark's renovated mill-style home, buying a bigger house after they had children. When they decided to go ahead with their wedding, a month later than planned, they knew none of that would ever happen.

ALS destroys nerve cells in the brain and spinal cord that signal muscles to move. It paralyzes and eventually kills most patients in three to five years. Heather's mother refused life support and died seven months after she was diagnosed. The doctors told Heather and her father then that the disease was not hereditary. They now know otherwise. Five to 10 percent of all cases are inherited.

When Heather and Mark rescheduled their wedding, for Dec. 19, 1999, Heather could not breathe on her own. She could not eat on her own. She could not talk.

She walked down the aisle of Holy Comforter Lutheran Church beside her father, Charles Mauney. She wore a floor-length wedding gown with a beaded bodice and scooped back, and from afar it looked as if she had a matching band around her neck. It was the cloth collar that held her trachea tube in place. When Charles gave Heather's hand to Mark at the front of the church, he also gave him her portable ventilator.

"I take you, Heather, to be my wife…," Mark said, "to be your faithful husband in sickness and in health.…"

Heather mouthed the words, silently, when her turn came: "I take you, Mark, to be my husband…to be your faithful wife…as long as we both shall live."

A WORRISOME DAY

"Are you OK, babe?"

Heather's thumb jerks. Once. Twice…Four times.

Mark jumps from the rocking chair.

"Babe, you're moving your thumb a lot tonight. Are you just moving it?"

He kisses her. Mark is worried. Heather's thumb has been spasming the way her other fingers did before the muscles finally wore out. He's worried her thumb is giving out. And then what? Mark doesn't want Heather to suffer, physically or emotionally. But if she can't tell him, how will he know when it's time to cut off her life support? Will it be when her lip no longer curls into a hint of a smile?

Heather senses the trouble with her thumb. A few nights earlier, she told Mark she was afraid.

Mark doesn't belittle Heather's fears. He's afraid, too. But he won't dwell on the negative. Heather could have died in the intensive care unit two years ago. Every day they're together is a miracle to Mark—and a joy.

"Your nose?"

Heather moves her thumb once.

"You need it wiped?"

Mark knew his time with Heather would be short. She's lived longer than expected. She didn't deteriorate suddenly like her mother, who was walking on a Friday and died on a Monday. Heather has declined gradually as the nerves that operate her muscles slowly waste away. One day, she no longer had strength enough to drive the car up and down the block. Another day, she quit walking. Then one day, she couldn't get into the wheelchair. She hasn't left the hospital bed in her parents' home since May 1, 2001. The time came when she couldn't lift her fingers to e-mail her friends. She couldn't tap her fingernail on the telephone receiver when Mark called. Finally, it became too exhausting to blink her eyes, once for yes, twice for no.

ALS does not affect the mind. Heather knows exactly what's happening, and she's powerless to stop it. There is no cure.

LOVING ASSISTANTS

Mark sits in a rocker beside Heather's bed, one hand wrapped around her left hand, side by side like any married couple, yet so unlike most couples. They don't have the physical intimacy of a shared bed, but Mark suspects their emotional bond may be stronger. When they're together, they focus every minute of every hour on each other.

Mark suctions Heather's airways. He wipes her eyes. Wipes her nose. Raises her bed. Lowers the bed. Heather's eyes follow Mark. At the end of every task, before he sits back in the rocker, he kisses her on the lips.

"I love you, babe. You're beautiful."

As he sits down, he takes her hand in his. Every minute of every hour that Mark is with Heather, he touches her in some way.

A lot of people help care for Heather. Her father, Charles, retired from his job as an Internal Revenue agent to be with her. He lost his first wife to ALS; now he is losing a daughter. He is home most of every day and sleeps in her bedroom three nights a week, waking whenever the alarm sounds to suction her airways. Her stepmother, Beverly Mauney, quit her job at Presbyterian Hospital and is home most of every day. She sleeps with Heather once a week. Mark works in the loan department of Belmont Federal Savings & Loan, but is with Heather at lunch, several hours every evening and most of the weekend. He spends three nights a week. Her sister, Ginger, spends Saturdays and Sundays. Others visit regularly: doctors, nurses, Hospice volunteers, a sitter, friends, family.

In September, Mark and Ginger took charge of the household for a weekend so Charles and Beverly could celebrate their 15th wedding anniversary in Charleston.

But when Charles and Beverly suggest that Mark take time for himself, he refuses.

My vacation is here, he tells them. This is my time with Heather.

A MESSAGE FOR MARK

And Heather? Her body is slowly shutting down, but she has something to say that she wants Mark to remember forever:

A? B?…I?

Heather's thumb moves.

Twelve more times through the alphabet. L-O-V-E H-I-M S-O M-U-C…

I love him so much?

Heather's thumb says yes.

"H-E S L-I-K-E A R-O-C-K," she says, letter by letter, thumb by thumb. "H-E G-I-V-E-S M-E T-H-E S-T-R-E-N-G-T-H T-O G-O O-N."

Lessons Learned

BY ELIZABETH LELAND

When I proposed a story about Mark and Heather, one of my editors moaned and said, "I don't want to read another story about someone with a disease."

It's all in your perspective, I learned.

I didn't approach it as a story about a woman dying from Lou Gehrig's disease. I saw it as a story about a husband and wife persevering against adversity. A love story.

But how do you tell a story like this without being maudlin? My approach is to get out of the way and let the people I'm writing about reveal themselves. Mark could tell me how he felt, the heartache he was going through. But what was Heather thinking? After an evening with them, I re-learned the maxim: Show, don't tell.

I watched Heather's eyes follow Mark around the room. When she looked up at him, the dull, glazed stare of a dying woman vanished; her eyes grew big and round and sparkled, a woman in love.

I reported this story as if I had a deadline. Heather's family thought she could die any day. (She lived four more months.) I wanted her to be able to read the story and I wanted the story to be about life, not death. Because Heather was confined to bed and couldn't move or talk, the action of the narrative would be defined by something as subtle as the jerk of her thumb.

My eyes became my camera.

I noticed Heather's thumb spasming. Mark saw it, too. He leapt out of his chair and went to her. A few days later, over lunch, I asked him about it. He explained that he was worried that the muscles in her thumb were wearing out the way the muscles in her other fingers had. If she couldn't communicate, how would he know when to pull the plug?

The first challenge in writing a narrative is reporting what's happening, getting the right detail to move the story forward. In most cases, you can't go back to find a missing detail. I've learned to write down as much of a scene as I can: the smells, the sounds, the tiniest movement. You may not know until later whether something as simple as the jerk of a thumb is significant.

The next challenge is to figure out the meaning behind those details, to uncover any insights they might hold for the reader. When Heather lifted her eyes to Mark, what did he see that I couldn't see? He told me he saw the woman he had fallen in love with: 5-foot-8, model-thin, full of life—not the shell of a woman I saw lying in a hospital bed. Understanding that told readers as much about Mark as it did about Heather.

Jonathan Tilove
Diversity Writing

Jonathan Tilove often envisions a theme for his news coverage during a particular year. The Newhouse News Service national correspondent finds that the use of thematic threads keeps him focused. Even though he has specialized in reporting and writing about specific topics such as immigration, ethnicity, and race since 1991, a particular theme enables him to explore topics from as many different vantage points as possible.

In the past, his themes have included the interplay between immigration and migration and its effect on communities, multiple perspectives on affirmative action, and the legacy of slavery. Such an approach makes it clear how stories simultaneously highlight similarities and differences.

"Even when they appear to be completely different, you realize they're the same," said Tilove, 48. "It's interesting to me how things tie together and how, even when you're starting off the year with what you think are a range of different stories, they thematically lead from one to the next."

His work on one theme led him to another he hadn't anticipated: an exploration of Martin Luther King streets around the country. The idea evolved over time. It led him to people and places he hadn't known. It immersed him in another reality of life he had been oblivious to despite his experience in covering race relations.

Tilove's exposure to racial issues occurred early in his life. He lived on the dividing line between a black community and a white school and witnessed racial conflict. And his politically active and socially conscious family made it clear that race relations was a compelling, moral issue. When he arrived in the Newhouse Washington, D.C., bureau, following stints at the Springfield, Mass., *Morning Union* and in a New York Newhouse bureau, he was asked one thematic beat he would like to cover. He chose race relations.

What's often missing from the news coverage of race relations is how complicated it is, he notes. He relishes teasing out views people don't see. "I do think there's something satisfying about just laying out something and explaining it in a way that makes people understand the complexity," he said.

His six-part series, "Along Martin Luther King: A Passage to Black America," examines the complexity of what he calls "a nation within a nation." He offers a rare glimpse of lives lived beyond the stereotypes and misconceptions harbored by those unfamiliar with a community in their midst.

—Aly Colón

[Editor's Note: Parts 4 through 6 of Jonathan Tilove's series have not been included here because of space considerations. The full text of those stories can be read on the CD-ROM included with this edition of Best Newspaper Writing. Photos by Michael Falco that accompany each story also are included on the CD-ROM.

The Diversity Writing award is funded by The Freedom Forum, which has partnered with ASNE on many diversity efforts.]

Martin Luther King streets map a nation within a nation

JANUARY 1, 2002

There is a road that wends its way through the heart and soul of black America. Sometimes it is called a boulevard, a drive, an avenue, a street or a way, but it is always named Martin Luther King.

It happened without grand design but with profound, if unrecognized, consequences. Together, the circumstance of segregation, the martyrdom that made Martin Luther King Jr. the every-hero of a people, and the countless separate struggles to honor him have combined to create a black Main Street from coast to coast.

Better than 500 streets are named for King in cities and towns from one end of the country to the other, with more added every year. Map them and you map a nation within a nation, a place where white America seldom goes and black America can be itself. It is a parallel universe with a different center of gravity and distinctive sensibilities, kinship at two or three degrees of separation, not six.

There is no other street like it.

The idea for a journey along Martin Luther King was born some years ago on a reporting trip through the Mississippi Delta. In town after town, directions to the black community had the sameness of a blues refrain: Just head on down to Martin Luther King.

Over the course of two years, a reporter and a photographer have done just that—headed on down to Martin Luther King streets of every size and description.

Our only mission was to see where a journey along these streets of a single name would lead. And we discovered that they lead to every facet of black life, politics, thought, belief, culture, history and experience.

We journeyed along King in Jackson, Miss., and on the south side of Chicago, the respective prime source and major destination of the great black migration north. We traveled King in Selma, Ala., and Atlanta, each in its way a mecca of the black freedom struggle.

We started one trip on Juneteenth in Galveston—

where that celebration began, marking the day when, 2-1/2 years after the Emancipation Proclamation, word finally reached slaves in Texas that they were free. We zigzagged halfway to Canada through East Texas, Louisiana, Arkansas, Oklahoma and Kansas—19 King streets in all, encountering black communities that one to another were still struggling to make good on that late word of freedom.

We journeyed to the rough-hewn Martin Luther King Boulevard amid the lush land and lean times of little Belle Glade, Fla., and to the most showy and celebrated Martin Luther King Boulevard of them all—125th Street in Harlem.

And in two West Coast outposts of the African-American diaspora—Oakland, Calif., and Portland, Ore.—our tales of our travels were welcomed like news from home.

Stretches of many King streets have a ragged, wasted quality to them. Comedian Chris Rock famously advised, "If a friend calls you on the telephone and says they're lost on Martin Luther King Boulevard and they want to know what they should do, the best response is, 'Run!'"

But pause on King, begin talking to folks, and you are transported beyond the sometimes battered facade into a black America that, with astonishing welcome, reveals itself. It's not only more separate and self-contained than imagined, but more tightly interconnected, more powerfully whole.

This black America is not hidden. But as the Harlem Renaissance writer Zora Neale Hurston wrote in 1950, in a piece titled "What White Publishers Won't Print": "For various reasons, the average, struggling, non-morbid Negro is the best-kept secret in America....His revelation to the public is the thing needed to do away with that feeling of difference which inspires fear, and which ever expresses itself in dislike."

And so we journeyed.

From the sultry rush of freshman week at Morris Brown College in Atlanta to the snow-wrapped funeral of the Chicago poet Gwendolyn Brooks.

From the ecstatic trombone shout music at the United House of Prayer for All People in Harlem to the furious throb of the Bay Area rappers RBL Posse, whom we encountered in Portland.

Craig Bowie, organizer of the Juneteenth parades in
Galveston, Texas, against a backdrop of his own design.

From the country-quiet MLK in Jasper, Texas—on
which James Byrd Jr. was walking when he climbed
into a pickup truck, to be dragged to his death—to the
prison on MLK in Oklahoma City where Wanda Jean
Allen lived until, the week before King Day 2001, she
became the first black woman executed in half a century.

Everywhere along the way, there are barber and
beauty shops, fast-food chicken franchises and slow-
cooked barbecue joints with sweet iced tea and standing
fans. There are the brilliant colors of murals paying
homage to King and other heroes. There are churches
beyond counting. And there is endless, ardent talk about
what it means to be African in America.

A very few big King streets—beginning with Chicago and Atlanta—were dedicated within months of
King's assassination. In the nearly 35 years since, the
grass-roots efforts to name streets for King have gained
momentum in the face of substantial inertia and resistance. It is a movement with no national organization, no
national attention, not even self-knowledge that a
movement is what it is—as if the transcontinental rail-
road had been built piecemeal by folks unaware of one
another.

These are streets united by struggle and circumstance, by history and happenstance. One leads to the
next and next and back again.

Many black people have moved beyond the neighborhoods where King runs (though there are now King streets in new black suburbs), but few live beyond the reach of the sounds, sentiments and stories rooted on King.

And for many, a street sign that says Martin Luther King heralds a home away from home.

When Dock Jackson, the park director in Elgin, Texas, arrived in Oklahoma City in need of a haircut, he simply headed down to Martin Luther King and found Robert Gates' barbershop. When Gates travels to a new place, he does the same. "When I don't know where I'm going," he says, "I'll find MLK."

The more communities that have one, the more a black community without one wonders why not. This often means a rousing fight, right up to last year's naming of a street for King in Waukegan, Ill., and the failed campaigns to do the same in Toledo, Ohio, and High Point, N.C. In 1987, voters in San Diego rescinded the naming of their city's MLK, and polls indicated that voters in Portland, Ore., would have done the same in 1990 had the courts not intervened.

Businesses don't like the bother. There are always some folks devoted to the history and significance of the old name. But in the hundreds of battles one also catches a glimpse of deeper white resistance and of the real King, the man with edge and meaning and not simply the dreamy King of grammar school coloring contests.

The biggest sticking point in these debates is usually whether the street named for King extends beyond the black community.

In Belle Glade, Harma Miller, who was on the city council at the time, said whites wanted the MLK to end before it reached their "beloved Elks Club." "I said, 'No,' and made a big fuss about it," and the whole of Avenue E now also bears the name Martin Luther King.

But when they did some street repairs in 1999 and replaced a few signs, Miller said, the print on the MLK signs was shrunk so small you had to stop and squint to make it out. That fall, when she became the first black mayor with a black majority on the council, the first thing she did was replace those signs.

Dock Jackson tells us that Elgin lagged 13 years behind the neighboring Texas cities of Bastrop and Smithville—dedicating its MLK on Juneteenth 2001—

because proponents wanted both the white and black ends of the street to bear King's name. Finally, he said, they settled for the black half alone.

It might have been the same story back in 1975 in Austin—just west of Elgin—were it not for J.J. Seabrook, an elder statesman of the black community, who suffered a fatal heart attack while imploring the city council not to treat King like that. He died and won. Austin's MLK crosses racial lines and borders the state Capitol complex.

The dedication on King Day 1993 of a Martin Luther King Boulevard in Americus, Ga., came after a year of ugly arguments, threats, protests and the memorable suggestion by a deputy fire chief that half the street be named for King and the other half for James Earl Ray, King's convicted assassin.

Occasionally, King streets turn up in unexpected places: a busy thoroughfare in Salt Lake City, a squib of a street in Newcomerstown, Ohio—a bucolic dot on the map midway between Columbus and Wheeling, W.Va., that was home to Cy Young and Woody Hayes. Sometimes there isn't one where you might expect it, like Philadelphia.

But for the most part, King streets are exactly where you would look for them: the densest swaths in the Deep South, from East Texas to Florida. Mississippi alone has at least 65, and King's home state of Georgia has the most, with upwards of 70.

At times the journey along King is like a pilgrimage along the stations of the cross for the martyred hero.

In 1958, Martin Luther King was stabbed while signing books on what is now MLK in Harlem. He led the 1965 marches in Selma beginning from Brown Chapel on what is now MLK there. Days before his own death, Malcolm X came to that same church to express his solidarity with King, who was then in a Selma jail.

Martin Luther King was tear-gassed in 1966 on what is now the MLK in Canton, Miss., on the Memphis-to-Jackson march along which Stokely Carmichael, tear-gassed as well, first roused a crowd to chant "Black Power."

The mule-drawn caisson carrying King's casket in 1968 rolled along what is now MLK in his hometown of Atlanta as it passed the Morris Brown campus, coming within shouting distance of the modest home where

King lived and his widow still does.

And for many years, Olivet Baptist Church on King Drive in Chicago took its address from its side street because the pastor, now dead, was such a bitter rival of King's in national black Baptist circles.

At times, we come upon the wholly unexpected on King.

Just a block south of Olivet Baptist in Chicago is the stately Griffin Funeral Home, where they buried Jesse Owens and Elijah Muhammad and where, each morning, they raise to half-staff a Confederate flag. It is a practice begun by the late owner, Ernest Griffin, when he learned that his mortuary stood on the site of Fort Douglas, a prisoner-of-war camp where more than 6,000 Confederate soldiers died, and where his own grandfather enlisted in the U.S. Colored Infantry during the Civil War.

On every new King we visit, we learn more about the last King we left, new threads in the tapestry.

Gwendolyn Brooks is waked at the same Chicago funeral home where they waked the hideously bruised and bloated body of the teen-age Emmett Till, killed while visiting Mississippi in the summer of 1955. In Jackson, we meet Charles Tisdale, who was a reporter for the *Chicago Defender* at the trial of the two white men acquitted of Till's murder.

And on the MLK in Oakland, we meet Lillie Luckett, who saw the famous photo of the murdered Till in *Jet* magazine and said, "That family always had trouble." Growing up in Mississippi, Luckett picked cotton on the land that Till's grandfather oversaw in the Delta.

Every step of the way, King streets are not just our destination but our guide.

We go to Oklahoma City to visit the well-kept women's prison where convicted murderer Wanda Jean Allen had been on death row.

But no sooner have we arrived than we stumble into the Miss Black Oklahoma pageant being held at a tumbledown hotel a few miles down King. The pageant is under the indomitable leadership of 78-year-old Clara Luper, who in 1957 took a group of black youngsters to Harlem to perform her play, "Brother President: The Story of Martin Luther King," an experience that began the Oklahoma City sit-ins the following year.

We go to Lanier High School on MLK in Jackson to see Robert Moses, who commutes every week from Boston to teach, part of the national Algebra Project, which he created to free black young people from the modern serfdom of math illiteracy. We also meet his assistant, Jolivette Anderson, "the poet warrior."

More than a year and a half later we are with Anderson in Harlem as she performs at the annual Show and Prove of the Five Percent Nation, a group that, teaching that each black man is God, is influential in the worlds of hip-hop and prisons.

That same weekend, on a radiant June day by the beach in Coney Island, Anderson performs at a numinous ceremony of remembrance of the black lives lost in the Middle Passage from African freedom to American bondage.

Lives are lived from one King to the next.

Almost every year, Charles Bolden, a truck driver in Oregon, drives his 1993 Mustang the 3,000 miles from the MLK in Portland to the MLK in Harlem—10 hours a stint, 3-1/2 days, 12 tanks of gas. On his arrival, he parks the Mustang at his sister's house in Brooklyn, and then it's into Harlem to hear "the drums" of black consciousness, which he says sound too faintly in his adopted hometown.

Shawna Holbrook, who owned the now-defunct Indigo Shack, an African arts shop on MLK Way in Oakland, used to spend summers with her grandma, who lives just off the MLK in Jackson.

The Rev. Daniel Stafford, pastor of Peaceful Rest Baptist Church on Martin Luther King Boulevard in Jasper, is also pastor of Starlight Baptist Church on Martin Luther King Drive in DeRidder, La.

Dolores Cross was president of Chicago State on King Drive before becoming president of Morris Brown on Atlanta's King Drive. She grew up in Newark, N.J., graduating from Central High School on what is now Martin Luther King Boulevard.

"It's haunting," Cross says.

NFL linebacker Ray Lewis led the Baltimore Ravens to a 2000 conference championship playing on the MLK in Baltimore, was the most valuable player in the

Super Bowl played on the MLK in Tampa, Fla., and spent the early preseason on trial on Atlanta's MLK for murders committed in the hours following the previous Super Bowl. (He pleaded guilty to obstructing justice.)

Jamil Abdullah Al-Amin, formerly known as H. Rap Brown, was arraigned in the same Atlanta courthouse on King, charged with the murder of a sheriff's deputy who went to Morris Brown.

When Al-Amin was captured in the Alabama countryside to which he had fled, he called the legendary attorney J.L. Chestnut, who on our Sunday in Selma presided over First Baptist Church on MLK, and whose law office is on Jeff Davis not far from its intersection with MLK.

A few blocks up King from First Baptist is the home of Marion Tumbleweed Beach, the gloriously cantankerous old woman with the beautiful garden, the black liberation flag and the lawn sign for Joe Smitherman, the white mayor defeated by James Perkins Jr., his black challenger. Beach knows Al-Amin as well. Back in 1990 he spoke at the funeral of her daughter, Carolyn Delores Beach Foucher, a former Black Panther in Chicago.

On Selma's King, we also meet Emmanuel ben Avraham, the Trenton, N.J., community activist (like many others, in town to help Perkins) who led the effort to name the MLK there and in his native Newark, N.J.

Earlier, on a visit to Belle Glade for King Day 2000, we had met Angela Williams, just moved onto MLK there from Trenton, where she had lived near that city's MLK. "Same damn street," she says with an ain't-it-a-shame scowl.

"Give a black man a black street in a black neighborhood?" she asks. "That's not the purpose. The purpose is to honor him."

But Annie Williams (no relation), who lives and works on Belle Glade's MLK, managing the Sudsy City Laundromat, disagrees. "Got to keep it black, got to keep this black, Martin Luther King got to be black," she says.

That's the way it is and ought to be, in her view, and not just in Belle Glade but in all the other places with MLKs—and that, she knows, is a lot of places, because every place she goes, she looks. "Every town," she says, "got a Martin Luther King."

Chicago and Jackson, Miss.: Heart and soul

JANUARY 1, 2002

The Martin Luther King drives in Jackson, Miss., and Chicago are about as different as any two King streets in America.

In Jackson, it's a big old country road, one that meanders a bit and doesn't seem to accomplish a lot, at least in terms of getting you anywhere other than where you already are. You drive by the Drummer house just once after being gone a year and a half, and when you finally get around to dropping by, Beola Drummer says, "I saw you were in town."

King Drive in Chicago is colder in every way. It's a big, broad, bricks-and-mortar straight shot as far as the eye can see. Stretches are grand. Patches are worn. But if it angled just a hair west and kept on for another 749 miles, it would run right into King Drive in Jackson.

And then the truth would become apparent: The two streets are connected by everything but tar and macadam, connected like before is to after, "what about" is to "you don't say," motherland is to colony and soul is to everlasting soul.

"We are not a tribe, we are a nation. We are not wandering groups, we are a people," the Chicago poet Haki Madhubuti, who teaches on King, wrote 30 years ago.

If Madhubuti's nation has a heart—a throbbing, vital center for its politics and pulse—it is Chicago, the chosen home of Jesse Jackson and Louis Farrakhan, of Muddy Waters and Willie Dixon, of *Ebony* and *Jet*. It is the poet Gwendolyn Brooks' "I Will city…ripe/roused/ready."

And the soul of black folks has got to be somewhere in Mississippi. It has the highest percentage of black people in the United States. Black life and culture everywhere in America are rooted in the South, and this is where the roots run deepest.

* * *

"I'm used to hard times," says W.L. Stokes, a man with a face of abiding eloquence, who grew up picking cotton "from can to can't, from can see to can't see,"

Men playing pool checkers at Brown's service station, MLK Drive, Jackson, Miss.

and now spends his days trading stories with the old-timers at Brown's gas station on Jackson's King.

These men, however, lived their lives along the arc from can't to can. They came of age at a time when "nothing and nothing could stop Mississippi," as Brooks put it in a poem about the death of Emmett Till, the 14-year-old Chicago boy who was visiting his uncle in Money, Miss., when he supposedly whistled at a white woman and ended up shot and drowned.

Stokes served in the segregated military. Johnny Mack Brown was a Pullman porter when that was about the best job a black man could have. Wardell Catchings fled the Watts riots figuring, "If I got to fight, I'd rather be home." The very day he returned to Mississippi he became one of the first two black men hired to drive a Jackson city bus. Quincy Brown, proprietor of Brown's Highway Service, marched for freedom.

They saw it all, survived it all, somehow intact, strong and sweet.

They play checkers at Brown's on a well-worn red-and-white board.

"I wouldn't do that if I was you," Stokes, cigar clenched in his mouth, warns Catchings, who is gently sliding his piece along.

"I didn't see that," says Catchings.

"You saw it," Stokes replies, raising and slamming his piece—snap, snap, snap, snap—a quadruple jump.

"You're just playing the wrong person. You know who I am, don't you?"

Charles Tisdale, owner and editor of the *Jackson Advocate*, now in his 70s, knows everybody. His career in black newspapers took him from Chicago to Memphis, Tenn., to Jackson—which, the way he makes it out, is like tumbling down a flight of stairs. "Mississippi goddamn," Tisdale says in his sonorous rumble, quoting singer Nina Simone. "Why did I come here? I am confused. Anybody who could escape should do so."

Tisdale is not confused. He is ornery, his newspaper's office a frequent target of attacks over the years. "If they hadn't tried to run me off, I probably would have left."

* * *

High up along an elegant expanse of King Drive in a part of Chicago's South Side known as Bronzeville is a beautiful statue dedicated to the great northern migration of black folks from the South. It's of a man both sad and jaunty, his back to Mississippi, arriving with a satchel tied with string, wearing a suit made up of shoe soles.

"When I got off at the train station, I saw all the lights and things, it was like entering paradise," says Rose Marie Black, who arrived in 1946 at age 12 from Summit, Miss.

Black is a vision in black and white—thigh-high boots, skirt up to here, hat out to there, all made by her own hand. When we first encounter her, we are driving south on King Drive and she is about to board a northbound bus. She must be used to the sound of screeching brakes, the swiveling salute of turned heads. She is Racetrack Rosie, the Bronze Temptress—at 66, Chicago's oldest stripper.

("The one with the hat out to there?" asks Jack Bennett back at Brown's in Jackson. After playing Negro League ball, he spent the shank of his life working for the post office in Chicago before coming home to Mississippi.)

Black's longtime boyfriend, Aaron "Stoney Burke" Johnson, is a Democratic precinct captain. On Election Day 2000, he was the dapper impresario greeting the faithful outside a polling place near King, an old church that looks more Mississippi than Chicago. (Johnson is

158

the superintendent of transportation for the Chicago Post Office, and Jack Bennett knows him, too.)

When Johnson delivered his precinct's tallies to Congressman Bobby Rush's office on King, Al Gore beat George W. Bush, 352 to 10.

It is poetic justice, Chicago-style, that Gwendolyn Brooks' very last public act—the last time she left her home before she died—was to vote in 2000. And, says Haki Madhubuti, "she didn't go out to vote for Bush."

Madhubuti is a professor at Chicago State University, a mostly black public college on King Drive. He saw to the creation of a Gwendolyn Brooks Center there with an annual writers conference, a hall of fame for writers of African descent and a professorship for Brooks.

"What does a son do for a mother?" asks Madhubuti, who says Brooks saved and softened him.

Madhubuti is also the founder of two Afrocentric schools—a public charter school and a private school—and of Third World Press, begun in a basement apartment and now occupying a former Catholic rectory with the quiet and class of some well-appointed Ivy League foundation.

He is a prolific and popular poet and essayist, "an interpreter and protector of Blackness," in Brooks' words, emerging, when he was known as Don Lee, as one of the sharpest figures of the black arts movement of the 1960s. His 1990 book, *Black Men: Obsolete, Single, Dangerous?* has remained a best seller in black bookstores.

"He was into that black stuff and he was as light-skinned as a piece of golden corn on the cob," he wrote of himself 15 years ago. So light-skinned that, in 1974, he decided to take a name as black as his consciousness—Haki, which in Swahili means "just," and Madhubuti, "precise" or "accurate."

In the years since, Madhubuti has become as profoundly influential in black America as he is invisible to white America. He is polite, reserved and deeply secure. He has presence—or, as we find traveling on King, omnipresence.

In 1989, when students occupied the administration building at Morris Brown College on MLK in Atlanta, they called Madhubuti for advice.

In 1995, Madhubuti brokered a peace between Louis

Farrakhan and Betty Shabazz, the widow of Malcolm X, that was publicly sealed at the Apollo Theater on MLK in Harlem. It was broadcast to a closed-circuit audience around the world.

A month after the 2000 election, Brooks died, Madhubuti by her side. She was buried in snowbound Chicago after a wake at Rayner and Sons Funeral Home on East 71st Street, a block and a half off King.

Rayner's most famous wake was in the summer of 1955 for Emmett Till. His grotesquely mutilated body was shipped back to Chicago, and his mother decided to leave the casket open for the world to see. Over three days, thousands filed by.

Jackson's Charles Tisdale, then with the *Chicago Defender*, was in Mississippi for the trial of the two white men who were ultimately acquitted. "We stood under a tree because they wouldn't let us in the courtroom at that time. Every morning the sheriff would come by and say, I think in his most benevolent tone, 'Good morning, niggers.'"

* * *

The Malcolm X Center in Jackson, a small, dark fortress of a building next to Lanier High School on King, was begun 10 years ago in the wake of protests over the police killing of a black man trying to clean drugs out of a local housing project. "We didn't choose the street because it was Martin Luther King, but we're happy that it was Martin Luther King," says Chokwe Lumumba, the revolutionary nationalist attorney who founded the center.

Lumumba arrived in the early 1970s as part of the Republic of New Afrika, a movement to create a black nation out of five Southern states, beginning here.

Later, after sojourns in his native Detroit, Chicago and New York, Lumumba returned to Jackson in 1988. Mississippi is the blackest place, he says, the place he is most at home and most challenged: "It is the center of the problem. If you can crack the nut here, you have done it."

The Malcolm X Center is a place for classes and lectures, for summer camp, for the New Afrikan Scouts—a national group whose first president was the late rapper Tupac Shakur, whom Lumumba represented in one scrape after another, most famously at a preliminary hearing at the courthouse on MLK in Atlanta when Shakur was charged with shooting two off-duty Atlanta police officers. The charges later were dropped.

The Malcolm X Center is also home to the Jackson Panthers, the very successful basketball team. And every spring, Lumumba runs a Black History Classic tournament for teams from throughout the South.

"I've reclaimed my interest in sports since I've been down here," he says. "Back in the '70s, I wouldn't have been bouncing no basketball. I would have been at the rifle range."

In the wake of Sept. 11, Lumumba, as head of the New Afrikan Peoples Organization, expressed his sympathy with the victims, but suggested that America must also be held accountable for its history of terrorism, at home and abroad, a view he says resonates in the barbershop talk of black America.

* * *

"The only thing that's changed is that for the first time in my life I've seen fear in the eyes of white folks," Haki Madhubuti says of the impact of Sept. 11. "For black folks, nothing's changed."

Lu Palmer concurs: "I don't think of anything that might be different."

Palmer is revered in black Chicago—for his writing, his newspaper columns, his radio show, his willingness to quit or be fired whenever one of his various employers over the years tried to shut him up for being too outspokenly black.

Palmer made a career of smiting white folks with his words. He was the "Panther with a pen." But he is an old man now, 78, and barely able to see.

He lives with his ailing wife, Jorja, in a 40-room castle where Chicago's King Drive intersects with a street named for himself. The castle—turrets, howling wind and all—is broken up into apartments, but renting them is a losing game.

For almost 12 years, Palmer had his own radio show—*Lu's Notebook*, a five-minute commentary sponsored by Illinois Bell on all four black radio stations in Chicago. It was in the basement of his castle that Palmer and a handful of others persuaded the reluctant Harold Washington to make the run that led to his election in

1983 as Chicago's first black mayor. The same morning that Washington announced for mayor, Illinois Bell canceled *Lu's Notebook*.

"They said, 'You have been too outspoken in pushing Harold Washington,'" Palmer recalls. "So they fired me."

From 1983 until his retirement in January 2001, he did talk radio. He rang in the 2000 election results denouncing both Bush and Gore.

There is something both heroic and forlorn about Palmer, devoting himself so wholly to his people. He considered himself a disciple of Martin Luther King Jr. in King's lifetime, but now believes King was wrong about two things—nonviolence and integration.

Palmer is campaigning to get black schools to quit having proms at white-owned hotels, but says, "These kids and their parents would rather die before they would hold a prom in their own gym."

* * *

Chokwe Lumumba's Black History Classic and Jackson's Lanier High School prom—being held at the Crowne Plaza downtown—are the same weekend in April 2001.

While the prom is all black, the tournament has a few white players. There are white Panthers.

"We're nationalists, not separatists," says Lumumba, who embroiders a little black nationalism into a pep talk mostly intended to encourage the players to stay on top of their academics.

At Beola Drummer's house just up King from the high school, her daughter, Jessica, is getting ready for the prom.

A piece of paper taped on the front door says, "No Public Restrooms. Don't even Ask!!!!!!!"

It's a joke of sorts. People are constantly in and out of the house, children dropped off and picked up. On our last visit, a woman sat on the porch enjoying a long drink of iced tea. When she left, we asked who she was. Drummer just shrugged.

When Drummer won big at bingo, she bought two large plastic swimming pools for the neighborhood kids to splash in. She provides a running commentary on life. She strips a tree branch and offers a lecture on the glory of switches. She has four children, three of whom have already graduated from Lanier.

Jessica—nicknamed Jessy—is in her room primping. The sign on her door says: "Keep out! Aja & Jessy only. Keep My Door Closed, my TV off. Do Not Sit on My Pillows (if I let you in). If I ain't here you shouldn't be here neither. RESPECT my property as you would yo' mammy!"

Aja is Jessica's baby daughter. Jessica's sister, Melissa, has a baby with W.L. Stokes' great-grandson, who is away at medical school. The baby's grandfather, Kenneth, is the city councilor responsible for getting this street named for King, and for the King Day parade that ends as it passes the Drummer front porch.

As she irons Jessica's powder-blue satin prom dress, Drummer is going on about "the laziest dog in the world," the one that put its paws over its eyes to avoid the light, that had to be dragged on its walks, that would give you this look like, "if you want that damn stick you better get it yourself."

"This dog was lazy!"

Outside, Mississippi is spread wide against the night but inside, the house is tiny, cramped and worn. The Drummers are poor, and fortunate. Here, in the soul of black America, Beola Drummer is a good soul.

"Life's too short to be sad," she says. "I enjoy life."

Figuring out what it means to be black in America

JANUARY 1, 2002

At 73, Marion Tumbleweed Beach is small and, in her pigtails and little African hat, at once captivating and ferocious. Few people have lived a life so sinuously intertwined, so passionately engaged, with the black American journey across the 20th century—as a teacher, writer, poet, reporter and editor, as an activist and intellectual. Her roaring, riveting recounting of her life comes fast and furious, with lyrical, spiky abandon. She is Miss Jane Pittman on speed.

So, how to explain that her home is the only one on Martin Luther King Street in Selma, Ala., with a red-and-white Smitherman lawn sign, advertising her support for the white mayor who has been frustrating black electoral ambitions since King himself marched here?

One hundred seventy-eight miles away, on Martin Luther King Drive in Atlanta, Kedist Hirpassa, a freshman at Morris Brown College, is by definition African American. She was born in Ethiopia and raised in the United States. But her first semester at a black college has been a twisting trek through the maze of her own relationship to blackness.

"It has helped me realize that I am black," she says.

But, after recalling the times her way of speaking or taste in music has been dismissed as "white," or remembering some irritating inefficiency at Morris Brown, she is back in the maze. Sometimes, she says, "being in an all-black school, I don't feel like I'm black. I feel like I have more in common with a white person than a black person."

The talk of Martin Luther King streets inevitably turns to what it means to be black in America. Marion Tumbleweed Beach and Kedist Hirpassa are living proof of just how tight the black community is, and how encompassing.

If that sounds like a contradiction, it's not. Like America, black America is endlessly, kaleidoscopically diverse.

"Wait until you see a congregation of more than two

dark-complected people," wrote Zora Neale Hurston in 1937. (She lived on streets in Harlem and in Belle Glade, Fla., that now bear the name Martin Luther King.) "If they can't agree on a single solitary thing, then you can go off satisfied. Those are My People."

The notion of a community speaking with a single voice is an invention of convenience. It comes from a broader nation and media that want to know what this separate piece of America is thinking and feeling, and it works backward from certain evidence—blacks preferred Al Gore to George W. Bush—to provide a quotebox of explanation.

What unites the black nation along King is a shared terrain, a sense of place and predicament. After that, anything goes.

About the only thing that all black folk in America have in common is contending with being black in America, figuring out what it means to be black in America. That turns out to be enough.

Marion Tumbleweed Beach, who defies the sense of the black community intuited from afar, who cannot quite be explained off King, makes sense, perfect and absurd, on King. And it's on King that Kedist Hirpassa can most freely, deeply and safely examine and cross-examine her own blackness.

* * *

When we first meet Tumbleweed—it's the name that suits her and sticks—it is September 2000 and she is storming toward the National Voting Rights Museum, citadel of civil rights history and gathering spot for out-of-town folks in Selma to help defeat Mayor Joe Smitherman. She's coming up the street from the Edmund Pettus Bridge, one of the movement's sacred sites, where two white women from New York stand sentry with signs telling passing motorists that "Joe Gotta Go."

Tumbleweed disagrees.

"Yankee go home!" she screams. "Yankee go home!"

"You're outside agitators," she says with a sneer. "You going to go back home and brag about how you freed us?"

Tumbleweed was born March 27, 1927, the 113th anniversary of the massacre of her great-grandmother's people, the Creek Indians, by Andrew Jackson. Her

Photo by Michael Falco, Newhouse News Service.

Marion Tumbleweed Beach, Selma, Ala.

great-grandfather was a free black man from Mali who had been told by his father that his destiny lay beyond the African stars. He made his way by salt caravan and silk ship to Mobile, Ala., arriving just after the end of the Civil War.

"I was supposed to die," Tumbleweed says of her birth—she was early and sickly—but her Creek great-grandmother said, "No, she's a tumbleweed."

She lived most of her adult life in Chicago, an activist in both the black and American Indian communities, godmother to other writers and artists.

Her late husband, Roscoe Beach, was a teacher and jazz musician. She was very involved with the DuSable

Museum for African American History, founding its
writers workshop and, after King's assassination, its annual Martinmas Day celebration of King's life. She
worked at the right hand of museum founder Margaret
Burroughs, with whom she maintains a fire-and-ice relationship.

"We're not speaking, but that's OK," Tumbleweed
says. "We would die for each other."

This is a woman with more feuds than most people
have friends.

"I've caught more hell from blacks than I have from
whites," she says. "I've lived with blacks. They had a
chance to kick my ass."

In 1965 Tumbleweed returned briefly to Selma to
help King find places to stay for the "outside agitators"
then swarming into town to support the voting rights
protests that, washed in blood and redemption, were in ret-
rospect King's crowning moment. Never before and never
again was the American public more moved to stand so
wholly and powerfully with the black freedom struggle.

"Confrontation of good and evil compressed in the
tiny community of Selma generated the massive power
to turn the whole nation to a new course," King said after
leading marchers across the Edmund Pettus Bridge and
on to Montgomery.

Compressed is right.

Selma seems in many ways a sleepy Southern town
where they keep time by the train whistle. But the car-
bon of black-white conflict has been compressed so
long and so hard here that the place is a gleaming, hard
diamond of racial antagonism.

Selma is a city of 20,000, 70 percent black. It is located in the heart of Alabama's Black Belt, so named for the
color of the rich earth, but also the stretch of America
with the blackest population. They are always commemorating battles fought here, whether King's or the Battle
of Selma, where Gen. Nathan Bedford Forrest was routed and the arsenal of the Confederacy fell, presaging the
rebellion's end.

* * *

Selma has remained a mecca of the civil rights movement. Kedist Hirpassa made the pilgrimage in high
school, on a Freedom Ride tour organized by C. Delores

Tucker, head of the National Political Congress of Black Women and a friend of the King family. Tucker is best known for her campaign against gangsta rap, one in which she enlisted Hirpassa, who nonetheless admits a soft spot for the late Tupac Shakur.

Hirpassa decided she wanted to try a black college, and when the tour headed to Atlanta, she knew where she wanted that college to be.

She was born to parents of two different, warring Ethiopian tribes—her father's urban, light-skinned and with European features; her mother's rural, dark-skinned, despised by her father's people. She came to the United States at 5 and grew up at a succession of boarding and later public schools, finishing high school in Washington's Maryland suburbs. Some in her Ethiopian circles considered her choice of a black college quite odd.

We meet her in August 2000 during freshman week at Morris Brown, which straddles MLK and is part of the Atlanta University Center of black colleges that adjoin it. In the late morning, Hirpassa, 18, is by herself in the nearly empty stands at Morris Brown's Herndon Stadium as the football team scrimmages and the cheerleaders thrust and shout in the pounding heat.

"I've never felt so much positive energy in my whole entire life from African Americans," Hirpassa says, and freshman week does pulse with what seems a deep and instant camaraderie and delight.

But she also notices right off that students at the other AUC schools—Morehouse College, Spelman College and Clark Atlanta University—"frown down" on Morris Brown as the "ghetto" school.

Morris Brown has its own distinction. While the other AUC schools were founded by whites for blacks, it was founded by blacks for blacks. Only a few years after they laid the cornerstone at Brown Chapel, the church that became home to the Civil Rights movement in Selma, the African Methodist Episcopal Church founded the Atlanta college, named for the same AME bishop. It prides itself on taking students as it finds them.

The Saturday night of freshman week, students from the AUC schools are brought together for an Olive Branch ceremony intended to dampen inter-school rivalries. Afterward, they march, thousands in all, to a party in the Clark Atlanta stadium on King, chanting their loyalties along the way: "Ashes to ashes, dust to dust. You got to be a Morehouse man to party like us." The Morris Brown reply is simple, direct. "We start it. We end it. MBC."

To be part of this dazzling parade of black youth, stretching as far as the eye can see, must be a nearly religious experience, though the soundtrack at the stadium is more Mystikal (the rapper) than mystical: "Shake ya ass. But watch ya self. Shake ya ass. Show me what you're working with."

Diagonally across King, 20,000 fans fill Herndon Stadium for a high school football double-header. The 440-strong Southwest DeKalb High School band is wailing brass, thundering drums. In the distance, the Atlanta skyline is set off against heavens of charcoal, blue and black. The intersection of Sunset and King is ablaze in light and motion, alive with the crosscurrent sounds of rap and football, of cruising and greeting, of Saturday night in a safe, happy, entirely black world.

King's funeral cortege marched past here. A few blocks up Sunset is the modest home that King, amid his Selma travails, bought in 1965 for $10,000. Coretta Scott King, his widow, still lives there, within distant earshot of the revelry.

* * *

On Sept. 12, 2000 in Selma, James Perkins Jr., the black candidate making his third run, defeats Joe Smitherman. The instant the news breaks, the streets are plunged into a delirium of celebration that lasts until morning.

Tumbleweed's phone starts ringing with excited calls from friends around the country. When she tells them she was with Smitherman, they are dumbfounded. She had, after all, been one of the organizers of artists and writers for Harold Washington, who in 1983, in the most triumphant political moment in black Chicago history, was elected that city's first black mayor.

Smitherman grew up poor, raised by an aunt who was the head waitress at the Splendid Cafe, where Tumbleweed's mother was the chef. "You noticed he talks black," Tumbleweed says. "He doesn't talk like a white man."

In recent years, Smitherman, a chain smoker, a bit

overweight, had taken a daily health walk past Tumbleweed's house. She'd be sitting in her chair under her sun umbrella and he would stop, sit. They would talk. It became his routine.

There came a time in Chicago, Tumbleweed says, when she voted for a black candidate over a better white candidate.

"It felt wrong," she says. "I'm bored with race."

Tumbleweed returned to Selma to live after her daughter, Carolyn Delores Beach Foucher, known as Polly, died of cancer in 1990. Polly had been a Black Panther in Chicago and at the funeral, former Panther Bobby Rush, now a congressman, read from Corinthians; Margaret Burroughs delivered the eulogy; and H. Rap Brown spoke. (The latter, now Jamil Al-Amin, is on trial at the Fulton County Courthouse on King in Atlanta, charged with the murder of a county sheriff's deputy, an alumnus of Morris Brown.) Tumbleweed's good friend, the poet Sterling Plumpp, read a poem he had written, "Panther Finder (for Polly)."

"Them old blues you got tumbling from a Tumbleweed.

"A wind song jumping from a hurricane."

With the wind song gone, the hurricane blew back to Selma.

* * *

In Atlanta, Hirpassa's freshman year is a whirlwind of activity. She throws herself into the middle of everything but remains a loner, reserved, observing—the calm in the storm of her own life.

She is elected freshman class president, but when the runner-up challenges the results, the election is left unresolved. She is Morris Brown's entry in the Miss AUC Freshman contest. She writes for the *AUC Digest*, a campus newspaper. She interns at the governor's office. She is the youngest and only black member of a socialist group that meets at Georgia State University. During her winter break, she works at C. Delores Tucker's office back home, providing the Bush administration with the names of black women qualified for top federal appointments.

At Morris Brown, she is intermittently enthused and exasperated. She loves the mix of black people and has come to appreciate black styles that once bewildered her. But she is also frustrated by "how things never get done."

In the fall of 2001, she transfers to Georgia State. But, even as she moves to a majority-white school, she starts a new organization with a few students from the various AUC campuses. It is called African Brothers and Sisters. They plan to create a magazine, to read to kids in the projects along King, to agitate for reparations.

* * *

Less than a month after Selma's election, a monument to Nathan Bedford Forrest, the Confederate general and founder of the Ku Klux Klan, suddenly appears on public land and the city is again consumed in conflict. On Martin Luther King Day 2001, protesters lasso the monument and try to pull it down, to no avail.

Tumbleweed thinks it would make more sense to place some sturdy wrought-iron benches next to the monument so people could sit and talk about it.

"Most of the people in Selma, white and black, have never had a conversation with each other," she says. "All people have to have their heroes and symbols. To attempt to take them away is to make an enemy."

At the end of February, with one white councilor crossing racial lines to break the deadlock, the council votes to move the statue to a private cemetery.

The trouble with her people, Tumbleweed says, is that they are both too bothered by other people's symbols and too readily beguiled by their own, like the Martin Luther King Street she lives on.

"All those damn streets are in the black neighborhood," she says. "No matter where you go in this country, there's a Martin Luther King street or drive or place or avenue. I say they still get us with trinkets. We go cheap. I resent it."

A conversation with
Jonathan Tilove

ALY COLÓN: What prompted you to write the series "Along Martin Luther King: A Passage to Black America"?

JONATHAN TILOVE: In 1994, I was doing a story on the 30th anniversary of Freedom Summer. I was in the Mississippi Delta. As I was traveling from one community to the next, I kept encountering the Martin Luther King Street. I knew there were a bunch of these streets, but I didn't realize how they were everywhere, even in really tiny towns. I thought it would be interesting to travel along these streets. It was a fantasy. I mentioned it when I got back, and my editors thought it was a great idea.

But how do you execute that without taking a year off? So it didn't go anywhere for a few years. I wasn't exactly sure what the story was, either. In 1999, I was in Jackson, Miss., doing a feature on Bob Moses, and I knew I was on Martin Luther King. We decided that I should spend a little more time there and check it out. They sent photographer Mike Falco, and he sent the photos of what we got. I think that was what sold the idea, because the photos were so good.

How did the photos help?

Most people are surprised by them. The photos are so contrary to people's first reaction of what they would expect to find along Martin Luther King. There's nothing depressing about the photos. What came through was that this was so much more heartening and alive than the kind of stereotype reputation of these places and these streets. So the fact that the images ran so counter to type, and the fact that both Mike Falco and I were so into this—we came back so excited each time—that sold it. Also, I've been doing this long enough so I had built up trust that this wouldn't turn out to be a waste of time.

How did you present this project to your editor, and

how did you make it work within the scope of all the other things you had to do?

It was done incrementally. There's no way I could have persuaded my editor up front to do what we ended up doing. It ended up being much more ambitious than anybody would have committed to, especially because it wasn't clear what the story was going to be. It wasn't as if we began by saying, "We've got to do eight different places." The ambition originally was much more modest. But because it was spaced over two years, and we were doing it intermixed with other things, it built and gained momentum. Then it was okay to commit to something grander. It really was the photographs and Torin Beefly, the photo editor, along with Deborah Howell, who had such enthusiasm for what they were seeing.

How much time over that two-year period did you spend on this?

We made multiple trips to some places. The Texas trip was two weeks. We went for two weeks to Portland and Oakland. We went on two weeklong trips to Belle Glade. It was about three months on the streets, three months of writing, about five weeks in the office researching, preparing. It got interrupted by Sept. 11. It was a hard thing to figure out how to write because there was so much stuff. And it wasn't as if there was a news story. It was a matter of just how to get a variety of people telling their stories and how to connect them and how to get the right kind of balance.

How did Mike help you connect with people?

The fact that photography has its requirements of seeing people in certain settings or needing a certain light kept us moving in a way that we couldn't otherwise. Or we would just be looking for something along the street, and a photograph would lead us into the story. I think people are much more obliged to say yes to Mike asking, "Can I make a photo?" Even though that would seem to be more of a commitment or more invasive, it's more welcome.

Can you give an example of how the photos led to fuller stories?

There are photos of these incredible faces. One was this classic scene of a gas station, Brown's service station, where old guys hang out and play pool checkers. They sit there all day. They look timeless in suspenders and smoking cigars, just sitting there, waiting for whatever, and talking. You start thinking, "This is just a bunch of old guys playing checkers." But one had been a Pullman porter, which was just the ultimate job for a black man from the South at one point. There was a guy who played Negro League ball. There was the guy who had left Jackson to go to Los Angeles, and then after the Watts riots came right back to Jackson, and then the next day he's driving the bus and breaking the color barrier there. This incredible history of the Civil Rights movement is told not by the people who would have any name recognition, but by people who experienced it firsthand and were pioneers. And this was just random—five or six people who were sitting by the side of the road.

Plus, people were open to telling their stories. You wouldn't learn all this stuff the first time you sat down with them. But in the course of a few days, a few visits, you would develop enough of a rapport so that you got this oral history. This is a block away from where Bob Moses, who's this incredible Civil Rights hero, is teaching class every day to kids who barely know his importance. And, it turns out, the woman who's working in the back of the classroom is this poet we'll end up encountering in Harlem and elsewhere. Quickly, it all weaves together, and you felt like you had gotten deeply into something with no other agenda but to just walk the street and talk to people.

Usually in reporting of any kind, but especially in writing about race relations, you're there to answer some very specific question, or to examine some particular phenomenon, or there's an agenda of some sort that has brought you there. There was none of that in this case. It was a real relief for me to just be saying, "Tell me about yourself" or "What happens on this street?" or "Who are you?" I think that transmitted itself readily because there was no kind of guard up.

174

Tell me more about how you decided to let the stories and voices unfold.

What I found was that, if you just keep going, people's stories are so compelling and intrinsically sympathetic that you identify with them. If you're able to just go with it, it makes perfect sense.

The guy who became one of the first bus drivers in Jackson was a very soft-spoken guy, so I listened to the other people first. But then he started telling his story. He was at a revival meeting in some rural place and a man dropped dead. He was so scared that he moved to Jackson at age 16 because he was freaked out. And then he ends up going from Jackson to Watts and loves it there. But he is there during the Watts riots and is so freaked out by that, he moves back to Jackson the next day. Then he goes for a job and he ends up being the first black bus driver in Jackson. So he's playing these heroic roles, but he's backing into them. He's telling me how nice the white bus drivers who trained him were to him and how satisfied they were to be training him to do this job, even though some riders wouldn't get on the bus.

It was so contrary to the normal text of the story, which is that he has to be a fearless individual blazing a trail, and he has to do it against uniform white resistance. In fact, it was just this mild-mannered guy with a slight stutter who told this completely self-deprecating story.

But when you look at the facts, he was a great figure. He was the last one I got to because I didn't see it in him. I figured he wasn't as dramatic a personality as some of these other people. And that kind of repeated itself in unexpected places. I was in Huntsville, Texas, where all the prisons and the death chamber are. Everything in Texas is on King. We were looking around, and there were these two sisters in their 80s and their brother, who had Alzheimer's. They would take him from the nursing home on Sundays. At first this interview was just a little too sedate. Then it turns out that his mother was pregnant with some of them while she was still a slave.

I'm wondering how that could possibly be? But they're 80, and he was 63 or something, and they were the last of 14 children. I did the math. You realize these people are only a generation or two away from slavery.

How did you choose the subjects you focused on?

They were the most compelling, and they also interacted with the photographs. When we were doing this, part of what drove where we went and when we went was having to turn these people and their stories into images. Mike would generally photograph them wherever we came upon them.

But then there might be something else he would do to more completely tell people's stories. Mike first photographed Johnny Brown, the Pullman porter who's in his 80s, at the service station where we found him. But then we went over to his house, and he ended up putting on his Pullman porter hat and telling stories. The second visit was much richer because it was like someone we knew and who opened up even further.

We had a second encounter for the people who emerged as the most important. The stories were much better having followed the photographs. There's no reason why I couldn't have returned if there'd been no photographs involved. But this required us to do it in a way that made more sense to the people we were dealing with. It pushed us.

It also made a big difference in terms of people's accessibility and openness. There's something about people being photographed that they respect or think you're making a certain commitment to them. And Mike is also pretty good at sending people photographs. When we went back the second time, his photographs from the first time were up at the service station. There's some really good faith there, and I think it showed. This would have been very different and not nearly as good if I had attempted to do something like this on my own.

As a journalist, what was it like for you to be white in black America?

What was interesting was how little that seemed to be a barrier. One exception was when we were in the middle of nowhere in Texas and a woman just back from church comes out and tells us to get off her street. We were kind of hurt. But then we recognized that we had expected that reaction to be much more common. The concern about being white and doing this loomed much larger in anticipating it, or thinking about it in the abstract, than in actually doing it. It's a matter of relaxing so we were not approaching it like, "I've got to get in there and get something and get out." We weren't starting out with some premise, demanding people tell us whether it was true or false. We were willing to spend a lot of time. We were there to listen and to photograph. We were happy to be doing this. Our excitement and interest came through. We'd start to tell them the things we did. And I think people were like, "Wow, that's interesting."

The fact that we were white almost was kind of a novelty. People gave us credit for doing it. I think our attitude about being open rubbed off.

And then knowing something. When people would tell stories with a certain history, I knew enough to be able to make connections, and I think that helped. Even showing up on a street and knowing a little bit about some things that had happened there was a sign of interest and good faith to people.

You picked the cities with a particular idea in mind, but they could have been other cities as well.

They could have been any number of others. What I wanted was different size places. I wanted geographic distribution. At first, I wasn't going to go to Harlem because I thought, "Everybody knows about Harlem." So why not go to Newark or somewhere? But then at some point I couldn't do this story and skip the most obvious places because then I'd be begging the question: "So, you didn't go to Harlem?"

After the one visit to Jackson, we picked Belle Glade, Fla., for Martin Luther King Day in 2000. I didn't know anything about Belle Glade. I researched it. I wanted someplace people wouldn't necessarily have a preconceived notion about, where it was a real struggle to name the street and to celebrate King's birthday. In Jackson, they said, "You've got to come back here; this is the biggest parade in the country." That was very attractive. But I was much more interested in what we ended up with, which was kind of a rag-tag parade in a place where they still had to argue over the parade route.

So you were interested in Belle Glade because it was a rag-tag place?

Yeah. It serves certain journalistic purposes. When Edward R. Murrow did "Harvest of Shame," that's where he did it. It's one of the poorest places. And we found out it also produces more professional football players than any community its size. What was interesting was that you realize there's more there than you realize. We compared Belle Glade with Harlem. Belle Glade seemed like it was this remote outpost of black America. But in fact, it was the source. Everything that was happening in Harlem had already happened in Belle Glade. If I hadn't been forced into having to construct some thematic connection, I wouldn't have realized that. What was nice about it was that we met people there who were talking about Morris Brown College in Atlanta, which I had never heard of, and it turns out it was on Martin Luther King. So we spent freshman week there that following August. One thing did lead to another again and again.

What kind of preparation did you do?

I did a lot. The Internet made it infinitely easier to arrive in places where I knew something about what had gone on there. If I already know a little bit about things people are dealing with and some of the players when I'm talking with people, that transmits itself. That's the virtue of doing this series after writing about race for so long. The thing that I would find intriguing would be based on things that I already knew and/or things that I didn't know but was interested in.

How did you come up with the voice that you used?

I was trying to get into the rhythm of the place. We encountered a lot of writers and poets along the way, so I was reading their stuff and listening to music that fit while I was working on the project. I also tried to read the stories out loud and be aware of the rhythm.

Did you read any particular history or poets beforehand, or did you learn those as you went along?

It was more as I went along. I hadn't read a lot of poetry. One of the things that impressed me was the importance of poets in playing other roles in the community. I met Haki Madhubuti in Chicago. I hadn't heard of him before. I had been writing about race for 10 years. How could I have not heard of him? What was I doing? He shows up everywhere, not just as a poet, but as a public figure throughout these communities. I just keep intersecting with him and the things that he'd done.

He was very close to Gwendolyn Brooks and that's what led us to go back for her funeral. So I read her. I read Zora Neale Hurston's novel, *Their Eyes Were Watching God*, because of Belle Glade. I had gone to Belle Glade without ever having read her. She captured the spirit of that place. I quote her several times, including her quote about what white publishers won't print and about how she says the average, non-morbid, struggling Negro is just invisible because either it's someone who's achieved great things or it is someone who's done awful things who make the newspapers. And this was written 60 years ago or longer. That could've been written yesterday. I read James Baldwin. I just kept encountering people along these streets in person or in their words. It wasn't like I had read a lot of the stuff before doing this, but it kept me in the right frame of mind.

Is there any particular framework you used?

It was letting people talk for themselves. Hopefully I allowed the reality to emerge as much as possible in their words. It was not something we felt obliged to sum up for the reader. That wouldn't have been true to it.

But you did have *some* point to make, right?

Right. I needed to deal with some themes to give the story structure. I was worried that we were going to try to superimpose some lessons, which I thought was not a good idea. But we tried not to overstate anything. We just have fairly simple themes that gave it a coherence it might otherwise not have had. There really is this enormously interconnected community, this nation within a nation. Once you went to one of these places, it really helped you to go to the next place and arrive there and not feel like you were arriving cold.

So did you mine the story and then step back from it to see what you had found?

I had to figure out some thematic connection. How am I going to explain this place in isolation? The pairing was nice; for example, being able to go back and forth between the King Drive in Chicago and the King in Jackson. The difficulty in writing it was just to say, "I can only give you a glimpse," because my tendency after meeting somebody was to try to find out everything about that person. I realized that part of what I had to do was to get back to that experience of the first encounter and not lose that sense of excitement. I think the danger with reporting too much, and then trying to write it, was losing the impact that had you so excited to begin with, which was learning something for the first time.

Did the experience change the way that you approach journalism?

It broadened my horizons, as someone who writes about race, in terms of who I would talk to. When you're writing stories about race for a mainstream publication, you often have to calibrate what the mainstream is thinking about this. Or you have some expert put this in context. But when I was there, I didn't worry about having to do that. I spent some time at the *Chicago Crusader*, a black newspaper on Martin Luther King Drive. I was there the day before the 2000 presidential election. Their election week issue was just the front page in addition to an interview with one of the relatives of James Byrd, about how Bush didn't support hate crimes legislation in Texas, and how that leads to Byrd's dragging.

It was the kind of thing most mainstream journalists would look at and say: "Oh, my God, and this is balanced coverage?" But in the black community the notion of the role of the newspaper, and what was considered the center of gravity, was entirely different. I was immersing myself in what people were saying and thinking and talking about, and not attempting to analyze it in that way. And it all kind of made more sense to me.

It gave me a chance to experience the rationality of what seems less rational looking in from the outside. For instance, Chokwe Lumumba in Jackson. He doesn't get written about much. He's a lawyer. He takes a lot of death penalty cases and he ends up in the paper. But it would be hard to explain in a conventional story that he's a guy who came from Detroit to Jackson to help create a separate black nation.

Now on the face of it, most white readers will say, "I'm not going to pay any attention to what this person has to say because he's either delusional or he's a fringe character." Well, he came there for that reason. He believed in that. He is also a pillar of the black community in Jackson. He's respected by people who might vote Republican or might vote Democrat, but they don't feel that they have an obligation to have it make sense to a white reader.

Any number of figures in the black community are written off because there's something about them that the white reader discredits. And that is just totally meaningless in the black community. If you tried to dot every "i" and cross every "t" to make sense to your mainstream audience, you've then made it *not* make sense within the black community. It's a struggle you're up against in writing about race. You've got these alternate realities so that you have to sacrifice one or the other. I feel a little bit less concerned about having it all make sense to every reader.

I'm still trying to figure out this woman I met in Selma: Marion Tumbleweed Beach. She has the most incredible life story of activism and firsthand connection with King and everybody else. When I went to Selma just before they elected a black mayor, she was the only one on Martin Luther King Street who had a sign for the white mayor. If I were there simply writing a story about this election for a daily newspaper, I could not explain her character in the context of that story without either discrediting her, or without her coming across as either disloyal or an aberration or weird. It was just too complicated to explain why she could be absolutely integral to that community and at odds with it, and yet that wasn't even problematic if you were part of that community.

How does that play out?

When you're trying to identify people in a news story about race, you've got to identify them in some way. She's conservative or he's a nationalist or she's affiliated with this organization or whatever. There's got to be something that places a person on a spectrum or in a place that people say, "Okay, that's why she does this."

The only way to explain Marion Beach was just to let her talk. But I don't know if, even in the confines of this story, you were able to get that. That's the problem with a lot of race coverage. You've got to distill it to a point of view or representation. Even if you have all these qualifiers, you've sort of emasculated the community because it's not saying anything. It has no particular point of view or can't express itself because you're generalizing. The attempt to fit people into the categories by which journalists either feel obliged, or are obligated, to explain the world, doesn't work. With the exception of writing more about communities and letting people speak at greater length, I don't know exactly how you solve that. It's just a matter of allowing for more complexity in the way they express themselves.

Were there any other particular things that you consciously did that you think others could do to help make that a more natural, comfortable experience for the journalist as well as for the subject?

I don't know if this is specific to race, but one of the things we tried to do was to go places when certain things were happening. We were in Galveston for Juneteenth. We were at freshman week at Morris Brown. In Belle Glade, we were there for Martin Luther King Day and then for a football game. We were in Chicago for the election. So we're finding ourselves in situations that are self-propelling. We're not standing there saying, "Okay, do something." We're talking to people along the way, but there's a built-in momentum to the occasion.

The people who held these communities together were just doing amazing things. But they didn't have any kind of title you could put after their name. They didn't have any kind of particular resources. They just functioned in these communities as important figures. I think these people get lost in daily journalism because, if you don't have an identifier that sounds official, then how is the reader supposed to know that they have some standing or legitimacy.

Do people have to have official status to get in the newspaper?

I think there's a natural tendency in a lot of daily journalism to approach the leaders of the community who have titles. Even if they're perfectly great people, they have a certain relationship with the press that then requires them to be guarded and deliberate, and to be the leader. Everything becomes kind of this official speak.

If you encounter them in a more natural way, they come across more naturally. For instance, when we were going down to Jackson, I was trying to reach Kenneth Stokes, who's the city councilman who represents that part of Jackson. He was responsible for getting the street named, responsible for the parade. So he was the official you'd want to talk to. He wouldn't return my calls. I left messages before we went and when we got there and could not get his call back. I was explaining this to Mike Falco. He told me the man in the gas station, Mr. Stokes, was Kenneth Stokes's dad. So Mr. Stokes called his son on his cell phone and he was over in two minutes and was giving a tour. He was great. But he wouldn't return my calls as a reporter calling from Washington, D.C. I was chagrined that Mike managed to find this guy I'd been looking for. The way I had to get hold of him was to call the gas station, get Mr. Stokes, get him to call Kenny, and have Kenny call me.

In a way you need a guide to get in, to connect the players.

Right, and that's a good point because the problem is the guide reporters usually use is the name. That person may be perfectly legitimate. Or he may be a joke in that community. But because Kenneth Stokes was introduced to us through his father at the gas station, we had legitimacy. He was open to us in a way that he would not have been if we had encountered him first. That was why we went back to Belle Glade for a third time. Even the images got better. It's tough because the more you do, the more you realize how superficial what you did was. And you thought that was pretty good.

Do you think that a good piece of advice for journalists might be that once is not enough?

By the time we went back to Belle Glade for the third time, we just felt so connected to people. When you first arrive in a place, there is a certain amount of being a little tense, or looking around a lot to figure out what you are going to do next. And by the third time, it was like we could just keep doing this.

There's so much about race in America that people get caught up in situations where they can't understand one another. You just know there's no good outcome. And feelings like that divide. But by sitting and talking to people, you end up feeling much better about people.

The classic is the O.J. thing. If you had people sit down and talk about it for three hours, they'd find that they weren't really that far off from each other in their total assessment of it. Or they would understand why the other person had a different point of view.

But people get cemented into antagonism when all they get is the single image of whites seeing blacks cheering, and blacks seeing whites horrified. The polarization is far more serious when you try to encapsulate it in a simplistic fashion in a news story.

That's the way these things happen in the community—by word of mouth and rumors. Then people get the wrong impression about what other people are thinking.

A lot of news stories are simply a refined version of that process. And what makes a good news story are the polar opposites, the extremes and the differences. The people I met on Martin Luther King wouldn't get quoted because they haven't had their passport to mainstream stamped. They're not part of the discussion.

But it's convenient for me to quote them now because I've developed a relationship.

Writers' Workshop

Talking Points

1) Jonathan Tilove wanted voices of authentic people in his stories about the Martin Luther King streets he visited. What did he do to find those authentic voices? Discuss whether he was successful.

2) Analyze the structure and themes Tilove used. Which were effective?

3) Tilove believes writing about race relations requires addressing the complexity that surrounds the topic. How did he tackle that complexity in this series?

4) Tilove and photojournalist Mike Falco, who are white, spent a lot of time in predominantly black neighborhoods. Do you get a sense of their race or of any racial conflict in the stories?

Assignment Desk

1) Tilove says he has a tendency to over-report his stories, to learn everything he can about his subjects. But in this series, he sought to convey to the reader the sense of fresh discovery he had experienced. In the next profile of a community you do, try to recapture and communicate your fresh experiences about that community.

2) Tilove focused on people without official titles. They were "ordinary" people who also were complex individuals. He allowed that complexity to become part of the story. Study some of the characters who are both at home—and at odds—with their community. Attempt to convey that complexity in describing people you have come across in your stories or beats.

3) Some of the stories Tilove found came about because he just sat and listened. He approached them without a preconceived story or set of questions he wanted answered. Try spending an extended period of time in your community or beat just listening and observing. See if you can "find" the story embedded in the conversations.

Portland Press Herald

Kelley Bouchard

Finalist, Diversity Writing

Kelley Bouchard has been a staff writer at the *Portland Press Herald/ Maine Sunday Telegram* since 1999, covering Portland City Hall, statewide immigration issues, and general assignment topics. She is a 1987 graduate of the journalism program at the University of Maine, and her studies included two reporting internships at her hometown newspaper, the *Lewiston Evening Journal*.

She started her career at the *Ipswich Chronicle*, in Ipswich, Mass., followed by stints at the *Beverly Times* and *The Salem Evening News*, also on Boston's North Shore. Previous writing honors include first-place awards from the New England Associated Press News Executives Association, the Pew Charitable Trust and the University of California Center for the Health Professions in 1998, and from the Maine Press Association in 1999 and 2002.

"Lewiston's Somali Surge" was part of a two-year series in the *Maine Sunday Telegram* about immigration's impact on Maine, past and present. Bouchard's story was the first in-depth look at how Lewiston, a struggling former mill town with a mostly white, French-Catholic heritage, was responding to such a large and rapid influx of Somali immigrants. For a follow-up story, Bouchard went to Georgia to find out why so many Somalis were moving from the Atlanta area to Lewiston. Her stories drew national attention to a simmering conflict that boiled over in the fall of 2002, when Lewiston's mayor asked Somalis to stop moving there, and white supremacist groups started recruiting members in Lewiston.

Lewiston's Somali surge

APRIL 28, 2002

LEWISTON—It is a driving force for the nomadic herdsmen who live on Somalia's vast, arid plains.

They move their livestock from one watering hole to the next, each a shrinking remnant of the *gu*, the monsoon season when most marriages and festivals take place.

For the rest of the year the herdsmen look to the sky, hoping to see clouds ahead. They send out *sahans*, young scouts who search for lightning, a sure sign that a storm is brewing on the horizon.

"We always go where the rain is going to fall," said Omar Hamed, 48, one of the newest members of Maine's growing Somali community.

Right now, it's pouring in Lewiston.

Hamed—formerly a schoolbook translator in Somalia, now a welfare caseworker in Lewiston—is one of 800 to 1,000 Somalis who have moved to this once-bustling mill town in the last year. Another 1,000 are expected to come this summer, most of them from Atlanta. Victims of Somalia's lengthy civil war, they have chosen Maine for its low crime rate. They are bypassing Portland for Lewiston's cheaper, more plentiful housing.

As a result, this largely white, Franco-American city of 36,000 may be on the cusp of its greatest social and economic change since the area's textile mills and shoe factories started closing in the late 1950s. Some are prepared for Lewiston to take its place in an American landscape that grows more diverse with each passing decade. Others don't like it at all.

The city has responded to such a large and rapid influx of newcomers. Signs offering translator services are posted throughout City Hall. The city's Web site now has a Somali information page. Social workers help Somalis find apartments, navigate massive supermarkets and understand the school and health care systems. Employment counselors take extra time putting together resumes and explaining the nuances of job hunting. Teachers and volunteers give classes in everything from English to American culture.

Somalis are working hard to settle in, too. They have opened a storefront Islamic mosque, a nonprofit community center and a variety store on Lisbon Street, once the city's main shopping thoroughfare. Women wearing colorful head scarves called *hijab* are seen everywhere in a city dominated by the spires of six Roman Catholic churches. Last Wednesday, the Somali community hosted an evening of food and culture at the Franco-American Heritage Center. More than 300 people attended.

Still, city officials estimate that only about 40 of the 400 to 500 Somali adults living in Lewiston are working. The local labor market offers little for unskilled workers who don't speak English well or lack high school diplomas. At the same time, the annual welfare budget for this financially strapped city has doubled to $200,000 in the last year because many Somalis are seeking rental and food assistance. Lewiston's Adult Learning Center, where half of the students are now Somali, is so packed that some classes are held in a stairwell. Lewiston has received $200,000 in federal grant assistance already, for additional caseworkers and an adult education teacher, but city leaders plan to ask state and federal officials for more help.

The Somalis' arrival has strained Lewiston's limited resources and rattled city and school officials who are trying to hold down taxes. It has stirred reactions among longtime residents that range from genuine support to outright bigotry. One Lewiston man shares his disdain for newcomers with signs posted in front of his house. Another man, 33-year-old Samuel Gaiewski, has been charged with a hate crime for using a racial slur when he allegedly threatened to kill a Somali man during a parking confrontation last January.

"There is an undercurrent of resentment of people who are coming," said Mayor Laurier Raymond. "I don't think it's racial. I don't think it's religious. I think it's dollars and cents. I think the citizenry is genuinely concerned about the impact on their taxes. We probably should be flattered they've picked Lewiston. Unfortunately, many of them don't come with any money and they don't have jobs, and there is some resentment of that."

Leaders in the Somali community are aware of the growing concern. When the *Portland Press Herald/ Maine Sunday Telegram* reported earlier this month that another 500 to 1,000 Somalis from Atlanta are expected to move to Lewiston this summer, one Somali leader went on Atlanta's Somali radio station and told them not to come. In response, Abdiaziz Ali, the Somali case manager in Lewiston's general assistance office, made a follow-up announcement saying that Somalis are welcome in Lewiston, but that they should meter their arrival.

"The problem is, as I see it, if they come too fast," said Sue Charron, Lewiston's general assistance director. "In the past couple of months, people have been more vocal about their concern. I think we need to simmer things down. We need to get the word out that we welcome you and we want you, but you can't come all at once."

Somalis started moving to Lewiston in February 2001, after they arrived in Portland and found that the only available housing was the city's family homeless shelter. Lewiston landlords started calling Portland officials to say they had plenty of apartments for rent.

In recent years, as Lewiston's population declined (4,000 people left in the last decade alone), rentals became increasingly available. Five years ago, before the city began tearing down substandard apartment buildings, the vacancy rate was as high as 20 percent. Now, by some estimates, the vacancy rate is closer to 7 percent. That's roomy compared to Portland's estimated 3 percent vacancy rate.

It's unclear how long Lewiston's vacancy rate will remain favorable. Many Somalis have found housing in Lewiston's downtown tenements. Others are renting through the Lewiston Housing Authority, where the waiting list for federally subsidized apartments has grown from 130 families last year to 230 families today. Somalis now occupy one-quarter of the 94 townhouse units in Hillview Apartments, one of the city's suburban housing projects.

"It has become the most popular destination (for Somali families)," said James Dowling, executive director of the housing authority.

The estimate that as many as 1,000 Somalis may

move to Lewiston this summer comes from a variety of sources within the Somali community. While some Lewiston officials and even some Somalis dispute or downplay the anticipated number of summer arrivals, officials in Portland and Atlanta have learned to respect the accuracy of the Somali rumor mill. Barbara Cocchi, a regional director of World Relief Corp., one of five refugee resettlement agencies in Atlanta, said Somali elders have told her that more than 1,000 are planning to relocate to Lewiston soon after school ends in June.

"It's not about being alarmist," said Gerald Cayer, Portland's director of health and human services. "From my perspective, it means how do we help Lewiston work on the issues that will arise."

Lewiston officials have reason to be concerned. If another 1,000 Somalis move here this summer, in less than two years Lewiston will have a Somali population that rivals the estimated 2,200 Somalis who have settled in Portland (pop. 65,000) over the last 15 years. And Lewiston has little of the social service or employment infrastructure that Portland, as Maine's largest city, has developed over the years to serve a diverse immigrant population. In comparison, there are 4,000 Somalis in greater Atlanta (pop. 3.4 million), and more than 50,000 in greater Minneapolis (pop. 2.8 million). A few Somali families have already moved to Auburn (pop. 23,000), Lewiston's sister city across the Androscoggin River.

Somalis say they are moving to Maine because they like its small-town feel, comparatively low crime rate and lack of racial conflict. Somalis have experienced tensions with established African-American populations in larger U.S. cities. They say Somali elders chose Maine after visiting several other states.

Statistically, Maine ranks 46th on the FBI crime index, while Georgia ranks 13th. Maine also is the whitest state in the nation, with a minority population of 3 percent, according to the 2000 Census. In Lewiston, black, Asian, Hispanic and other minorities represent about 5 percent of the population, including a handful of French-speaking Togolese families who moved here in 2000.

"In Atlanta, we were concerned the whole day what we would find when we got home," said Mohammed

Abdi, the Somali community/parent specialist in Lewiston schools. "Here, our children can go out in the afternoon and ride their bicycles and come home when the sun goes down, and we do not have to worry."

Most Somali refugees in the United States came from refugee camps in Kenya. Many Somalis in Portland were initially settled by Catholic Charities Maine, the state's primary, federally funded refugee resettlement agency. Many Somalis who are relocating to Lewiston from other states are no longer eligible for federal refugee assistance. As a result, those who cannot find work rely on city, state and federal welfare programs.

Since February 2001, a total of 210 Somali families (more than 600 individuals) have been served by Lewiston's general assistance office, Charron said. At this time, 200 Somali families (563 individuals) are receiving food and housing vouchers. Among them, 339 are children, 224 are adults.

The adults include 16 Somalis who are in the country illegally and have applied for asylum. While they wait for their cases to be decided, which could take more than a year, they are prohibited from working and ineligible for any public assistance other than the city's welfare program.

Charron said Somalis now make up 22 percent of the people getting welfare from the city, and she expects general assistance spending to continue to grow if the Somali population increases as predicted.

Another 48 Somali families in Lewiston are getting Temporary Assistance for Needy Families, said Pierrot Rugaba, the state's refugee coordinator. Temporary Assistance for Needy Families is a federally funded program administered by the state that provides monthly stipends of about $125 per family member.

Financial costs aside, various agencies in the city are stepping up efforts to coordinate services for the Somali community. City officials have been meeting with Somali leaders to get a better understanding of how many are coming and what services they will need. Police have held similar meetings to explain local laws and better understand Somali culture and family life.

One place Lewiston is benefiting financially from the infusion of newcomers is in its schools, where the city is spending an extra $250,000 on staff and programs for Somali students.

Lewiston's student population had dropped from 5,196 in 1990 to 4,439 in 2000. With its lower property values and the addition of 205 Somali students during the last year, Lewiston's state education subsidy increased $1.2 million this year to $18.2 million. Portland, which lost some students and saw its property values skyrocket, lost $1.8 million in state aid.

What worries Lewiston school officials is that federal grant funding has grown scarce for education programs like those that helped Portland establish a nationally recognized multicultural center in its schools. Still, Lewiston school officials say they are doing their best to welcome Somali students, with diversity training, civil rights teams and cultural heritage events.

"It's not something we planned for or encouraged," said Leon Levesque, Lewiston's school superintendent. "We're mandated and obligated by state and federal law to provide an education to all students in our community and that's what we're going to do."

If the Somali community continues to grow, Lewiston officials expect it to become more difficult to maintain services for all children. That time may arrive sooner than hoped. By some estimates, there are about 200 Somali children already living in Lewiston who are under school age but will soon be entering the system.

While Lewiston is attracting Somalis from various U.S. cities, most are coming from greater Atlanta, which lost 60,000 jobs after the Sept. 11 terrorist attacks. Lewiston-Auburn hasn't fared much better.

Business leaders say good jobs are still available in the Twin Cities, but the manufacturing jobs that attracted thousands of French Canadians in the late 1800s and early 1900s are gone. Lewiston-Auburn saw its job market shrink 2.9 percent last year—the ninth largest percentage decline in the country among metropolitan areas, according to CBS Marketwatch. Lewiston-Auburn's unemployment rate is 4.5 percent, compared to 2.9 percent in Portland and 6.1 percent in the United States overall.

Rose Hodges, an employment and training specialist at Lewiston's Career Center, said the local job market is tight. A year ago she typically had two or three pages of job openings. Now she has only one page. And the available jobs usually require applicants who speak English and have a high school diploma or can pass a test that requires high school reading and math skills. While some Somalis are well educated and are attending the University of Southern Maine in Lewiston and Portland, others have no education at all. Some are willing to commute to find work, but that prospect is difficult if they don't own a car.

"We have jobs available, but they may not be suitable for some Somalis," Hodges said. "Some (Somalis) are very employable. Some of them are not. We are making every effort to find them employment. Those we have placed have had good results."

Several large employers in Lewiston-Auburn have hired Somalis, including Gates Formed-Fibre Products Inc., Bell Manufacturing Co., Tambrands Inc., St. Mary's Regional Medical Center and Central Maine Medical Center.

Charles Morrison, president of the Androscoggin County Chamber of Commerce, said results have been mixed. While some Somalis have worked elsewhere in the United States, those who are unfamiliar with the American workplace require extra training. Some Somalis have become model employees. Others have had a difficult time adjusting to new concepts such as showing up on time, calling in sick and giving two weeks notice before leaving a job. So far, the need to pray during the workday and the safety hazard of long clothing worn by most Somali women haven't become problems as they have in other cities.

"This is a long-term adjustment for everybody," Morrison said. "People who do good work and maintain the standards are going to keep their jobs and be promoted, no matter who they are."

Despite the lack of jobs in Lewiston, Somalis are coming because they want to find a safe place to live. Many endured years of violence and famine in their home country, which still has no functioning government.

"Safety comes first," said Abdiaziz Ali, 32, who is married and has five children. Ali left a high-tech manufacturing job in Atlanta that paid $16 an hour to find work in Lewiston last spring. He was hired by the city four days after he arrived. He said those who are motivated to work will find jobs, even if they must first learn to read and write English.

Somalis deny they are coming because they have heard Maine's welfare system is easier, a perception state officials say is unfounded. Since 1994, the number of Maine families on welfare has dropped from 23,200 to 11,000 because of welfare reform, said Judy Williams, the state's director of family independence. Somalis say they want to work and are ashamed to be on welfare.

"Many people believe Somalis come to Lewiston for the welfare, but it's not true," said Mohamed Hassan, 34, one of two Somalis who work at Bell Manufacturing Co., a clothing label maker in Lewiston. "We come here because it is a good place and because the people who live here are very, very nice people."

Still, some Lewiston residents wonder why the city bends over backward to make Somalis feel welcome when their French, Irish, German or Italian ancestors were mistreated when they arrived more than a century ago.

James Teehan has posted two large signs in front of his Sylvan Avenue home that have drawn widespread notice. Orange letters neatly stenciled on plywood ask why the city helps Somalis when veterans and homeless people go without and American soldiers fight in the Middle East.

"I was so irritated, I had to do something," said Teehan, a 33-year-old flooring contractor. "Why are we taking care of them before we take care of our own?... Immigration had its place at a certain time. That time has come and gone."

People with that mindset only get so far with Phil Nadeau, Lewiston's assistant city manager and point man on the Somali issue. Nadeau is preparing a report on Lewiston's rapidly growing Somali population in an effort to win support from Gov. Angus King and Maine's congressional delegation for expanded job training, adult education and general assistance programs.

Nadeau acknowledges a certain amount of pride in the fact that his French-Canadian forebears overcame great odds to make it in America. In Lewiston, some children were beaten for speaking French in school.

Workers who couldn't speak English often got the lowest-paying jobs. But Nadeau rails against the idea that immigrants today should face the same trials. He notes that the social service programs available to Lewiston's Somalis are available to any American, no matter where they live. And he sees obvious benefits from an infusion of culture and residents in a city that has been losing population for decades.

"God bless the tenacity of our grandparents and great-grandparents," Nadeau said. "But the fact remains that laws have been created because we've learned that putting up barriers isn't the best way to integrate newcomers into our community."

So far, that integration has gone pretty smoothly. Observers marvel at the way Lewiston has accepted the challenge of welcoming such a rapid infusion of newcomers. The next step, most agree, is getting them working.

"Right now, I don't see a problem," said Sgt. Michael McGonagle, spokesman for the Lewiston police. "But if the Somali community continues to grow and they don't find work, there may be conflicts within the Somali community and with the community at large."

Somalis who are already in Lewiston downplay the concern over those who are expected to follow. Eventually, they say, if housing in Lewiston-Auburn gets scarce and jobs remain hard to find, word will spread to the Somali community outside Maine.

"Down the road, the reality will set in and people will stop coming," Abdi said.

And they will look elsewhere for signs of rain.

Lessons Learned

BY KELLEY BOUCHARD

It's always important to get both sides of a story. It's even more important to seek that balance when the story is multifaceted and the complicating factors are prejudice, bigotry, and racism. Providing thorough information without passing judgment leaves the reader to do the work of understanding an issue and reaching his or her own conclusion. Being fair and balanced was the challenge I faced in writing "Lewiston's Somali Surge," about the growing unrest over a rapid influx of Somali immigrants in Lewiston, Maine.

We were a year into our "American Journey" series about immigration's impact on Maine when I turned my attention to Lewiston. Until then, the series had focused on Portland, Maine's largest and most diverse city, because that's where most political refugees and other immigrants had settled in the last 20 years. But housing is expensive and scarce in Portland, so Somalis who had decided to move to Maine from other American cities simply headed on up the turnpike to Lewiston, a 45-minute drive north. They found plenty of inexpensive housing in Maine's second-largest city, and they sent word to other Somalis that Lewiston was a pretty decent place to live. By the spring of 2002, about a year after the influx began, Lewiston officials estimated that 800 to 1,000 Somalis had moved to the city and some expected that figure to double over the summer.

I wanted to find out how residents in that mostly white, French-Catholic community felt about sharing their streets, schools, and workplaces with newcomers who were black and Muslim. It was clear from the start that I would encounter a wide spectrum of opinions in a struggling former mill town. Some people were eager to welcome diversity and the possibility of economic revival. Others worried about the cost, both social and economic, when many of the newcomers needed help to resettle and assimilate. Still others said they wanted nothing to do with the Somalis and hoped they would leave.

My task was further complicated by the fact that I grew up in Lewiston and still have family there. I knew the community well, and I was surprised that so many Somalis were choosing to move to Lewiston. It hasn't been a go-to city since French Canadians and other immigrants came in the late 1800s and early 1900s. And because Lewiston's once-thriving textile mills had closed during the last few decades, good-paying jobs that don't require a college education are hard to come by. So I was a bit skeptical as well. More than 4,000 people had left Lewiston since the 1980s, looking elsewhere for economic prosperity. Why did so many Somalis want to move there now? And how was Lewiston responding?

Ultimately, those questions formed the core of my story. I interviewed a lot of people, and I let their answers tell the story of "Lewiston's Somali Surge." I envisioned myself writing the story right down the middle, pulling together threads of information to give readers an overall understanding of the people and the issues involved. I took the same tack for "A Thousand Miles," when I went to Atlanta to find out why Somalis were moving to Lewiston, and for other stories in the "American Journey" series.

I was gratified when people said they enjoyed my work on the series, whatever their reasons. I was most proud when they said the stories were fair.

Argus Leader

Stu Whitney

Finalist, Diversity Writing

Stu Whitney has been a sportswriter for the Sioux Falls, S.D., *Argus Leader* since 1992, covering a variety of issues that stretch beyond the playing field and illustrate how the games people play can deeply affect their lives.

A native of Grosse Pointe Park, Mich., Whitney received a journalism degree from Michigan State University and worked for *The Lansing State Journal* before arriving in South Dakota, where his columns and enterprise reporting have established a standard of excellence.

Whitney, 36, has been named the state's Sportswriter of the Year three times and he is a six-time finalist in the national Associated Press Sports Editors contest, including a second-place finish in the enterprise category in 2003.

Whitney lives in Sioux Falls with his wife, Lisa, and 3-year-old daughter, Emily.

In the series "Bright Hopes, Dashed Dreams," Whitney examined the unique challenges faced by Native-American athletes as they try—and often fail—to make the transition from high school to college.

While researching the three-day series, he traveled to Indian reservations in South Dakota and visited several college campuses—including Haskell Indian Nations University in Lawrence, Kan.—to add poignant detail to a powerful story that struck a chord with many readers.

Squandered chances

SEPTEMBER 15, 2002

POTATO CREEK—After weeks of trying to track down the elusive Jess Heart, this is where the trail finally leads.

It's a tiny village on the Pine Ridge Indian Reservation, where dogs come snarling over dirt-rutted roads and children chase each other in a jagged little line, the smallest girl crossing the rubble on roller skates.

This is where you find the 22-year-old Heart, staying in a two-bedroom house with seven members of his family, which on this day includes his 4-year-old son, Latrell, born when Heart was a high school junior.

The former Little Wound High School basketball star also has a 1-year-old daughter, Erika, who is staying in Rapid City with her mother, Heart's former girlfriend.

"It's good to have little ones around," says Heart's father, Narcisse. "It keeps you on your toes."

Behind the house, a twisted, rusty basketball rim lies forgotten—a salient symbol amid the desperation and debris of one of America's poorest communities.

For Heart, a 6-foot-4 scoring machine who flunked out of three colleges, this seems like the most sensible place to disappear. Like many Native American athletes, the first-team All-State guard and 1999 Mr. Basketball finalist has failed to make a transition from high school to college sports.

Heart hasn't played officially since leading Central Community College of Columbus, Neb., to the National Junior College Athletics Association tournament in 2000, and he will not play this season.

"I think most people have written me off, except for those around me," says Heart, sitting in the dark at a kitchen table while his 15-year-old brother, Tyson, naps on the couch nearby. "It's tough to explain, but I just like being around my family and the people I've been with my whole life."

For the rest of South Dakota, though, Heart's absence from college basketball seems like a waste of potential. Few fans have forgotten his heroics at the 1999 Class A state tournament, when he scored 48 points in a semi-final overtime loss to eventual champion De Smet.

"I don't know that I've seen a better performance," says former Huron University coach Fred Paulsen, who helped guide Custer High School to a win over Little Wound in that year's third-place game. "I've seen a lot of basketball, but it seemed like he played with a passion that was unbelievable. I mean, I was awestruck.

"I've talked to several coaches who think Jess Heart was big-time. His fluidity was unbelievable, and he had the ability to know where he was on the floor. But if someone has a passion for the game and knows that there are other responsibilities involved with being able to play, at what point does the fault lie with him?"

At least on the surface, Heart's future seemed fine when he lifted Little Wound into that televised showdown against top-ranked De Smet.

After playing for Pine Ridge as a junior, Heart had transferred back to Little Wound, which he had attended as a freshman and sophomore. Both schools are based on the Pine Ridge reservation, but Little Wound is in Kyle, just 15 miles from Potato Creek. That makes it Heart's hometown school.

But perhaps the biggest reason to return to Little Wound was the presence of legendary coach Dusty LeBeau, who had moved to the school after a successful stint at Red Cloud.

"Somebody once asked me what Heart added to our team," recalls the coach. "I said, 'Well, to start with, about 30 points a game.'"

Finishing the season 16-3, the Mustangs routed Winner in the regionals to advance to the state tourney for the first time in 20 years. They slipped past Cheyenne-Eagle Butte 55-50 in the first round to reach the semifinals against De Smet.

"We followed them all year, and we knew they were No. 1," says Narcisse, a former basketball standout who coached his son from fifth to eighth grade. "No one ever gave Little Wound a chance to stay in the game. That's what all the sports reporters were saying. But we figured we could play with them."

Despite a severe case of nerves, Heart came out gunning and turned in one of the greatest shooting displays in tourney history—a performance that inspired his teammates and filled the Oglala Lakota people with pride.

"Once Jess starts hitting, you know he's not going to miss," says Cory Shangreaux, a forward on that Little Wound team. "He just throws it up, and it goes in."

Heart hit 19 of 33 shots from the field—including six 3-pointers. But De Smet kept its composure in the face of full-court pressure and forced overtime when Heart's 3-pointer at the buzzer bounced off the rim.

The comeback spelled trouble for LeBeau's underdogs, who had encountered foul trouble and had only one player other than Heart scoring in double figures.

"It was a classic Indian vs. white battle," says Narcisse, a former Flandreau Indian School standout who played at Haskell Indian Nations University.

"We pressed them the whole way, but they were disciplined enough to handle it. They played smart, and it showed what a disciplined team can do to you. Little Wound depended on Jess too much."

Heart, who scored his team's only seven points of overtime, drew his fifth foul while trying to steal an inbounds pass during the extra session. He left the court with his head buried in his jersey as fans from both sides of the arena paid tribute to his effort. Heart then watched helplessly as the Mustangs failed to manage another point and fell 81-78.

For some, though, Heart's heroics stirred memories of Cheyenne legend Freddie Knife, who led the Braves to a Class B title in 1959 and drew thunderous cheers with his basketball artistry.

But unlike Knife, who succumbed to alcoholism and faded into obscurity, this new hero seemed to have a chance to keep his career alive in college.

Heart's senior success had drawn Division I recruiting interest, including serious overtures from Kansas State University. But his commitment to classes, never strong to begin with, became nonexistent as soon as basketball season ended.

"His problem was definitely on the academic side," says LeBeau, who guided Red Cloud to the 1995 title and is now back coaching Pine Ridge. "Kansas State was offering him a scholarship, but I told them he wasn't academically prepared. They wanted to put him in a junior college close to their campus. He was aware of all that, but the next thing I heard he was headed to junior college in Nebraska."

Heart had enrolled at Central Community College in Columbus, which has about 1,000 students. Longtime coach Jack Gutierrez initially recruited Little Wound's Ted Standing Shoulder, but he became smitten with Heart when the two Pine Ridge friends visited the campus together.

"When we signed Jess, Kansas State called and wanted to know where he was so they could keep tabs on him," says Gutierrez. "I'm sure there were a lot of Division II schools that also liked him.

"But when we recruited him, it was nip and tuck whether he was even going to graduate (from Little Wound). He didn't attend high school on a regular basis. But he was such a quality basketball player, they let him do whatever he wanted. And that carried right over to college."

While Standing Shoulder rented an apartment, Heart lived in the dormitory at Central and immediately felt restless on the mostly white campus, located about 280 miles from Pine Ridge.

"It got boring at night," recalls Heart. "The campus was five miles out of town, so there was nothing to do. I came home every other weekend, and I was making it back and forth for a while. But then I got tired and lazy, and I'd stay home a few extra days and fall behind in my classes."

Those close to Heart insist the lack of fellow Native American students at college contributed to his longing for home.

"When you're on the reservation, you're surrounded by that Indian atmosphere," says Narcisse, whose other children include daughters Jessica, 17, and Kiesha, 5, and sons Tyson and T.J., 8. "There are Natives all over, and so when you go into the outside world, it's a culture shock. Kids have that link to the reservation that they can't get rid of."

By the time basketball season arrived, Heart was soaring on the court and sinking in the classroom. He averaged 25 points a game as a freshman, but Gutierrez and his staff were constantly dragging their star player out of bed to keep him eligible.

"He loves his sleep, I guess," says Narcisse. But Gutierrez was running out of patience.

"It was a real travesty, because he's as good a talent as we've ever had here," says the coach, who has seen dozens of players transfer into NCAA and NAIA programs.

"I tried to tell him, 'This is your opportunity to move off the reservation. You can improve your life and go back to help your people.' But looking back, I don't think that's what he really wanted.

"He'd get financial aid money, and the next day it would be gone. He'd buy his girlfriend a $150 ring and then scramble for money the next two weeks. His friend (Standing Shoulder) tried to keep him on track, but after a while, he got tired of it, too."

On the court, though, Heart's high-scoring skills helped the Raiders reach the national Division II junior college tournament in 2000. In that setting, any doubts about his status as a legitimate college talent were erased.

While setting a four-game tournament scoring record of 108 points (that mark was later broken), Heart drilled nine 3-pointers in one win and 10 trifectas the next night.

In the semifinals, Heart had 30 points and nine rebounds but couldn't prevent an 86-72 loss to eventual champion, Dundalk Community College of Baltimore.

Rather than fueling his ambition to transfer to a larger school, though, Heart treated his team's fourth-place national finish as more of an end than a beginning.

"Everyone went home for spring break, and then we didn't see him the rest of the semester," Gutierrez says. "I'd call him up at home, and he'd say, 'I don't have a ride.' He would have been a junior college All-American, but I didn't even nominate him. I didn't feel like he was a true All-American."

With his academic status for 2000-01 severely damaged, Heart severed ties with Gutierrez that summer, announcing he was transferring to Northeast Community College in Norfolk, Neb. But he had to sit out the first semester and never retained his eligibility. He left without playing a game.

Heart enrolled at Huron the following season to try to get his grades in order and revive his career. But again, he skipped classes incessantly, testing the patience of coach Shane Warwick and well-wishers such as state Sen. Ron Volesky, who lives in Huron.

"Shane told me, 'Anything you can do to try to encourage this kid would be most appreciated,'" Volesky, a Harvard-educated Lakota, recalls. "But Jess' attitude was, 'I'm not going to do it. I don't care how good I am or how good you think I am or what you think I can become. I'm just not going to do it.' And he didn't."

According to Heart, his departure from Huron was hastened by a fight with teammate Joe Allen at a preseason practice.

"I was doing pretty good there, but (Allen) and I had a little confrontation, and the coach told me to leave practice," he says. "Me and the coach and my teammates weren't really getting along, so I just decided to quit."

Back home in Potato Creek, the ever-elusive Heart still comes and goes. Sometimes he lives with current girlfriend, Stacee Valandra, in Mission. She is expecting a child with Heart in October.

Heart has mentioned someday attending United Tribes Technical College in Bismarck, N.D. But for now, he is content to hang out with former teammates on the reservation, where he is hailed as a hero.

"He's like an NBA star around here," Narcisse says. "People see him, and they want his autograph."

Heart stays active by playing in independent tournaments on reservations, many of which feature prize money and could further damage his eligibility. He played a few tournaments with the Iron Five squad from Standing Rock, led by former University of Minnesota and Huron guard Russ Archambault. This season, he will compete with Pine Ridge's Thunder Valley team, which is sponsored by Roger Mills and travels to games in a Chevy Tahoe equipped with TVs so players can watch movies or play video games.

"We go all over the place—Oregon, Wyoming, Oklahoma," says former Little Wound center Jay Jacobs. "I'd say Jess' game is even better now than it was. He's going up against a lot of good players and averaging 30 points a game."

Such independent tournaments have long offered a competitive alternative for Native American players, many of them former high school stars.

"We used to call it the circuit, because they were all over the place," says former Huron standout Terry Dupris. "Kids get caught up in playing those tournaments, but it's just not the same as competing against top talent at the college level."

Heart, though, is running out of chances to show that he is serious about finding the next level. At times, he seems determined to disappear.

"If Jess had played four years of college basketball, he'd probably be known as one of the top five players who ever played in South Dakota," Volesky says. "I told him, 'Well, now I guess you can be the greatest independent Indian basketball player of all time.' But what does that really mean?"

Lessons Learned

BY STU WHITNEY

As a sportswriter in South Dakota, I have often been fascinated by the athletic vitality of Native-American athletes from reservation high schools—usually basketball players or cross country runners whose sporting spirit at state tournaments fill their fans with pride.

Why, then, do so few of those students make the transition to college to pursue greater athletic and educational challenges, setting the stage for a brighter future?

That question became the thrust of a three-day series, and "Squandered Chances" was an examination of a Lakota athlete named Jess Heart who seemed to symbolize the tug of war between collegiate ambition and reservation life.

Heart had virtually disappeared after captivating South Dakota basketball fans at the 1999 state tournament, where he scored 48 points for Little Wound High School in a thrilling overtime loss to the eventual champion, De Smet.

After flunking out of three colleges and fathering several kids, the 22-year-old local hero was living with his family on the Pine Ridge Indian Reservation—one of America's poorest regions with an unemployment rate of nearly 80 percent.

To gain a better understanding of why a vibrant young athlete was willing to settle for such a seemingly stagnant existence, I knew I would have to pay a visit to Heart's Potato Creek village.

I finally reached his father on the phone and established a day for the trip, imploring him not to let Jess leave Pine Ridge for one of his frequent forays into other reservations.

A photographer and I made the five-hour drive from Sioux Falls to Pine Ridge. Once we got there, I decided not to scribble away in my notebook but rather to rely on visual memory to describe the desolate surroundings that Heart called home.

In the first few paragraphs of the story, I relied on

these images to paint a picture for the reader—the dirt-rutted roads, the snarling dogs, and the little girl walking in roller skates over the rubble.

But equally important were my efforts to make Jess and his family feel comfortable with my presence, which might lead to more genuine revelations than reporters receive in more structured interview sessions.

I basically spent a day with them, chatting in the dark at a kitchen table, strolling through the tight-knit neighborhood, and watching a pickup game involving Jess and his former high school teammates in the hard-hitting August heat.

None of the players from that storied Little Wound basketball team are in college, and few have jobs. It's easy to conclude that their reservation existence has not prepared them to make a contribution anywhere else.

But as we sipped sodas that day, they talked of feeling out of place off the reservation, and how the familiarity of family and tribal heritage was one of the few aspects of their lives that they could truly trust.

That's why so many Native Americans who participate in mainstream college athletics frequently find themselves struggling to find success or quickly heading home. Simply put, their basic human need to belong has not been fulfilled.

Driving back that night through the Badlands, as a soft rain started to fall, I caught up on my notes and felt energized by my visit with the elusive Jess Heart, who helped me understand that it's possible for people to have varying definitions of ambition, and disparate notions of despair.

Michael Kelly
Commentary

When Mike Kelly left the University of Cincinnati ready to parlay his American history degree into a journalism career, Omaha looked like a good place to spend a little time. That was 33 years ago. Now the veteran columnist calls himself "a piece of the furniture" at the *Omaha World-Herald*. He is embraced by his readers and benefits from the gifts of their ideas.

That's a good thing, too, because he needs lots of ideas to produce four columns each week, including a Saturday "notes" column. He has held the metro columnist job since 1991, moving back to the news side after spending 10 years as sports editor and columnist. Before then, he covered police, courts, and city hall, journeying outside of those beats periodically for enterprise stories.

He and his wife, Barbara, have four children: Laura Brus, 30; Kevin, 29; Bridget, 26; and Nicholas, 15. Kelly is an avid reader and keeps his sports life alive by playing golf and maintaining, at age 54, a respectable hook shot on the basketball court.

His writing, which has won numerous local and state awards, keeps him in constant contact with his readers. That conversation is animated through strong reporting, Kelly says, because "we're able to ask people questions that you would never ask in a normal social setting." He saw that principle come to life early in his metro columnist career when, acting on an idea he'd carried around since the December 1969 draft lottery, he tracked down the story of Reggie Abernethy, a North Carolina native who had the misfortune of being born a day earlier than Kelly. Abernethy, whose lottery number placed him near the front of the line, was drafted to serve—and who died—in the Vietnam War. Kelly's Memorial Day piece got a tremendous response from readers.

That reaction, though, paled in comparison to the way hundreds of readers responded when he told a story that hit much closer to home. In his winning columns, Kelly unveiled the chilling details of how his daughter Bridget was robbed, raped, shot three times, and left for dead. The stories underscored the breadth of his connection to readers and catapulted his writing to national prominence. The issue represented one of those times, Kelly says, when it's okay for a columnist to write about his own life.

"If you're constantly just writing 'I, I, I,' that just wears on people," he says. "But when there is a personal story that has power to it, go ahead and write it and just trust your instincts."

Kelly's columns celebrate the heroes, excoriate the rapist, debate the ethical issue of identifying rape survivors, and give his readers sometimes-unfettered access to his family's painful journey from trauma to healing. The columns put on display Kelly's careful use of words and sentence structure as tools of persuasion and show the great power of the personal story.

—Keith Woods

Family's tragedy
becomes a miracle

JUNE 30, 2002

KILLEEN, Texas—June 21, the longest day of the year for daylight, became our family's longest, darkest day.

Our daughter Bridget, 24, a first-grade teacher for the Killeen Independent School District, was kidnapped by a stranger, robbed, shot repeatedly in the back and left for dead. But, at least for now, it is a story of her triumph.

Police are amazed she is alive.

But she will need to heal from severe physical and psychological wounds. Saturday, she was in fair condition at Darnall Army Community Hospital at Fort Hood, the world's largest active-duty military installation.

Imagining the terror she endured fills us with tears. The will to live that she displayed leaves us in awe.

Bridget underwent 6-1/2 hours of emergency surgery. I was the first in the family to arrive. She looked up at me, tubes down her mouth and nose to her lungs and stomach. Her eyes looked lifeless.

Unable to speak, she motioned with her hand. I pulled out a reporter's notebook, and she penned words I will never forget: "Dad, I was thinking about you and Mom and my whole family when it was happening. I just wanted to see you again.…I didn't want to die."

Bridget had picked up a girlfriend at the airport in Austin at midnight and driven the 80 miles back to Killeen. She dropped off her friend and returned to her own apartment complex. She locked both dead-bolts.

Getting ready for bed, she heard a terrifying sound—someone kicking at her door. She looked out the peephole and the door hit her in the nose, knocking her down. At gunpoint, a young man forced her to her car and to an ATM, making her withdraw $200.

He drove on, and she prayed quietly but audibly: "Hail Mary, full of grace, the Lord is with you.…"

She tried to make a human connection, telling him she was a teacher and that she loved teaching children to read. The man told her to shut up.

He drove her 1993 Nissan Maxima to the edge of a

housing development and into a deserted area. He eventually made her turn around—and shot her in the back. She fell, and he shot her again and again.

She played dead, and he left in her car. She began crawling and felt the blood on her fingers and lower abdomen. In danger of bleeding to death, she thought about life: "I might not be able to have babies."

She screamed for help, but no one could hear her. She was scared she would black out. She walked but fell down.

Then came a miracle. She said she felt as though God lifted her up. She got up, walked and began running the 200 yards to a new subdivision. She pounded on a door, and a terrified woman called 911 at 3:50 a.m.

Not knowing that the woman had called for help, Bridget slumped to the house next door and fell on the welcome mat, pounding on the door and screaming for help. Frank James, 43, a retired Army veteran of Desert Storm and Somalia, opened the door and said, "Oh, my God!" He called to his sister-in-law, Aquita: "Get a blanket!"

He checked to see if the attacker was nearby, and knelt next to my beloved, beautiful, bloodied daughter, his hand on her back. Police arrived quickly. The rescue squad helped save her life.

The Killeen Police Department reacted magnificently. A helicopter, a canine crew, patrol cops—officers everywhere. Several hours later, about 14 members of a SWAT team, guns drawn, surrounded a house and arrested a man as he ran out the back door. Jamaal Adrian Turner, 18, has been charged with attempted capital murder.

There is much more to tell, but that can wait for other days. My editors are giving me time off to focus on helping Bridget and dealing with the stress to our family, as well as with the numerous details you don't think about until faced with this horror.

What I want to say for now is thank you.

For the past nine days, we have focused on Bridget. Our far-flung family arrived from Ohio, Florida and Nebraska. Fellow teachers and administrators from Bridget's school at Fort Hood kept watch for days. *World-Herald* readers sent words of care and concern.

Dr. Clinton Beverly, her surgeon, and other doctors, nurses, counselors and staffers showed great skill. The Army brass, including Lt. Gen. B.B. Bell, commander of Fort Hood and III Corps, showed great compassion.

To all, our family is forever grateful.

Bridget has had ups and downs. She went from critical to serious to fair condition, definitely the right direction. But she has battled nausea, depression and anxiety. At times she has smiled, and the sparkle has returned to her eyes. She faces a tough road ahead, including post-traumatic stress and major follow-up surgery in August.

Late in the week, the James family, who opened their door to Bridget, visited the hospital. Frank and Denette, natives of North Carolina, celebrated their 25th wedding anniversary in March. He builds modular homes and she works at an Army commissary.

They have two beautiful children—Dont'e, 13, and Nikkiya, 11. Bridget said that as soon as she saw the reaction of the man who opened the door at their house, she knew he was a father.

"Your dad is my hero," Bridget quietly told Dont'e and Nikkiya from her hospital bed. "When that door opened, for the first time I thought I might make it. He was so brave."

When Frank visited the hospital Friday night, he hugged Bridget and said he was glad to see her. We were grateful he opened the door that night. The attacker could have been nearby.

"I wasn't going to leave her there, no matter what," he told us. "Even if the guy returned."

Some have said that people always think these horrible crimes happen only to others. I have never felt that way. I've written enough stories the past 32 years to know that these things can happen to any family—and this time it happened to ours.

Bridget Ann Kelly, third of our four children, graduated from St. Cecilia Elementary, Duchesne Academy and St. Louis University. My wife, Barb, was her Girl Scout leader. Bridget backpacked Europe for a month in college, and spent her spring breaks working with the poor. She intends to pursue a master's degree in reading education.

We used to call her "Midge," as in Bridget the Midget, but now she stands 5 feet 9-3/4 inches—tall in stature, as well as in spirit.

A Killeen police detective, Sharon Brank, found my

work number in Bridget's address book and called me at the *World-Herald* at mid-morning June 21. It was the type of call every family dreads. I soon was on an airplane, wondering if Bridget would live.

How she survived the urban terrorism, the gunshots and the 200-yard trek for help, I don't know. All I know is that our brave daughter is alive.

A plea for more openness on rape

JULY 25, 2002

Now you don't have to read between the lines and wonder: My daughter was raped.

Since she was attacked June 21 by a stranger who kicked in her locked apartment door, *World-Herald* news stories and two of my columns have said that she was abducted, robbed, shot and left for dead.

That's in keeping with this newspaper's long-standing policy not to name rape victims. It's a good policy, grounded in the notion that much of society still attaches a stigma to rape victims and that printing names might discourage victims from going to the police.

The policy remains, and victims need not fear that their names will be printed in the paper. They should report a crime that is believed to be the most underreported of crimes.

My daughter's attack in Texas made news in Omaha because of its horrible nature—she was shot in the back with 9 mm bullets—and because she grew up in Omaha. Editors say an additional factor, and one causing Bridget's name to be published initially, was that she is the daughter of a longtime columnist.

A grand jury in Bell County, Texas, indicted a man Wednesday on five counts, including attempted murder and aggravated sexual assault. Because Bridget's name had already been reported in connection with the shooting, the sexual-assault charge created a policy dilemma for editors, who decided—with the concurrence of my daughter, my wife and me—to make a rare exception and report it.

In the hospital more than a month ago at Fort Hood, Texas, unable to speak at first, Bridget wrote that in news coverage of her case, "It's OK if they say rape."

She says she wasn't speaking for others or suggesting how they should feel. But she adds: "Why is it more shameful to be a rape victim than a gunshot victim?"

Surely, it is not. But there is shame in rape, and it rests squarely with the attacker, not the victim.

Historically, though, society unfairly has made many rape victims feel either that they contributed to the attacks or that they are somehow diminished—stigmatized—merely by being victims.

The stigma from this awful crime should be on the predator, not on the prey.

In conversation, our family has spoken openly about our daughter's ordeal. We honor her courage in not only surviving her attack but also in not being ashamed.

To be sure, she has wept. So have my wife and I. So have our daughter's grandmas and brothers and sister and aunts and uncles and cousins and friends and colleagues and, in some cases, kind people we haven't met. The circle of anguish spreads widely.

Our 25-year-old daughter has endured extreme physical pain from her brutal attack as well as mental pain—post-traumatic stress and anxiety, which will continue. She has benefited from physical and psychological care, and is determined to return to a full life and her career as a first-grade teacher.

But there have been moments of near despair.

"This should never have happened to you," I said painfully at her bedside that first weekend. Crying, she replied: "This should never happen to anybody."

But it does. And the silence about rape may add to the feelings of victimization.

Geneva Overholser, then editor of *The Des Moines Register*, made that point in 1989. "I believe that we will not break down the stigma," she wrote, "until more and more women take public stands....Rape is an American shame. Our society needs to see that and attend to it, not hide it or hush it up."

Sexual violation is not sex, it's violence. It's not love, it's hate. It's not so much an act of lust as of power and control.

Because rape is such a personal and despicable act, it is natural for victims and their families not to talk. But perhaps, in the long run, that works to the advantage of the attacker and to the detriment of the victim.

Justice Department figures indicate that one woman in three is a victim of some form of sexual assault during her lifetime. Since our daughter's attack, that statistic is no longer static—it has come alive, all around us.

Dear friends of ours for 20 or 30 years, several of them, have revealed that they were raped. We had no idea. Some never told police, counselors or even family members.

"If you or your daughter ever need someone to talk to," an Omaha colleague told me quietly, "I'd be happy to do so. A man broke into my home 11 years ago and raped me."

People we met in Texas told us painful and harrowing stories—a 9-year-old daughter, now 23, beaten nearly to death in an attempted rape; a wife, now in her 40s, abducted in her 20s, chained to a pig sty and raped; an airline supervisor's daughter, now 15, raped by a stranger when she was 12.

The news reports of my daughter's abduction and shooting, and of her 200-yard trek to a subdivision seeking help, produced a comforting wave of sympathy and encouragement. The cards, e-mails and prayers had a tangible result for us and for her—they are helping us all get better.

We are so grateful. But at the same time I hold feelings bordering almost on guilt. Why? Because most rape victims must go it alone. They don't get all that moral support.

The walking wounded from the crime of rape try to move on. They rebuild their lives, return to their jobs, rejoin society, caress their children and try to smile—hiding the horror they experienced.

Some victims suffer for years. Some families break up.

And all of that is in addition to the immediate fear of impregnation, HIV or other diseases. (My daughter is not pregnant, and her first HIV test was negative; more are needed.)

Because my daughter's attacker had a gun and was a criminal, he made her feel helpless. But not hopeless.

She tried to talk with him, saying she was a teacher and didn't he remember his teachers? He reacted coldly, telling her to shut up.

Her strong religious faith strengthened her spirit. As he was about to rape her, she told him: "God doesn't want you to do this."

He ignored her. Even as she feared for her life, knowing what might come next, she offered her suffering up to God.

When the man was finished with her, he got dressed and told her to turn around. He shot her in the back, and she fell. He shot her twice more.

He thought she was dead and left in her car.

The Catholic faith, which Bridget practices, honors a saint named Maria Goretti. A century ago this month, Maria was stabbed 14 times in an attempted rape and died the next day.

By coincidence, according to an account I read, she had used words almost identical to my daughter's. Trying to rebuff the man, Maria said: "No! It is a sin! God does not want it."

God does not want rape, and neither does our society. And yet it continues, and we rarely talk about it.

Rape survivors deserve no stigma

AUGUST 11, 2002

I'm still angry. On national TV recently, a guy called my daughter "damaged goods."

I was invited on MSNBC to discuss when, if ever, it is appropriate to publish or broadcast the names of rape victims. On June 21, a stranger raped my daughter Bridget, 25, and shot her in the back three times.

Opposite me was Ted Kavanau, 69, a former CNN vice president, who said the stigma of rape victims will never go away.

"It's always going to be there," he said. "Women who are raped, in almost every single culture, are considered damaged goods."

He and I were in different cities, which was good—because I wanted to damage his nose.

But what I said, my voice rising, was, "The stigma is going to continue because of attitudes like that. They're so backward."

The exchange took place nine days ago on *Nachman*, former New York newspaper columnist Jerry Nachman's nightly show. A California sheriff had disclosed on CNN's *Larry King Live* the night before that two abducted teen-agers had been raped.

Most news organizations, including the *World-Herald*, don't normally disclose the names of rape victims. The names and faces of the California teens had been broadcast widely because they were abducted.

Fortunately, deputies killed their abductor. When the sheriff disclosed the rapes, news outlets began withholding the girls' names and faces—trying to put the toothpaste back in the tube.

It's a dilemma. This newspaper faced it in my daughter's case because her shooting had made news, and a month later a man was indicted for attempted murder and aggravated sexual assault.

Editors decided, with Bridget's concurrence, to report the indictment. In a column, I pleaded for more openness about rape and for placing the stigma and the shame on the attackers.

The California sheriff shouldn't have blabbed to Larry King about the rapes. My daughter isn't saying, and neither am I, that every rape victim's name should be published.

But on the issue of rape, this country needs a sea change, a "paradigm shift." We need to move out of the Dark Ages in which rape victims are whispered about and stigmatized.

My daughter is a rape *survivor*, and she is not diminished or embarrassed one bit. I admire her courage because she is standing up not just for herself, but also for many others who are raped.

The U.S. Justice Department says that one in three women will be a victim of sexual assault of some kind. That means millions and millions of women—the crime is widespread, but we mostly treat it as a dirty secret.

The California teens gave an interview to NBC's Katie Couric. And even though rape wasn't discussed, everyone knew they had been raped. The *Los Angeles Times* quoted experts as saying the TV appearance points to a shift in how people view sexual-assault victims.

The girls must know that we rejoice in their survival and don't consider them, in Ted Kavanau's Neanderthal term, "damaged goods."

Chicago Sun-Times columnist Richard Roeper last week cited my daughter's case and the California girls in questioning whether the news media policy on rape is outdated.

The policy is grounded in the notion that much of society still attaches a stigma to rape and that printing names might discourage victims from going to the police.

Roeper says we quote experts who say rape is a crime of violence and the victim shouldn't be blamed "but then we withhold the names of victims, lest they be blamed or stigmatized."

It's a difficult issue, and there are arguments on each side. But there are no immutable laws that societal stigmas can't change.

Less than a man

SEPTEMBER 1, 2002

BELTON, Texas—I looked into the eyes of the beast who raped and shot my daughter, and I saw nothing.

Not a flicker of remorse. Not sadness. Not cockiness. Not even self-sorrow or apparent regret that he won't be eligible for parole until June 21, 2052, if he lives that long.

Just...nothing.

In a Texas courtroom Friday, I stood at a wooden lectern, six feet in front of him. He sat shackled and wearing an orange jail jumpsuit. The beast had just pleaded guilty and received sentences that require him to serve at least 50 years in prison.

I'll be long gone by then. He would be 68. Friday we met face to face, but certainly not man to man. He is much less than a man.

Ten weeks earlier to the day, Jamaal Adrian Turner, 18, had kicked in Bridget's apartment door, stuck a gun in her chest, terrorized her, robbed her, raped her and shot her three times in the back. She waited for him to drive off in her car, and then she made it 200 yards to nearby houses. Surgeons saved her life.

Turner had returned to the scene with two friends to gloat and show off the body. When he got within a half-block, he saw emergency vehicles and ran.

But one of his buddies froze, and the police in Killeen, Texas, six hours later found where the attacker was staying. They surrounded the house with 14 armed SWAT team officers and arrested him as he ran out.

As a father, what do you say to the creature who savagely, mercilessly attacked and tried to kill your daughter? I got the chance to speak because Texas law provides for a victim-impact statement—a laudable opportunity that Nebraska and other states should provide.

"We stand in the presence of evil," I began, looking at evil and hoping for eye contact.

I spoke for five minutes, and he looked at me two or three times. Once was when I invoked his mother's name, which seemed to surprise him. (She was not present.)

"I feel sorry for your mother, Pearlie. She never wanted this. You were a baby once, a little boy, and you turned into a monster. What was the origin of your evil?

"I know you're sorry you were caught. Are you sorry for what you did to my daughter? Have you any remorse for the pain your depravity caused her, her mother, her sister, her brothers, her cousins, her aunts and uncles and her grandmas?"

No response.

"Bridget, in effect, survived her own murder," I continued. "From what I read, the only truthful statement you made to police is that when you left her, you thought she was dead. In your mind, you had committed murder.

"The great irony of all this is that if Bridget had died as you intended, you surely would have been caught and received the death penalty. So to whom do you owe your life? Bridget. She saved hers and thereby saved yours."

Twelve days ago, Bridget underwent follow-up surgery. But now doctors have diagnosed her with something else—stress-induced diabetes, which they say was brought on by the attack.

She didn't attend Friday's court session, preferring never again to lay eyes on the attacker. So I stood there in her stead.

Friday was a milestone, putting the beast away for good. But it's been a long summer. I'll never be so glad to see the leaves turn.

In a month or so, Bridget will return to teaching in her first-grade classroom. Her spirits are good, and she is healing in mind and body. She laughs. The sparkle is back. I can see it in her eyes.

Her eyes are full of life.

An extra reason to give thanks

NOVEMBER 28, 2002

On the eve of Thanksgiving, I called a man to give thanks.

Our family, like most, has much to be grateful for on this day set aside for that purpose. But for us, it's a most special Thanksgiving—because our daughter is alive.

And one of the reasons she survived horrible violence is a kind man, a husband, a father and an Army veteran named Frank James.

"I'm just glad," he said Wednesday, "that a life was saved, not taken."

In the middle of the night on the first day of summer, he opened his door to Bridget and protected her until help came.

In Killeen, Texas, where she teaches first grade, she had been abducted by a stranger who raped her, shot her three times and left her for dead.

Bridget somehow made it 200 yards from a field to the door of the James home. As I slept unaware hundreds of miles away in Omaha, Frank covered her and comforted her.

On the 911 tape, he says a woman on his doorstep was raped and shot and is "bleeding all over the place."

Bridget, now 25, had many heroes that night, including police officers, rescue squadsmen, nurses, doctors and others. And many in the days and weeks afterward, such as fellow teachers, therapists and relatives.

But that first hour made all the difference.

Dr. Jon Bruce, then a surgeon at Fort Hood and now in private practice in Georgia, said that in the emergency room Bridget's blood pressure plummeted. If she had arrived at the Army hospital five to 10 minutes later, he said, it would have been too late.

He opened her up and saw intestinal contamination and massive internal bleeding, which required replacing five units of blood.

He said he thought: "If this girl has a chance to live, I need to call in another surgeon."

Dr. Clinton Beverly arrived, and in 6-1/2 hours of

surgery, the pair saved our daughter's life.

I've written about Bridget's ordeal and recovery, and her decision to stand up for rape survivors and reject the so-called stigma and shame. Her attacker, in swift Texas justice, was sentenced to life plus 40 years, ineligible for parole until 2052.

Bridget had a colostomy removed in August. She has received psychological counseling. And she now deals with juvenile diabetes, which two physicians have said was brought on by the stress of her attack.

She returned to teaching at her school in Texas on Sept. 30—by coincidence, Frank James' 44th birthday.

On a recent Sunday afternoon, she and a friend made an unannounced visit to the site of her attack—her first since that awful night.

They drove past Frank James' house and parked. Bridget said she returned to the site to conquer any lingering fear, to see for herself that there was no longer anything there to be afraid of. She stood at the edge of the field and quietly wept.

Months earlier, bleeding and bent over in pain, she had screamed for help where no one could hear. Feeling as though she was lifted up by God, she improbably made her way the length of two football fields to seek help, ending up on Frank's doorstep.

The field, once jagged and sharp and mean, now looked so different. Construction equipment had graded it, smoothing it over in preparation for new houses, new life—a perfect metaphor for Bridget's own life.

A neighbor saw her and asked, "Can I help you?"

"No, thanks," Bridget replied. "We're just looking."

The neighbor figured out who she was and called Frank, who stepped outside. Bridget saw him, called his name and ran to him. They hugged.

She and her friend visited with Frank and his wife, Denette, for an hour. Frank says he and Bridget have "a lifetime bond."

The Jameses have two children, Dont'e, 13, and Nikkiya, 12, and Bridget told them their dad was her hero.

Even heroes endure tough times. Frank, a veteran of the Persian Gulf War and Somalia who retired from the Army five years ago, has lost his job. The Oakwood Homes manufacturing plant was shut down two weeks ago, laying off almost 300 workers.

It was especially bad timing, right before the holidays. But there's never a good time to lose your job. A mechanic, Frank has applied at numerous places and attended a job fair.

Brighter days will come, but Thanksgiving will be tinged with a bit of sadness at Frank's house. Our family, Bridget included, will pray for him and remember that he responded in her time of greatest need.

We give thanks for Frank and for all who helped her survive.

A conversation with
Michael Kelly

KEITH WOODS: First, how is Bridget?

MICHAEL KELLY: Mentally and emotionally she just amazes me. I can't imagine anyone who could have dealt with this better than she has, and she certainly has received professional counseling and help. But she was in Omaha a couple of weekends ago and spoke at her high school about rape and violence. It's an all-girls school and they were pretty mesmerized. She's just such a wonderful speaker. She's only 26 years old and it's just a pleasure as a parent to watch your children grow up and surpass you. She says she feels like she's aged 10 years in the last several months—not physically; she just looks wonderful. But in wisdom, I think, probably she has. So, thanks for asking. She's doing really well.

What concerns did you have about telling her story?

My main concern was in telling it in a way that would not merely be venting my grief or anger, but telling it in such a way that it had an impact on other people; both on people who have been victims of this horrible crime of rape and on the male society. Any time I'm in a group now I know that there are survivors of rape there—just statistically plus anecdotally. But then I wonder, "Well, if that's true, does that mean there are rapists in this room as well?" I guess I wanted to tell her story in a very powerful way yet with a measured tone. People have asked me, "Was this therapeutic for you?" It probably was. But that in no way is a journalistic reason to do this. There are lots of other ways I could have vented. I did not want to abuse my position as a newspaper columnist. I was just inspired by Bridget to do this.

Were you worried about what impact your writing would have on her?

Certainly. We talked about it quite a bit, and I think

some of my editors were worried about that as well because, as you know, most newspapers—most news organizations—have a policy of not naming people who are raped. It's not just a matter of sympathy and respect for privacy—those are good reasons—but also because police say if you start printing the names of victims who are willing to be named, it will have a chilling effect on others coming forward. I don't happen to think that's an especially strong argument, since so few come to police as it is. You always worry about the effect on your daughter, on your family, writing about something personal. But this just seemed to be about an issue of such overarching importance. We thought about it a lot and talked about it as a family, and we decided we wanted to do it. Of course, deciding we wanted to do it didn't mean it would get done. That took approval from editors of our newspaper to make an exception to policy.

Was that difficult to get?

When I first brought it up, our executive editor, Larry King, who's a contemporary of mine and a great editor, said yes right away. A couple of other good editors chimed in that we were moving too fast. I know they had our best interests at heart and really wanted to put the brakes on the idea. So we saw that there was no harm in waiting. Bridget asked me fairly recently, "Dad, when this happened, did you know right away that you would write about this?" I said no; I was just reacting as any father would. But it was on about day four in the hospital and Bridget had the tubes in her nose and mouth and couldn't speak, and she wrote in this notebook, "Why is it more shameful to be a rape victim than a gunshot victim?" A rhetorical question, but a powerful question. We didn't right away say, "Okay, let's go public with this." It just evolved. But I knew from that moment that it was a possibility. Then we waited. The newspaper was in kind of a dilemma in that, five weeks after the attack, her attacker was indicted on robbery, kidnapping, attempted murder, and rape.

So at that point, you had written twice about the attack, but not about the rape.

Exactly. We had a news story that Bridget had been shot multiple times and was in critical condition. My first column ran nine days after the attack. It did not mention rape, and I thought that people would read between the lines and see that she was raped. But I talked to friends, even colleagues, who were shocked to know that. In one column I said that she showed up naked on the doorstep of Frank James, and then I think people started to get the idea. Then we went public with it the same day we reported his indictment, and that, you might say, forced the issue. We had to decide: Are we going to ignore the fact that he's being indicted for rape?

What was the feedback like from your readers about these columns?

It was wonderful. It was supportive. They were shocked. There was almost no negative feedback from our readers. But even before we went public on July 25 with the rape, the outpouring we received was so heartening. I mean, her hospital room down in Texas was like a floral shop—cards and prayers and good wishes.

Part of our discussion was that most victims of rape go it alone, and here we are, even though we haven't said rape yet publicly, benefiting. Bridget felt it was just a tremendous benefit to her healing emotionally and physically. I was almost feeling guilty that, because I have written a column for a long time and some people know me and they feel like they know our family, they wanted to do something to help us. I thought, man, everyone should have this.

Give me a sense of volume in terms of letters, e-mails.

I would say—we still have them all—500 cards. I wrote a piece for *The Dallas Morning News* in November at their request, because it happened in their back yard, and that produced 300 e-mails. It's just a horrible crime, but a compelling story, and her survival is just such an amazing story that it gives her a kind of platform. She said to me a few weeks ago, "Dad, I didn't ask for this, but I feel like I've been given a life assignment and I'm not going to shirk my responsibility."

In your first column you bring a writer's eye and ear for detail to what is a very personal piece of writing. When you were crafting this column, how did you summon those details?

You know, the police detective asked Bridget two days before her grueling 4-1/2-hour statement to police, "Do you think you remember details?" And Bridget said, "I remember everything." And talk about an eye for detail, you should see her statement to police. I mean, it's pretty heartbreaking. At that time we were on something like hyper-alert. Everything is vivid, and it's like you notice everything and remember everything. Of course, our perspective and Bridget's are totally different. It happened to her. But from everything I experienced firsthand or what I heard from Bridget, I guess it wasn't difficult to recall the details.

I hear your voice twice in that first column. You use the words, "…my beloved, beautiful, bloodied daughter," and then you come back again a few sentences later and talk about how the police department reacted "magnificently." There are places where I hear you loud and clear emotionally. So you do let yourself into the column, don't you?

I don't think to be totally detached would be the best way to convey the power of the story, because readers try to imagine this happening to their families—and some, of course, have had this happen to their families, unfortunately. There are times when you let it show and there are times when you're telling the detached narrative. I think if it were just the narrative, it would be too sterile. Or, if it were just an emotional outpouring of grief and anger, that wouldn't convey the power of the story either. So I hope I was able to successfully combine the elements.

Let's talk about beginnings and endings. Your five pieces begin with blunt, declarative statements and end with a wistful kind of air. What guides you when you're deciding how to start and end columns?

You've heard the theory that one way to write a piece is

to figure out the beginning and the ending, and then figure out how to get from the beginning to the end? That's not how I write. I love that theory. I think it makes great sense, and if I could figure out how to do that, I would probably do it. I'm somewhat of a plodder as a writer. I do think in advance about the entire piece, but first things first: How am I going to attract readers and make them stay with this, sentence by sentence? Every paragraph is a chance for them to go do something else. But I guess the one lead that was the most blunt was the July 25 column: "Now you don't have to read between the lines and wonder: My daughter was raped." A lot of times I'll try something and delete it, and on the 20th try I'll think, "Well, maybe that's about it." That sentence was my first try, and I just put it on the screen and startled myself. I thought, "Oh, my gosh, I think that's what I want to say." So then I started. I build brick by brick, one on top of the other and hope I have good mortar in between so it holds together strongly.

And your endings?

I usually figure out an ending when the end is in sight. I never want a story or a column just to end. I want it to have an ending, and I want the ending to give the reader a sense of completeness, a sense of tying this up with a ribbon, that this is a complete package; something that's memorable. The ends of sentences are important because what the reader remembers most is what was last. So when it comes to the column, what they're going to remember most, I think, is what you said last. One technique is that you look back and say, "How did I start this?" or "What is the nut graph and how can I somehow tie back in to the lead or to the nut graph and give that sense of completeness?" On the July 25 column, I use the little story about the saint and the Catholic Church. That piece ended up with the saint supposedly saying, "God does not want it," and I said, "God does not want rape, and neither does our society. And yet it continues, and we rarely talk about it."

In two of the columns, and the July 25 column was one of them, you seem to ask something of your

readers. What were you hoping they would do when they read "A Plea for More Openness on Rape" and "An Extra Reason to Give Thanks"?

Well, let me take the first one first. We were hoping that this was going to encourage readers just to talk more about this crime and to lift the veil of secrecy that I think inures more to the benefit of the rapist than it does to the rape survivor. Anecdotally, it certainly appears to have had that effect. Part of the reaction—a large part of it— was that many, many people have come to us, including close, dear friends whom we have known for 20 or 30 years, and told us that they were horribly raped, sometimes with objects and hideous things. These are people who were good friends of ours, and it had never come up. But because we went public, they felt like they could talk to us. Sunday at church a woman came up to me and hugged me and said, "I just want to thank you for Bridget. My cousin was raped, and my sister and I are survivors of incest." This is not rare for me to hear. I've had colleagues at the *World-Herald* tell me their experiences of someone breaking into their home and beating them and raping them. I'm now past the point where my jaw drops because the one thing that has hit home with us, perhaps more than anything else as a result of these columns, is that this crime is all around us.

There's a surprise waiting for readers in "An Extra Reason to Give Thanks." Why did you save the information about Frank James's job until the end?

Well, he doesn't live in our area, so it's not like I was trying to help him get a job. He does have a job now, by the way. Anyway, we love Frank, not only for what he did but for the kind of man he is. I can get choked up pretty easily talking about Frank James and his family. But because Frank had appeared previously in the column and been pictured, and I felt so bad that his plant had closed and he was out of a job, I did want readers to know about that. That Thanksgiving Day column also served the function of tying up some loose ends. I guess you'd say, "It's Thanksgiving. I'm grateful my daughter is even alive." I wanted to pay tribute to this wonderful man who helped her and all the other people who helped save her life and helped her in the recovery. But I just wanted people to know, "Oh, by the way, sorry to say, Frank is out of a job." I wasn't trying to get readers to set up a fund or anything like that, but some did ask how they could help him.

Did it have that impact?

Oh, yeah. It wasn't like tons of people sent money into a fund, but some people did. A lawyer in Omaha, whose niece was murdered a few years ago, was very moved by Frank's actions and she asked me for his address. Bridget's school at Fort Hood took up a collection and had Frank and his family over to the school.

I don't want to give the impression that the Jameses are poor because they're not. They have a beautiful, newer house. He was in the Army for 20 years, so they're not destitute or anything like that, but it'd be just like anybody else. All of a sudden you're out of a job, and it's the holidays. They're very dignified people. In our eyes, no one has greater dignity than Frank James. He would tell you that he didn't do much. He would say, "I just opened the door, and there she was." He said he wasn't going to leave her no matter what, even if the guy came back. Well, guess what? The guy was on his way back, and that's how he ended up getting caught. This is so horrible, and yet so many wonderful things have happened from it.

How has your thinking about reporting on rape changed since this began?

I guess it struck me much stronger than ever before how pervasive this crime is, and then it struck me that there is not a whole lot of outrage in our society about it. Now, you can easily say, "This is a very wounded father and so he's taken up this cause because it happened to his daughter, but there are lots of other important issues in society." Well, all that is true. This is a cause that I'm not going to write about every day or every week in my column and abuse my position. But this is an important issue, and to my mind the proof of that is the response that we have had from it. How can you not be affected when you continually get that kind of response?

You say often in your columns that you would prefer more openness about rape, and yet you didn't mention rape yourself in the first two columns.

Right. And that's because of our newspaper's policy.

Would you have been inclined even then to do it were the policy not in place?

Yes. I would have been inclined on that first column, June 30. We had talked about it enough, but that was when other editors suggested that we delay. It was because of the policy that we didn't mention it in the news stories or in my first two columns. From that point on we were talking about it the whole time; and when her attacker was indicted on rape, that brought it to a head. We had to make a decision, column aside: Are we going to report the fact that Bridget Kelly's attacker is being indicted for rape? The decision was yes. And that left the door open. But I do hope our policy evolves on that.

If these columns are a fair gauge, the force of your anger about the attack on Bridget doesn't emerge in print until two months later, first when you faced Ted Kavanau on TV and then when you faced Jamaal Turner in court. Was it intentional to wait before letting out that level of anger?

Only in the sense that I was conscious while writing of not using my columns merely as a platform to vent grief and outrage. I thought my columns would be more powerful if, for the most part, I let what happened speak for itself. What could be more powerful than that? She was being executed. He told her to turn around because he didn't want to look her in the face when he killed her.

Your strongest language was reserved for Jamaal Turner in "Less Than a Man." You called him "beast," "creature," and "monster." Strong words. What was going through your head at that time?

The writing was kind of in two stages. First, I had to write the "victim impact statement." I was going down to the courthouse to represent Bridget and our family, and I felt like I've been a writer for 32-plus years and that this is the most important thing that I'll write. I wanted it to be powerful, and I knew I had only five minutes to say whatever it was I wanted to say. I wanted to respect the dignity of the court by not using vulgar or vile language, but believe me, I had many vulgar and vile thoughts about this guy. So I spent a lot of time writing and rewriting that statement. I got the victim impact statement done and I thought, "Well, this is an important chapter. I'm going to write the column about it." I think that one started off with his non-reaction.

I want to focus on your decision to use such words as "beast" and "monster" because you could have used them any time and you didn't. You pulled them out for this column. What went through your head in making those specific decisions?

I suppose there was some kind of an evolution like with the previous column about venting and showing some emotion. So many people are stunned and shocked by what we went through, I guess if I didn't characterize him in a way that I think most people would, they might think either that I'm trying too hard to be detached or that I'm more stoic than I am. I feel as though I'm just like our readers. You know, good days, bad days. Your kid gets hurt, you've got stresses at work. And I feel like after 21 years of writing columns in our community, I not only have a feel for our readers, but they know me.

When you began that column you focused on Turner's eyes. Did you already know that you would end with the image of Bridget's eyes?

I don't think I did. I saw it on the horizon. I'll never forget walking into that room in the ICU that first time I saw her and her eyes were open. Tubes everywhere; her eyes were open but looking lifeless. And I think I wrote about kissing her and talking to her and then she started writing and so on. But then the contrast between her and the eyes of the beast just couldn't have been greater. This was Sept. 1 or Aug. 30, the day of the sentencing, and she had just had her colostomy taken out 10 days earlier. By that time, we had time to see her laugh again and smile and think about the future. But I think the image of his eyes and Bridget's eyes as a contrast came about halfway into the column.

There's no escaping the undercurrent of race in the overarching story: a black teenager raping a white woman; a black man coming to her rescue. Have you explored race as a subtext in your writing about Bridget's case?

No. This has never been about race, for Bridget or for us. When we were in the hospital, just a few days after this happened, Bridget had a big envelope and I could see she was looking at it and was distressed and she said, "Dad, what is this?" And I looked at it, and it was from some racist organization in North Carolina. They already had Turner's picture on their website and it was just vile, stating that if you're raped by a black male, you're 14 times more likely to get AIDS.

Based on that piece of mail, it's fairly safe to say that your readership is thinking about race. They're wondering how you're feeling about this and maybe how they should be feeling about this in terms of race. But you don't take it on in the columns.

Well, let me give this as part of the answer. A good friend of mine, a black woman, works in the government here in Nebraska. She told me that before she saw his picture and she heard his name was Jamaal Adrian Turner, that her heart sank because it sounded to her like it was probably a black guy. And it was interesting to me that this black woman took it personally that it was a black guy who did this to my daughter. I guess it's just that we're all human. But the way Bridget has looked at it and the way we've looked at it is: What difference does it make what his race was? What he did was horrible and disgusting, and, by the way, the man who came to her rescue and protected her is a black man. And one of the two surgeons who saved her life and stayed with her every day for the next 15 days, Maj. Clint Beverly, is a black man. And the first Army psychologist who spoke to Bridget was a black woman. And a friend from school who came into her room and prayed with Bridget and me spontaneously, the most beautiful extemporaneous prayer I've ever heard, was a black lady. And there were lots of white and Hispanic friends there.

So it may be a failing of mine that I have not specifically explored this. I've thought about doing it, and I'm not sure why I haven't specifically done so. But I was very curious that the contest judges picked up on that. What's the citation say? It says something about "provides insight into other issues such as crime and race." I never said Jamaal Adrian Turner was black. That's never appeared in print. And I guess I just didn't think it was germane. I could have written something that said, "Although the guy who attacked her was black, look at her rescuers and the people who saved her life."

I guess I thought it was not necessary to do that because I did write about her rescuers. I never said Frank was black but we ran his picture a couple of times. I don't know that I ever said Dr. Beverly is black. Some people say we should have a colorblind society. I don't know that that's possible or even desirable. But race was never an issue to us in this crime. The crime was the big issue.

I think that point comes out very clearly in the evenness with which you talk about Jamaal Turner and Mr. James. I asked the question not so much to ask whether you, as a white person, explored race for yourself or your family as much as whether you, as a columnist, explored it for your readers, who probably were mulling over these thoughts themselves.

As I say, there have been times when I thought maybe I should explore it specifically. I guess I just thought I didn't need to. But I may still write about it some day.

You have written about family members before. Talk a little bit more about what guides you in deciding when to bring your family into your writing.

Only if I can make a universal point that applies to other families; if I think I can get readers to see that I'm not just being a self-absorbed columnist writing about my family. I think that's my standard. You have to use your instincts. Like a lot of local columnists, I am not a pundit, I am not an op-ed page columnist. We specifically do not take positions on legislative bills or proposed city ordinances or endorse candidates. Everybody's going to do it differently; but the way I see it, it is not primarily intended as an everyday, hard-hitting opinion column. Certainly it should have a point of view and sometimes should have an opinion and make fun of things in public life.

We had a local city administrator in one of our suburban towns here of about 20,000 people, a real growing area, and we found out that he had negotiated a clause in his contract that no one in city government was allowed to criticize him publicly. Well, it's just a columnist's dream to get a story like that. I mean, you can't wait to get to the terminal and just have fun with it. And by the way, they ended up changing his contract. I enjoy writing about local politics sometimes, but they're not op-ed page type columns, even though I enjoy reading those. They require reporting most of the time, getting out of the office, talking to people, taking your readers into all corners of your community.

How do you get your ideas, Mike?

By just constantly keeping my antenna up. And from readers calling or writing and telling me stuff. That is one of the great benefits of having the column job where they put your picture in the paper. Also, I've been in this community for so long and have covered so many different kinds of things. I know all the sports people, I know the political people, and I think our readers feel as though they know me. So I'm part of the furniture here. I think they feel comfortable, like they can call. You listen carefully to each person. I really appreciate the fact that we get so much reader feedback. You get your ideas from a variety of sources. Mainly just by being interested. That's what I have said to students and young writers. Be interested in what's going on around you.

Do you do much revising of your copy?

Yes.

What form does it take?

Hating what I write. The form is looking at structure a lot. I read so many columnists, and I admire their ability to use beautiful metaphors and similes, which I'm not especially adept at. But I think I know how to get the juice out of a story. What's the best information you've got? How do you organize it for maximum impact? How do you arrange your sentences for emphasis? So when I'm revising, that's usually what I'm doing. I'm rearranging for emphasis. I like to use this phrase when I'm looking at it: Does this hang together? Does this have a good beginning, middle, and end? Does it have a point? It doesn't have to have the most colossal, important point in the world; but can somebody read it and come away with something?

I don't have any exaggerated idea of how important my column is in the day of my readers. But I have had a lot of people over the years say they hang in with the column because they know there's something for them at the end. That's one of the things I'm happiest to hear, that they know I'm going to do something at the end that either surprises them or ties things together somehow in an interesting way. I don't know. Don't you think writing is like putting a jigsaw puzzle together? I mean, you've got all these different parts. How do they fit? I think that's the essence of writing.

How do your editors help you?

My direct editor is Anne Henderson. Anne has worked in Chicago and at *The New York Times*. And she's from southwest Iowa, which is near here. She came back 10 or 12 years ago to be near her mom and her family. I love having Anne as an editor. I always say that one of the great functions Anne serves is to keep me from embarrassing myself. Isn't that a great function for an editor? She's my first reader, and she's going to read it on behalf of everybody else first. There have been times when she'd say, "Okay, one too many cute phrases." As a columnist you try to be interesting and have cute phrases or interesting plays on words and so on. Whenever she says that, I say, "Thank you." The older I get, the more malleable I am. The only thing that counts is what's printed. I have so much less ego at 54 than I had at 27. It's the old saying that the more you know, the more you know what you don't know. You just want the piece to be as good as it can possibly be. Whether it's Anne or the copy desk or anyone along the way who has a suggestion, I just say, "Thank you." It's not that I won't stand up if somebody questions something. But I appreciate the editing and definitely don't feel like anything I write is sacred. There's nothing that can't be improved. But eventually the deadline comes and you turn in what you've got, and you hope that that's good enough.

What writers do you read?

Well, I like Leonard Pitts of *The Miami Herald* a lot and Dana Parsons from the *Los Angeles Times,* who writes in the Orange County edition. He's a friend of mine and I think he's a great writer whom not everybody knows about. I really enjoy Laura Pulfer of *The Cincinnati Enquirer*. I like reading a lot of the op-ed people: Maureen Dowd of *The New York Times* and, of course, Tom Friedman, who is not only a columnist for *The New York Times,* but it's like he's the columnist for our time.

Mike, is there anything I've failed to ask that you think is important to know about column writing?

It's a job that I am very fortunate to have. I don't think it's the most important job on the paper. In some ways it's the best job. But being a good reporter is the most important thing. Most columnists get to be columnists because they were good reporters and good writers before that. On my business card it says, "Reporter/Columnist." I had it put there as a reminder to me that I'm not going to be a good columnist unless I'm a good reporter, too. So that's what I try to be.

Writers' Workshop

Talking Points

1) When writing about themselves, columnists have to walk a very tricky line between serving readers and seeming self-centered. Like many columnists, Michael Kelly says he reserves personal columns for those times when his experience seems to have broader meaning. Beyond this extraordinary personal story, what might those experiences be?

2) How do you feel about the ethical issues raised by Kelly's decision, and that of the newspaper, to reveal that his daughter had been raped? Go to Poynter Online and read the work of Kelly McBride of the Poynter ethics faculty on identifying rape victims ("Rape and American Journalism"). Discuss how that debate resonates today.

3) Michael Kelly does not explore race relations in any of the columns, though, as he points out, the contest judges' comments suggest that they thought it was part of the story. Should a columnist inject such a volatile subject into the unfolding story even though no one had brought it up?

Assignment Desk

1) In his first column, Kelly uses straight narrative to tell the early story of his daughter's attack, adding the bulk of his voice at the beginning and end of the story. The technique gives the column momentum and drama. Try it out. Write a column in which you sandwich a narrative between opinion.

2) Kelly says he would have been misleading his readers had he not revealed in his column the depth of his anger at society and at the man who raped his daughter. Step into the shoes of a metro columnist. Write something that gives your readers a look at your deeper emotions.

3) Writers use different paths to get from lead to ending. Read Kelly's version of that process in the interview. Then go back and deconstruct your last few stories. Write an analysis of your writing process. How do you determine the focus? How do you develop the lead? How does the ending emerge?

Kate Nelson

Finalist, Commentary

Kate Nelson is a columnist and writing coach at *The Albuquerque Tribune*. A native of Overland Park, Kan., she graduated in 1981 from the University of Kansas in Lawrence and joined *The Kansas City Star* in 1985. She moved to New Mexico in 1989, working at the *Tribune* as a political reporter, assistant city editor, and editorial writer before becoming a full-time columnist in 2001.

In 2002, she was inducted into the Scripps Howard Hall of Fame for excellence in deadline, editorial, and column writing. She has won numerous statewide writing awards and was given the 2001 governor's award for outstanding New Mexico women. She was a member of the reporting team that produced the *Tribune*'s "State of Our Children" project, a 2002 finalist for public service in the National Headliner Awards.

Nelson is an occasional commentator on National Public Radio's *Sunday Edition*, hosts a weekly public-television program, and teaches studio-cycling classes. She lives and gardens in the foothills north of Albuquerque.

In "There Was a War Within," Nelson pulls the reader along in a column about late-blooming love. She drops a surprise toward the end, then charges forward with a simple point that is made powerful by a tightly packed narrative and an ear for the lyrical.

There was a war within, then peace, embraced by love

NOVEMBER 2, 2002

Neither expected to be at Caravan East that night. Neither expected to two-step with a stranger. Neither expected to fall in love.

Maria Chavez should have been home, cooking Thanksgiving dinner. But a girlfriend called, begging for company.

Richard Rocco fought with his roommates, stormed out, strode past the lounge, decided to get a drink.

They locked eyes. They talked. They danced. And they found out they needed each other—although not in the starry-eyed way that would come.

Maria was assistant director of New Mexico AIDS Services. Richard was a military hero who organized programs to help veterans.

Her new office needed plumbing. His veterans needed work.

Not exactly a match made in heaven, but it gave him an excuse to ask her out.

"He took me to Los Cuates," Maria said. "I'm used to Scalo, and he took me to Los Cuates."

As he drove her home, she thought, "Once is enough."

Then he began to sing, "Tú, Solo Tú"—the same song Maria's father had used to court her mother.

She melted.

Love in the later seasons can be a foolish risk or a timely rescue. Both Maria and Richard had grown children. Three failed marriages stood between them. They had loved and lost.

The odds seemed distant.

But salvation had arrived.

Linda Hastings, Maria's daughter, blushes at what she thought when she met her mother's new beau: "Isn't he a little short for you?"

She can laugh about it now, "because I came to learn that he was a man of such huge stature."

Louis Richard Rocco earned the Medal of Honor, our nation's highest military award, for his service in Viet-

nam. He had saved three comrades in the middle of enemy fire, despite his own injuries.

He came home angry at the war, angry at his country
and angry at the way his fellow veterans were treated.

But he used that anger and that medal to leverage
money and attention for programs that would help.

That story has been told. What hasn't been told is the
postscript, the happy ending, the falling away of anger,
and the falling in love with Maria.

By the time they married, they had given too much of
themselves to people in need. They were worn out.
They fled to San Miguel de Allende, Mexico. They held
big parties, cooked, gardened, played with their dogs on
the beach.

They let go of stress and grabbed onto love. Maria
had heard tales of Richard's anger, the explosive aftermath of Vietnam.

"I've never seen it," she said. "His daughter says that
I got the best of him. Maybe we both just mellowed."

They moved to San Antonio, Texas, in 1998. Richard
was having a few health problems, nothing serious, but
it helped to be close to good care.

Even there, they laughed well, dreamed big, reached
out and lived large.

Sometimes, they fell into one of those snappish ex-
changes common to couples: That's not what happened.
Yes, it is. You're wrong. No, I'm right.

Their eyes would lock. What happens in that moment? In the worst of couples, vengeance. In the best,
remembrance, the echo of love.

They would take a breath and move the conversation
onward and away.

On Thursday morning, Maria held Richard in her
arms to keep him warm. Ten months of his cancer treat-
ments and her unwavering care seemed to be helping.
But as the sun rose, his heart stopped. A hero died. A wife
became a widow.

For the skeptics and the cynics, the ones who have
loved and lost, this is the story of Richard and Maria. It
roars with passion, murmurs in intimacy, thumps in a
heartbeat. Love is, love heals, love lives.

Lessons Learned

BY KATE NELSON

Richard Rocco was dying by the time I met him. He had deteriorated so badly that my plan for a tidy three-hour interview turned into two days of Q&A scraps snatched between naps. During that time, I watched him and his wife, Maria, exhibit the full range of love—from tender devotion to gentle teasing to silly spats.

Moving as that part of their story was, it wasn't part of my job. Instead, I was there to write about Richard's lifelong heroism, so I focused on that and wrote about that.

Case closed. Or so I thought.

I often tell young writers that they won't blossom until they live. Let yourself fall in love. Let your heart get stomped on. Let yourself grapple with a loved one's death.

Let yourself sample joy, grief, and every other flavor so you can taste the epic quality of ordinary lives.

In the earlier years of my career, the story of Richard and Maria would have passed by with barely a shrug of my shoulders. Just another couple, I would have thought then. But in the years that led me to now, I endured the breakup of my own marriage. I helped bury a dear friend, killed far too young by breast cancer. I stood by my father's deathbed, wrenched by grief and guilt and love.

News happens not only when brave men and women perform heroic acts, but when every one of us experiences the wonders that form the themes of our greatest literature: birth, love, failure, coming home, going to war, winning, and dying.

Standing on my own cache of emotional rubble let me see the love story of Richard and Maria.

The day after he died, I took a sunrise hike from my house. At the top of a high hill, I said a prayer for him, and the words of this column fell into my head. That simply. That naturally.

I trusted the universal reach of the story's theme and

tried to avoid blatant sentimentality by stripping it down to what it was—a tale of love found late in life.

The image of Maria trying to keep her husband warm as his heart stopped inspired the rhythm of the final paragraph. I wanted to take readers into their bedroom and into their love by mimicking the sound of a heart-beat.

"You made me cry all over again," Maria told me after she had read it.

And then we hugged, and we let ourselves hold on tight.

Seattle PostIntelligencer

Robert L. Jamieson
Finalist, Commentary

Robert L. Jamieson is a metro columnist with the *Seattle Post-Intelligencer.* He writes three times a week, focusing on a wide range of matters, from the hot-button local issues of the day to stories of everyday people navigating through life with hope and dignity.

After graduating from Stanford University in 1991 with a degree in political science, he worked for *The Wall Street Journal* in the newspaper's Houston bureau. He joined the *Post-Intelligencer* in October 1991.

At the *Post-Intelligencer* his assignments have ranged from covering higher education and city hall to enterprise reporting and long-range projects. In 2000, the *Post-Intelligencer* nominated him for a Pulitzer Prize for a feature story about David Ballenger, a homeless man who was fatally stabbed more than a dozen times by three Seattle teenagers.

In 2002, Jamieson won first place for column writing and commentary in the American Association of Sunday and Feature Editors competition. He also was named best general columnist in the regional Society of Professional Journalists contest.

Jamieson has fun with "the battiest story yet," cleverly introducing an interesting cast of characters, including a writer for the hit comedy *Seinfeld*, in a real-life sketch about nothing more profound than a used baseball bat and the lengths fans go to to possess it.

This may be the battiest story yet

MAY 14, 2002

Our wacky tale involves the Mariners and Red Sox, a mortgage broker who writes comedy, a Greek restaurant owner and a minister with major muscle.

There's also a heartbroken teen, a Seattle cop, attempted bribes, a cash payoff—and one curiously sticky baseball bat.

Add it all up, and you get this: Batgate.

The whole shebang took place during Friday's game at Safeco Field. In the middle innings, Boston designated hitter Brian Daubach took a swing, lost his grip and flung his wood into the stands.

Fans shrieked, scattered and ducked.

The bat spun, whirled and richocheted before it landed in Section 122, Row 15—close to where Jessica Maus was sitting with her best friend.

"I reached out and grabbed it," Jessica, 18, said.

But an opposing force with a surprisingly strong hold pulled back.

It was an "old woman," Jessica said, "who looked like she was 50."

Actually, it was Penelope Thomas, a minister from Everett, whose business card touts "weddings…& counseling" and shows pink flowers.

"I had the bat. She grabbed it!" Penelope said. "Imagine that. A young girl trying to capitalize by yanking a bat out of an older lady's hand."

Wait, there's more.

A third pair of hands clung to the bottom of the bat, at the nub.

They belonged to Perry Panagiotu, a mortgage broker who has used those very same hands to write *Seinfeld* scripts on the side.

Perry, 41, is brawny on the outside, but he's a softy at heart.

"Yeah, I had a hand on the bat," he said. "But what? Like I'm gonna fight a woman over it?"

Perry left it to the ladies to duke it out. Youth was not

served.

Penelope, inspired perhaps by a higher authority, out-muscled sweet Jessica.

"It was mine," Jessica said, marshaling support from other fans who hooted, "Give it back!"

Our tale could have ended right there, with Jessica moping. With fans chanting.

Then the money started to fly.

Penelope, who was sitting right behind Perry, leaned over.

"I have no attachment to this bat," the minister said. "You really want this?"

Perry did—but not for himself. It would be a cool gift for Johnnie Dimakis' 11-year-old kid. Johnnie, who sat next to Perry at the game, owns a Greek cafe in Lakewood.

"Twenty bucks?" Penelope asked.

Faster than you can say Andrew Jackson, a dead president was in Penelope's hands.

And Perry had a game-used bat.

Other people saw the unfolding market speculation. Within minutes, the section of Safeco became a stadium version of eBay.

One Red Sox lover from Boston offered $100.

A nearby Yankees fan caught wind of the Boston bid and raised the ante.

Perry wasn't selling. He held the bat and watched the game.

He should have kept an eye on the Red Sox dugout, where serious talks were going on.

A Boston official chatted up a Mariners rep. The rep talked with a Safeco guest host. Before you knew it, Perry and Johnnie had company—the guest host asked them to give the bat back, citing Major League rules.

"Here it is I paid $40 for a ticket," Johnnie explained. "$25 to park. $5 for peanuts. $6 for a hotdog. $8 for beer. The Mariners make millions. And you can't allow me to keep a bat? No way. It's ours."

The Mariners employee vanished. More pacing in the Boston dugout. The stadium host returned to Perry and Johnnie, bearing a gift: a replacement bat.

Perry and Johnnie said nope. Not good enough. How about a baseball glove signed by pitcher Pedro Martinez?

A bat signed by all of the Red Sox? A…

The Mariners representative walked away.

Johnnie dashed to the bathroom. Perry stayed behind with the bat.

Then someone in blue—not Mariners blue, either!—started looking Perry's way.

It was Mike Hargrave. Officer Hargrave of the Seattle Police Department.

Perry made off like Seattle Slew. I caught up with him, mid gallop, at a stadium exit. He had stuffed the bat into a black jacket, where it poked out from a sleeve.

"Look at this," he said, pulling out the Louisville Slugger. "Feel this part."

The wood was covered in pine tar, a substance players use to get a better grip.

The pine tar wasn't where you'd expect to see it—on the handle—but slathered up on the "fat part" of the bat, a section between 17 and 20 inches from the nub. "I'm confident this bat is illegal," Perry said, but he wasn't about to take chances by showing anyone with the Mariners.

A spokesman with Major League Baseball said a bat can have pine tar on it so long as the substance is no more than 18 inches from the nub of the bat. Failure to, um, stick to those rules "shall cause the bat to be removed from the game."

Which, ironically, is what happened when Brian Daubach, for whatever reason, lost his grip.

His bat was out of the game.

Out of the stadium.

Out of sight.

Like a bat out of hell.

Lessons Learned

BY ROBERT L. JAMIESON

Life happens and, sometimes, being in the right place at the right time yields wondrous fodder for a good yarn. I was lucky enough to experience this firsthand at a Major League Baseball game, after a player's bat, flung into the crowd, ignited a commotion.

"There might be a column in it," a friend sitting next to me suggested. I embarked in lukewarm pursuit, unsure whether this was a story. After I started to talk with people, I realized how wrong I was. The subtext of the tale was how folks in the middle of watching the most American of pastimes had regressed to their primordial, selfish, and cantankerous selves. Decent folks turned into a pack of humans—and all because of a bat. Once that broader theme dawned on me, it was clear the scene in the stands was like a petri dish of the human experience. Looking back, here are some lessons I learned during a night at the ballpark:

■ **Think visually.** Let readers feel as though they are seeing the action unfold right before their eyes. Re-create scenes based on careful reporting, but write to give readers the sense you were there the whole time.

■ **Capture the emotional thrum.** The bang-bang pace of what occurred was best served by short, rapid-fire sentences. Such a structure helps capture a sense of the frenzy and chaos.

■ **Lasso dialogue like a bull.** I learned that stories live or die not only by what people say but how they say it—and in what context.

■ **Don't fear humor.** Funny things happen in life, but sometimes we become too serious about our craft. I almost edited myself from pursuing the story because I did not feel it had gravitas.

■ **Listen to outsiders.** Other people can offer great perspective on what is a story. Trust their instincts, if not your own.

■ **Be prepared.** The Boy Scouts got it right. You never know when a story is going to leap right out at you.

James H. Smith
Passion for Journalism

Now happily married, Jim Smith had once been divorced and included that detail in a column that earned him ASNE's first Passion for Journalism award. He was defending his newspaper's decision to write about the divorce of a state senator, and, if public revelation was newsworthy in the case of the politician, it was worth applying to the executive editor of the local newspaper.

The seeds for Smith's passion for journalism were planted early. He is the son of a weekly newspaper editor from upstate New York, a man who served as newspaper janitor, ad director, Linotypist, and top editor. When Smith was 8, he watched his muscular dad work the Linotype machine. He fell in love with the musical rhythms of that process engine, and still keeps on his desk his own name set by his father in lead type.

Smith's journalism career spans 34 years, with his

longest stint a 14-year stretch at *The Hartford Courant* as a reporter, city editor, general assignment editor, and sports editor. For the last decade he has been at the *Record-Journal* in Meriden, Conn., where he is executive editor and senior vice president. He is one of a vanishing breed of newspaper editors who write a regular column.

Smith's passion for journalism includes a love of language and storytelling, which can be reflected in both his management style and his own writing. Through praise and coaching, he encourages good writing at his paper, including such experiments in descriptive journalism as "A Short Walk: A Closer Look at Where We Live and Work." Smith wrote the first installment of this feature and managed to cite Led Zeppelin and Henry David Thoreau in the same paragraph.

In winning a Society of Professional Journalists First Amendment Award, Smith's columns received this praise from a judge: "Smith doesn't preach. He treats the free press discussion as a dialogue, not a sermon. He explains without condescending, and often invites the reader into the world of decision-making to demystify the process. He is not shy about fiercely promoting the traditional marketplace of ideas."

—Roy Peter Clark

Little white lies erode credibility

MARCH 10, 2002

Some readers are after us for writing the truth. I am always dumbfounded when people can't bear the truth. A newspaper deserves criticism when it errs. When we get it right, I don't completely understand the condemnations.

The American public expects the truth from its newspapers, but last month several subscribers told us that we ought to be ashamed for writing in his obituary that former Wallingford Police Chief Carl A. Grasser pleaded guilty to obstruction of justice and resigned his position in 1969. He tried to cover up the arrest of a man accused of assaulting one of his own officers.

Mr. Grasser was a high public official in Wallingford and the career of a public official is just that—public. If he had retired with laurels instead of being forced to resign, we would have reported the laurels. But he didn't. Can you imagine leaving out of Richard Nixon's obituary that he resigned from the presidency? Can you imagine when Sen. Ted Kennedy dies, ignoring the bridge at Chappaquiddick?

Those who called or wrote asked why we couldn't concentrate on the good in Chief Grasser's life. We did. We wrote that he was "an innovative chief," a "devoted family man," a "devoted husband," an "active parishioner" in his church. We quoted a former town attorney who said he was "a good police officer," "very kind," and "led a very exemplary life" after he left the department. We quoted former Mayor William Bertini that he regretted having to take action against the police chief.

This is one disconnect between the press and the public that is difficult to resolve. There seems to be a feeling that we should not speak ill of the dead. Certainly, not every misdeed in a person's life has to be recorded in the last story written about him or her. Minor blemishes are not newsworthy. If a police chief, for example, had been suspended for a day only once back when he was a sergeant over a small departmental violation, it probably shouldn't be included in a story about his whole life.

The New York Times Manual of Style and Usage, a highly regarded reference work in the industry, gives this guidance for obituaries: "If a crime or indiscretion was the subject's main claim to fame, it should of course figure in the lead (first paragraph). But an early indiscretion should be kept in proportion—subordinated or omitted, depending on its ultimate significance in a life."

I sympathize with family and friends who do not want to read about Chief Grasser's resignation, but it was a wholly significant event in his life and my responsibility is to the tens of thousands of readers of this newspaper who expect the *Record-Journal* to present truthful accounts. If we receive 10 complaints, it means some 65,000 other readers did not complain, so perhaps this is a sermon to the choir.

Someone's life is not black and white. To trot out only platitudes, to pretend that unpleasant things never happen in a life, to deny the complexity of life is almost an insult to a human being.

I should mention that this newspaper has a paid obituary policy whereby a family submits an obituary through a funeral home that includes information they choose and leaves out information they do not want. These notices appear on the obituary page for a fee which allow a family to virtually dictate what will and will not be in the obit.

The *Record-Journal* also assigns news obituaries on prominent people. It is in these news articles that we are duty bound to follow the dictates and judgments of sound journalism. We simply would not be upholding our responsibility to our readers if we started withholding significant information about prominent public officials. That kind of editing leads to erosion of trust with our readers.

Everything offends somebody

MAY 5, 2002

Here's an idea. Let's take all the accountants and have them do the judging and take all the judges to do all the accounting. The accountants will decide what justice is and the judges will decide what is good financial practice.

We could take all the political operatives and have them do the journalism and have journalists do all the politicking. The politicians will decide what news is and the journalists will run our governments.

Farmers could do the engineering and engineers do all the farming. Teachers could do the policing and cops do the teaching. Diplomats could do all the fighting and soldiers do all the diplomacy. Probably wouldn't work, though. For sure, editors could not run our town, state or federal governments.

You may have noticed that a political operative, and others, wrote to us last week that a state senator's divorce is not news and how dare we print it. It is hard enough finding good people to fill the ranks of politics and government without them having to worry if their divorce shows up in the paper, says he. David Fordiani is a skillful political operative and was a key player in the Democrats' loss of the Meriden mayorship. But I would suggest he stick to politics and we'll stick to what is news.

Since 1776, in this country it has been a given that if you become a public official or public figure what you do and say will become news. That is our system. That is our democracy. Anyone who wants to get involved should understand that. America stands for journalists deciding what is published—not anybody else deciding, certainly not the government.

Inside a newspaper, we have deep and long discussions about what to print and what not to print. Often that gets into how much of a public person's private life should the voting public know about. We have been told that a president having sex in the Oval Office is nobody's business. We disagree. We have been told that a governor's divorce is nobody's business. We disagree. And we disagree that a state senator's divorce is not news. It is.

Sen. Thomas Gaffey, D-Meriden, has said his divorce has held up thousands of dollars in reimbursements for his personal expenses to his employer, the scandal-wracked CRRA. Sen. Gaffey himself did not object to the *Record-Journal* reporting his divorce.

Because a state senator makes the laws under which we all live, because a state senator has power over you and me, because a state senator, like a governor or a president or a city councilor, decides policy—his or her character, his or her thinking, his or her makeup is important for the public to know.

Marital status is part of a person's makeup. Divorce is not good or bad, it can be both. I was divorced. I have written that my four daughters are a melded family. I do not make policy, but I make decisions on how much you will know about the policymakers. If the policymakers don't like that, they are living in the wrong country.

If you don't like a certain story, turn the page. I guarantee you will find something you like. It is sort of like listening to the radio. If a song comes on you don't like, change the station. Every day a newspaper prints things that are upsetting to someone. And every day a newspaper prints things that are satisfying, even uplifting to someone.

Life on this planet is troubling, exciting, uplifting, sad, happy, horrifying, beautiful. If a newspaper is supposed to reflect life and if you are reading a newspaper that does not portray horror, beauty, happiness, sadness, excitement or trouble—if it doesn't uplift you and make you laugh or make you cry—what kind of newspaper is that? It is an irrelevancy at your doorstep every morning. It is not worth your time. It is bland and blank and missing the parade of life as it goes by.

Don't tread on my freedom

SEPTEMBER 8, 2002

Last Sunday we published nearly 5,000 words on a dispute this newspaper is having with the Meriden Police Department. We retained a respected freelance writer to research and write the piece and arranged for Associated Press editors in Hartford to edit the story. We could have written and edited it ourselves, but chose to engage outside journalists to scrutinize the issue in order to present the most objective account we could.

Freelancer Alan Bisbort of Cheshire, who has written for *The Washington Post* and *The New York Times* and has authored 14 books, interviewed city police officers, *Record-Journal* personnel, and independent experts. The different points of view—that police think they can arrest reporters for harassment; that journalists think covering news cannot lead to harassment charges—were presented fully.

I believe that most of our readers see the value of telling them the story of this dispute and understand the importance of a free press. It troubles me when some readers write letters about how we are "hiding behind the First Amendment" or that we are "veiled in the cloak of First Amendment rights." Such language cheapens the Bill of Rights. It makes me wonder if some Americans don't understand how crucial those rights are to our way of life.

We all need to consider how dangerous it is to let armed police handcuff journalists for asking questions in the pursuit of news. Writing news is no easy task. Minions stand in the way, do everything they can to prevent the truth from coming out. Reporters must ask questions, they must ask tough questions and they often have to ask the questions repeatedly in order to do what our society has appointed the news media to do: inform. You cannot have a democracy without a free press. You cannot have a free press if the police can round up reporters for doing their job.

We hear much lately about the right to privacy. There

is no right to privacy listed in the Bill of Rights. You will not find the word privacy anywhere in the U.S. Constitution. The Founding Fathers enumerated the peoples' rights in the first ten amendments—from freedom of speech to the right to a fair trial—but were silent about privacy.

The modern legal theory of privacy began with an 1890 *Harvard Law Review* essay co-authored by Louis Brandeis, who later became a Supreme Court justice. He argued that people have the "right to be left alone," but also held "the right to privacy does not prohibit any publication of matter which is of public or general interest."

We should welcome the balancing act of conflicting liberties but we should not let the police make those decisions. It is in the civil courts, not criminal courts, where Constitutional disputes are settled.

We were mindful of the privacy of Fire Chief William Dunn's wife and family after the tragedy of his suicide, offering the opportunity to comment if they chose. But some criticize us even for asking the chief, after he took a leave, why he did. The fire chief is charged with protecting city residents from danger. He manages a $6 million budget and a staff of 114. Of course the public should know why he needed a leave, and the way the public finds out is by the newspaper asking why.

In a 1988 Washington State case where an official sued a reporter (he did not try to have him arrested) on harassment grounds, the judge ruled in favor of the reporter because to find otherwise "would constitute an unwarranted interference in the newsgathering process in violation of the First Amendment."

In Meriden last month, the fact that the state's attorney tossed the warrant out should be proof enough that the police were off base in seeking to arrest our reporter.

Do the police have a right to censor the news?

SEPTEMBER 15, 2002

Meriden Deputy Police Chief Jeffry Cossette asked me for a retraction on the last paragraph of my column last Sunday.

I wrote: "In Meriden last month, the fact that the state's attorney tossed the warrant out should be proof enough that the police were off base in seeking to arrest our reporter."

The arrest warrant wasn't submitted to the state's attorney, the deputy chief wrote to me in an e-mail.

I'm not sure how crucial it is whether the warrant formally went to the prosecutor or not. Clearly the cops went to the prosecutor.

The deputy chief was quite incensed, however. He called it a "fabricated statement," a "cheap shot" with "no factual basis" and said I was unethical and unprofessional for writing it.

I should have been more precise in that last sentence. Instead of writing that it was a *fact* that the state's attorney threw the warrant out, I should have pointed out what was reported in this paper the week before: "The legal matter is unresolved. It *appears* the state's attorney's office has rejected a police application for the arrest of (a reporter), but officials refuse to confirm or deny that."

Deputy Chief Cossette is now denying it. "The arrest warrant was never submitted to the state's attorney. Therefore, it was never 'thrown out,'" he wrote.

Free-lance writer Alan Bisbort, in his Sept. 1 story, quoted the deputy chief saying that the police "had sent the matter on to the state's attorney." Mr. Cossette says now that he wasn't referring to the warrant affidavit.

I asked Mr. Bisbort if the deputy chief or the chief, William Abbatematteo, said anything else on the subject. The writer checked his notes. In the hour-long, wide-ranging interview with the two top Meriden cops, one or the other also said: "Legally, it's in the hands of the state's attorney's office, whose job it is to enforce criminal law." Also: "Whether it's a criminal matter is not up to us. We send it on to the state's attorney…" Also: "Normally we send these matters on to the state's attorney." Also: "The state's attorney suggested that we get the family's attorney to send a letter to the newspaper."

That last point interested me, because it is exactly what I suggested to Deputy Chief Cossette, that if someone is upset with the newspaper, he can always take civil action, which is not a matter for the police. It then goes directly to a judge.

Once more, for the record, here is the crux of the controversy: The police tried to arrest one of our reporters because he contacted Meriden firefighter Ryan Dunn. The reporter called him to offer him the chance to comment on the official police report on the suicide of Fire Chief William Dunn, Ryan's father. The newspaper maintains that out of fairness and sensitivity, reporters must do everything they can to give those involved in news stories the opportunity to comment. The police have called it alleged harassment and say that if they receive a complaint, they can arrest reporters for doing it.

Chief Dunn's widow had told us she preferred not to comment, so we never contacted her. His son Ryan said at various times that he wanted to, and that he didn't want to, comment.

Assistant State's Attorney James Dinnan told Mr. Bisbort that if his office rejects an arrest warrant application, he will not comment. He refused comment except to say there is no legal case pending against a *Record-Journal* reporter.

The stance Abbatematteo and Cossette are taking should be troubling to everyone. If you follow their logic, anytime someone is upset at being asked questions by a reporter, they can call the cops and get the reporter arrested.

So let's say Monica Lewinsky didn't want reporters asking her questions. Just call the cops and charge harassment. Stop the story in its tracks.

But this case is about a human tragedy. Both police officers and reporters serve essential functions in society, especially in times of tragedy. Police and reporters work in tragic situations often. Tragedies like the deaths of thousands in two towers in New York. Tragedies like the death of one fire chief in Meriden. In order to do their work, police must ask a lot of questions in the midst of tragedy. In order to do our work, reporters must ask a lot of questions in the midst of tragedy.

So consider the Abbatematteo/Cossette stance that if someone is upset in a tragedy over being interviewed by a journalist, all they need do is complain to the cops, who then can go after warrants for the arrest of the journalist. How, then, could reporters write about what happened at the World Trade Center? How can reporters help a community, a nation, comprehend, understand, fathom what is going on, if cops can carry them off and prevent them from telling the stories?

It is difficult to interview grieving people. It is sometimes difficult for grieving people to express their thoughts and feelings. But journalists give them the opportunity to do that. Quite often, grief-stricken people want to; they find it cathartic; they want to say something important about the loved one who is gone. They honor the deceased by sharing with others what was good and meaningful about them. Read the poignant "Portraits of Grief" in *The New York Times* about the victims at the World Trade Center and you will know the power of good reporting. Or read the compassionate coverage in words and pictures in this newspaper of a courageous fireman, William Dunn.

Our reporters do not harass people who are grieving, they give them a chance to express themselves. In doing that, they allow the public to read a more human story and a more comprehensible story.

In his e-mail to me, the deputy chief wrote, "The complainant did not want to pursue charges at this time…If you had obtained a copy of the police report, this factual information would have been available to you." And "If you had done the proper research and obtained your information as to how the case was closed, you would have learned the truthful conclusion to the case."

I was gratified that the complainant withdrew his complaint, which Mr. Bisbort reported on Sept. 1. The police provided us their report Friday. It left out an important fact about the "truthful conclusion to the case." It didn't mention that City Manager Roger Kemp told the chief and deputy chief to stop any and all action against *Record-Journal* reporters until the city attorney (who is different from the state's attorney) looks into it. In other words, until City Attorney Larry Kendzior examines the constitutional—civil, not criminal—case law, the police are to stand down.

Mr. Kemp hired Chief Abbatematteo. The city manager is the police chief's boss and he told him to cease and desist. It is always a good idea in a democracy to have civilians in charge of police.

Deputy Chief Cossette told me that his department is "a professional organization committed to public service." So is this organization.

Anyone who breaks the law, including journalists, should be arrested. But no one here is breaking any laws, and the police should have known that from the very beginning. This newspaper and the police department have served this community together for more than a century, and the relationship has historically been a good one.

Recently, Deputy Chief Cossette organized a media relations seminar for his command staff. Some of our staff participated. That's a good step. I have told him and the chief that we are willing to meet at any time to discuss differences.

Given Mr. Kemp's directive, I am hopeful this dispute is behind us.

Teaching the wrong lessons

DECEMBER 15, 2002

Maybe you read the other day that Southington School Superintendent Harvey Polansky kicked a reporter out of his office. Harvey is a big bear of a guy who has told us he runs an open administration. Caroline Porter is a smidgen, but she carries big questions. Too big for the superintendent, apparently.

Meanwhile in Wallingford, a usually reasonable public personage asked a reporter not to talk to any members of the town's Wooding-Caplan study committee. He should limit himself to writing only what is discussed at formal committee meetings, this committee member said. The Town Council appointed the committee to figure out what to do with the uptown property, which has sat dormant since the town bought it in 1991 for $1.5 million.

This disregard by public officials for informing the public is frightening.

Educators especially have a heavy responsibility to teach the American way of life—the importance of a free and unfettered press to Americans. It is a basic freedom, isn't it, that we all stand for and fight for and die for, in how many wars, when our way of life is threatened?

Isn't it the First Amendment—the first!—in our Bill of Rights?

What does it say to our students when our leading educators decide that what happens in the public schools is private, none of the public's business? Dr. Polansky not only kicked a reporter out; he chastised her for interviewing teachers and students about issues in the schools.

Now tell me, who else should reporters talk to about what is happening inside the schools other than teachers and students—and, of course, administrators, if they choose to answer questions? The saddest thing in Southington is that it was merely about why the police officer assigned to the high school was suddenly re-assigned. Will somebody tell me why that is such a sensitive topic?

Maybe we all just want the official versions, the spin, the half-truths of officialdom—no need for independent scrutiny by an inquiring press. Never mind that a vigorous and inquiring press is one of the foundations of our free society.

"Freedom of the press belongs to the people. It must be defended against encroachment or assault from any quarter, public or private," states the American Society of Newspaper Editors' "Statement of Principles," which has stood since the 1920s, when it was adopted.

"The American press was made free not just to inform or just to serve as a forum for debate, but also to bring an independent scrutiny to bear on the forces of power in the society, including the conduct of official power at all levels of government."

If this isn't being taught in Dr. Polansky's schools, it sure ought to be.

Translate the Wallingford official's idea on how to cover the local committee to Henry Kissinger's committee looking into the failures of our national security apparatus. What if the rules were that reporters could not ask Dr. Kissinger any questions, that reporters could not talk to committee members, all they could do was listen at their official meetings?

What kind of media would sit back and publish only the official version? The Iraqi press, for one. The German press in the 1930s and 1940s for another.

The ASNE code also dictates that "journalists must be constantly alert to see that the public's business is conducted in public." We take these principles seriously because so many people who rise to high public office forget so easily that the American system is all about freedom, including the independent scrutiny provided by a free press.

A conversation with
James H. Smith

ROY PETER CLARK: In these pieces your passion for journalism and the First Amendment is right on the surface. Tell me about the sources of that passion. Where's all this coming from?

JAMES H. SMITH: First of all, it's renewed almost every day. Every time some public official says, "No, you can't learn that," I say, "Yes, we can, and it's our obligation to let the public know." On the other hand, I think it goes way back. One of the jobs my father had was as a Linotypist, and he took me to work one day when I was 7 or 8 years old. He sat down at that Linotype machine and typed out my name. That piece of lead sits on my desk today. So I think way back in my own memory I got molten lead and printer's ink in my blood.

Was your dad a journalist?

He was a lot of things. He was a janitor, he was a Linotypist, he was the editor of several small weeklies in upstate New York. He was also an ad director. So he was on every side of newspapering in the weekly business.

So this passion is both wired and nurtured.

Yeah.

Jim, the writing editor seems less common and less prominent than he used to be. What does it mean to be a writing editor, to be in charge of the news operation but also to have a prominent spot in the paper?

I spend my time running a newsroom, and that's a hard job. It's making sure the publisher is happy, and interfacing with other department heads, and corporate hocus pocus and budgets. I edit other people's words all the time; it's wonderful to work with reporters and other editors to make stories better. But writing my column is like my island of sanity. It just means something to me to be able to sit down and write my own stuff. Writing brings editors back, I think, essentially to the reason they got into the business and it reminds them about the value of words. And if you are doing that, the community and readers you serve can only be helped, because what you're doing is making the message clearer.

Are you a confident or an anxious writer? Where on that spectrum would you put yourself?

I'm probably more confident than anxious. I love writing and, if you love something, I think you have to have some confidence in that effort.

Are you a fast writer or a slow writer?

I'm more fast than slow.

What are some of the things that help you be fast?

My fingers. I came across something you wrote about trusting your fingers, and sometimes I do. When I have half a thought, I just let my fingers go. Writing is thinking and your fingers help you think. That helps me, helps the words flow.

On most of the pieces that you write, do you wind up with the lead that you want at the beginning of the process?

I usually wind up with the idea of the lead. I almost never end up with the words in the first two or three sentences that I've written. I always have to go back and fix things. I know marvelous writers who have to get it right in the beginning, but I don't. I can go back to it.

Do you ever write with your ending in mind?

Yes, I do, and that goes to outlining a beginning, a middle, and an end. With columns you want to make a point, so I'm wending my way to what I hope is a good conclusion.

You said beginning, middle, and end. Is that the basic framework from which you think about the story? Or is it more elaborate than that?

It is more elaborate. A story has to pull the reader along, so you can't get lost in a labyrinth. When you're done, there is a beginning, a middle, and an end, but there's an awful lot of meandering to get it right.

Do you do a lot of revising? Do you revise as you go along, or just at the end of the process?

Both ways. I go along, then I put it aside, and if there's time, I go back to it and go through it again. I read the *Paris Review* interview when George Plimpton asked Hemingway about rewriting. Hemingway said he rewrote the ending to *A Farewell to Arms* 36 times or maybe 39 times, and Plimpton asked why. And Hemingway said it was to get the words right. So that's what I always remember. Get the words right. Hemingway was a genius, and every time I read *A Farewell to Arms* I cry because it's such a powerful, powerful ending. But it took him 36 times to get it right.

So if I could see your plan, what would it look like? Would it be written on a blotter, on your napkin, on your sleeve, on a piece of paper, on the clipboard?

I think a lot of it is just banging around inside my head.

We sometimes talk about rehearsing—the story cooks in your head while you're gathering stuff and preparing to write.

Absolutely. I do that all the time, partly because I have a lot of other things to do besides write a column. So I'm walking around managing a newsroom, but somehow this stuff is banging around in my head, or I'm out walking and I sort things out in my head. That's rehearsal.

For the rest of the conversation, Jim, I'd like to get into your arguments, your passionate defense of newspapers and editorial prerogatives and the First

Amendment. Let's talk about "Little White Lies Erode Credibility." You wrote, "Those who called or wrote asked why we couldn't concentrate on the good in [Police] Chief Grasser's life." Journalists seem to lose credibility when we are seen as treating people insensitively. Yet you say that if we don't tell the truth about people, flaws and all, that we will lose credibility. But the complaint is not that we're telling lies about people. The complaint is that we're telling *truths* that hurt people. Help me think that through.

Right; the truth hurts sometimes. I don't think we should be vicious. Think of H.L. Mencken's column after William Jennings Bryan died. I mean, he savaged the guy. I go back and I read it because it's such wonderful writing, but he called him a mountebank and a fraud. It was wonderful, and, of course, Jennings Bryan was a hugely public person at the time. So fair is fair. But I don't think we should savage people, and that's why I think it was important to point out all of the good things Chief Grasser did. That's why I tried to point out that we wrote about his whole life, not just the good and not just the bad. Life is complex, and people should understand that.

Do you think there's a case to be made that the news media are too insensitive and intrusive? There seems to be a lot of that kind of criticism out there.

Yes, there's a case to be made. We have to explain ourselves more. It has gotten worse since television images show the pack with its microphones and television cameras chasing after whomever, and it's not a pretty sight. People don't see a newspaper reporter out gathering information. What they see is the end product. But there is often ugliness in going after the news, in going after the truth. You have to be tough, you have to ask tough questions, you have to use all sorts of intelligence and intrigue to get to a fair, balanced, and accurate account. And if people saw that process, they would say, "He's being impolite." You know something? So is the one who's trying to hide the information. We have to be professional about it, and we have to be respectful about it, but we have to get the information and publish it.

There's a long tradition in American journalism of going to the house of the family and asking for the photograph of the dead child. That's traditionally one of the jobs reporters say they hate. You make the case that, quite often, grief-stricken people want to express their feelings, "…they find it cathartic; they want to say something important about the loved one who is gone." What if you confronted a study that suggested that people are in a state of shock as victims, that they're vulnerable, that they're not in a position to make informed consent; from a legal standpoint, they're not public figures?

I want to answer that in a two-pronged way. I think if you're presented with evidence that people are in shock, you also have to consider the value of storytelling to society. Is compelling writing of equal value to society so that, in order to provide good storytelling, you have to perform some unpleasant tasks? I would ask that we weigh those things.

When my wife, Jacky, was a reporter, she had to go out and interview the best friend of an 18-year-old girl who was just senselessly murdered on her own street. The friend was standing next to her when she was shot. So Jacky went out and knocked, and the friend's mother came to the door. Jacky told her who she was and the woman said her daughter "couldn't talk right now; maybe later." So Jacky just said, "I'll come back later." So Jacky went to the high school and got some year-book information, and some assistant principal called her ghoulish or some terrible thing. Then she went back to the house and she knocked on the door again. And this time, Jacky put her foot in the open door so the woman couldn't close it on her. And she said, "Please, just let me come in. I want to hear what your daughter has to say about her friend." There were a lot of people in the house. And in the end Jacky spent two hours in that house, talking to the friend and her parents, but she just sort of blended in, and she came back with just an incredible picture of this young 18-year-old girl who was murdered. And I didn't hear directly from the family and friends, but we heard later that that story helped them.

A lot of it is how you approach people who are facing tragedy. You can't stick a microphone in their face and say, "How do you feel?" You have to be empathetic, you have to sincerely try to understand what they're going through, but you have to try to do it. In the end, like in this police case when the fire chief's wife made it clear to us she could not talk to us, we never contacted her.

If I were working for you, Jim, and I showed up once and they said no, and I gave them some time and I showed up twice and they said no, would that be good enough for you?

I think twice is okay. Edna Buchanan [famed former police reporter at *The Miami Herald*] once said that she does five murders a day, and a lot of it's by phone. She says, "I call and they'll hang up." And she says, "Sometimes I call back and you might get someone else and then you've connected." And I've always remembered that. I think trying twice is worth it. Three times, it gets a little murky.

Here's one of the things that I think is a hard problem for journalists to solve: If we could watch you or your reporters work, we would see that they include in their stories a small percentage of the material that they gather. Is that fair?

Oh, absolutely. Yeah.

So reporters are making decisions regularly to exclude from stories material that is deemed inappropriate, more harmful than the general value of the story would warrant.

We always gather, I hope, more information than we're going to use. The more information you gather, the richer your story can be, and decisions are made at the reporting level and at the editing level about what's appropriate for the story.

Let's say you've written an obit about a person, and there is an embarrassing piece of information in his past, but you deem that it's not relevant to his public life, so you leave it out. You don't get any points for doing that. Your restraint is invisible—invisible virtue.

How do you solve the problem in which people think that all the decisions are going in one direction when, really, many of the decisions are going in the other direction, to exclude?

You know, we did that yesterday. We had a story about a couple of guys going into the high school wrestling hall of fame. They had spent years being referees in high school wrestling matches. One of them pleaded guilty to felonies and had to resign his other job. So we asked ourselves, "Is that relevant to a story about him going into a high school wrestling hall of fame?" In the end, we decided it's not relevant: It happened 15 years ago, it has nothing to do with his role as a wrestling referee, and so we left it out. So we left out some truth but, to me, that's an irrelevant truth to this particular story. And you know something? You're right. The readers are never going to know that we wrestled with that.

And you can't write a column about it.

Right. But you can write a column, without naming the person, about how we wrestle with these decisions. And when you do that, people are amazed.

Let's go to "Everything Offends Somebody." You open it with a very clever argument about account- ants and judges and engineers and farmers, and it's funny, it's interesting, it has a kind of immediate, powerful, common-sense logic. I want to test your log- ic with another set of arguments: I'm not the doctor, I'm the patient. I'm not the parish priest, I'm the parishioner. I don't give out communion, I receive it. Right? But I'm a stakeholder as both a patient and a parishoner. I want my priest to be as good as he can be and I want my doctor to be as good as she can be, and I want my editor to be as good as he or she can be. So

doesn't that argue for a more activist and reformist role in dealing with a variety of professions, as opposed to: "I'll just leave those decisions to the editor because the editor knows how to do that."

We shouldn't ever close our ears to what people are trying to tell us. I feel, though, that we have to remind people, "Thanks for your input, but it's our decision." If I'm an engineer and I'm building a bridge, I have people who are going to go over that bridge say, "Gee, I don't like that design." At some point I'm going to say to them, "Well, thank you, but if you don't do it my way the bridge is going to collapse." And so I'm an editor, and I know words, and I know journalism, and I know fairness and balance and accuracy and what bias is, and it's my decision. The founders of this country said there should be free speech and a free press.

But they gave that right to the people and not just to the editors. You don't have any special privilege.

I think that's arguable. Certain people in America decided to become writers and editors, and they have the right and the responsibility to do their jobs as well as they can. That includes listening to other people who have the same right in this country but who choose *not* to be an editor or a journalist. I choose to be an editor, and so I say it's my decision because that's what I do in life.

Okay, that's fair. If you don't like a certain story, turn the page. But I guess I'm troubled a little bit by that sort of "love it or leave it" argument. Why don't you say, "If you don't like a certain story, mark it up where you think it's inaccurate and send it to us, and we'll take a look at it"? I'm wondering if you actually believe readers should turn the page.

I do believe that, because it's true. If you turn the page, you will find something that you like. A newspaper every day is just filled with wonderful, diverse stuff. I don't mean to say, "Don't tell me you don't like that story." I listen to complaints all the time, and I try to respond to those complaints, and I think complaints are good because they help us get better. But we can't ignore that on any given day in my newspaper there are 90,000 words and dozens and dozens of articles and photographs and comics—the parade of life. We have to present everything, and however many readers you have, some of them aren't going to like that George Bush said "X" last night at a news conference, but some are going to like it.

Let me ask you about the line between public and private. If a mayor gets a divorce, is it newsworthy?

Yeah, and that's ethical decision-making. We draw lines all the time. If a policeman gets a divorce, it's probably not news. If the mayor gets a divorce, I think it is news.

How about a city council member?

I think so. When somebody has policymaking power over a constituency, then I would opt to delve into his private life more than someone who doesn't.

All right, so that's a line. One of the things I thought was interesting and, I'm sure it gives force to your argument, is that you say, "Marital status is part of a person's makeup. Divorce is not good or bad, it can be both. I was divorced. I have written that my four daughters are a melded family. I do not make policy, but I make decisions on how much you will know about the policymakers." Tell me more about why you thought it was a good thing to include your own divorce.

Certainly the executive editor of the local newspaper is fair game and a public person, and so if my state senator is a public person, so am I. If I'm going to write about his divorce, I think mine is also public.

The son of my former publisher, Frank King, at *The News-Times* in Danbury, Conn., was arrested. Instead of a blotter item, Frank insisted that his son's arrest be put on the front page.

Tell me about the decision to hire an outside reporter

to cover the public disagreement between the newspaper and the police department that you write about in "Don't Tread on My Freedom."

What we tried to do first was have meetings with the police chief and the city manager and other high-ranking police officers and resolve this privately. It was something I felt that we could sit down and have a meeting of the minds on. But it didn't work. So at one point I called our First Amendment lawyer, Ralph Elliot, in Hartford. And he said to me, "Well, Jim, maybe you should write about this." So the editors sat down and I said, "Let's write about this," but someone said, "It's hard to write about ourselves." So I said we should find a freelancer. The coup was calling Elaine Hooker, the AP bureau chief in Hartford, and asking if she would have her staff edit it. I could have assigned a reporter, and we could have edited it, and I think it would have been fair and balanced, but a lot of people wouldn't believe it. So I hired an absolutely respected writer, and he was writing it for the AP. I told him he could interview anybody here and interview all sorts of people in the police department and just write it straight. My publisher, Eliot White, thought that was a terrific idea and, looking back on it, I think so, too.

You write: "I believe that most of our readers see the value of telling them the story of this dispute and understand the importance of a free press. It troubles me when some readers write letters about how we are 'hiding behind the First Amendment' or that we are 'veiled in the cloak of First Amendment rights.' Such language cheapens the Bill of Rights. It makes me wonder if some Americans don't understand how crucial those rights are to our way of life." Who's complicit in the failure of American society to make people more aware of the value of their rights?

The press itself. In the last decade or two, people just seem hypercritical of those of us who practice the First Amendment. It's been exacerbated by the present administration with the Patriot Act and all of the secrecy that's going on and questioning people's patriotism for being critical. The First Amendment is just so utterly, absolutely basic to what America stands for. If newspapers don't make that argument, if we don't help educate the public to the value of our rights and freedoms that, my God, so many men and women have died for, who is going to make that argument? I hope teachers are, but we play an immensely important role in that.

I want to go to your essay, "Do the Police Have a Right to Censor the News?" First of all, this is an essay in which you seem to make a correction. You say you should have been more precise when you talked about whether the state's attorney threw the warrant out. Can you tell me about your sense of responsibility for correcting even small misunderstandings or errors.

It was an error. And I kick myself. I should have read the damn story more closely. The deputy police chief called me on it and, to a certain extent, he was right. I had to acknowledge that. But that's why I asked the reporter to look in his notebook, and I chose to use all of those quotes that essentially said the same thing. I think as a writing device it was persuasive. There's no question that the cops went to the state's attorney on this.

If my daughter were coming to work for you, what would be the ways in which she would absorb your passion for freedom of the press, First Amendment rights, the role of journalism in a democracy?

It just has to permeate the newsroom, the people I choose to be my editors, the leaders in the newsroom. I believe they have that passion, too. And a lot of it is my own demeanor. I'd never want to undercut the city editor because it's his job to manage his staff. But that doesn't mean I can't sit down next to his education beat writer and ask her, "What are you working on?" and just talk about the stories. Show them that I'm interested in how they put words together and how they go about their jobs. It has to be at absolutely every level. You have to praise the photographer who just took a remarkable picture. You have to shout it in the middle of the newsroom:

"That was marvelous, that was wonderful." You have to praise people publicly and when you have to criticize someone, you do that privately.

You sound like someone who is inclined to stand strongly behind your reporters when they're being enterprising and aggressive. Have you ever been in a circumstance in which you had to publicly admit that your reporter was wrong?

I just did that, and, God, I hated doing it because I think we made a terrible error. A reporter and his editor let a story go through in which we held a 16-year-old girl up to ridicule. A local girl had just won some presidential scholar prize so we were going to do a feature on her. She's an incredibly articulate young lady. And she said during the interview with the reporter that George Bush is an idiot and then she had the presence of mind to say, "Oh, gee, you probably shouldn't put that in the newspaper." This is a 16-year-old girl. So what we put in the newspaper is that she called George Bush a dope.

A dope?

Yeah. And we started getting letters to the editor. So I had to call in the reporter, and I went over with him how you can't embarrass children like that; and I talked to the editor, and then I wrote a column about how we have a policy in dealing with teenagers and how we take care with what they say because they don't always know what they say. So that's one of the very few times when I've publicly held up a reporter and an editor saying that we did the wrong thing.

But if you're willing to say you were wrong, it increases your credibility. If all you did was defend your reporters, I think people would think you just did it reflexively and that was your one move.

On the other hand, powerful public figures at the local and state level are constantly complaining about reporters, and I think it's very, very important to defend reporters to those people. We need to do that.

Is there some territory we didn't get to that you want to talk about?

I'm a little bit concerned that the credibility movement can make us too timid. We allow the phrase, "They're just trying to sell newspapers" to be pejorative. My response to that is, "You bet I'm trying to sell newspapers, because the more newspapers that are sold in this society, the better off society is." I think that we have to remember that writing the news is noble and writing the news and photographing the news mean we are going to offend people, because the world is offensive. I buy into the whole credibility thing about being sensitive to people, but I think some of us are taking it too far, and we're becoming too timid, and we're leaving too much out of our newspapers when our job is to tell the truth. And that's where these columns come from.

Writers' Workshop

Talking Points

1) James Smith writes about "one disconnect between the press and the public...that we should not speak ill of the dead." Discuss which of these details might be included in the obituary of a public figure, and why: death by AIDS, death by suicide, death by alcoholism, an arrest for indecent exposure 20 years earlier, a spouse's suicide, a child's drug overdose, four marriages. Would your decisions change for someone not considered a public figure? How?

2) Smith argues that newspapers that fail to tell important truths risk their credibility with readers. But he also acknowledges that readers consider the media insensitive when they print inappropriately private details. Is there a way out of this seeming contradiction?

3) Discuss this controversial proposition: Reporters should cover public figures as aggressively as necessary; but private figures, especially victims not accustomed to dealing with the press, should grant the reporter an "informed consent" before becoming the object of coverage.

Assignment Desk

1) Read some of the feature obituaries in "Portraits of Grief," published by *The New York Times* of those killed on Sept. 11, 2001, noting especially the ways in which negative details about the dead are handled. Try writing or rewriting the obituary of a controversial public figure using the same sensitivity.

2) In his interview, Smith argues that those in society who choose to be journalists receive special constitutional protection, the freedom of the press clause in the First Amendment. Research this argument and write about your own conclusions.

3) Why are some journalists more interested in the First Amendment than in the Second or Sixth amendments? Write a column about what happens when rights collide, when freedom of the press, for example, threatens the right to a fair trial.

Chicago Tribune

N. Don Wycliff

Finalist, Passion for Journalism

N. Don Wycliff has been public editor of the *Chicago Tribune* since July 2000. He moved into that position after serving nine years as the *Tribune*'s editorial page editor. During his tenure as editor, the *Tribune* editorial page won one Pulitzer Prize, was a finalist for another, and took several other major awards, including two Distinguished Writing Awards from the American Society of Newspaper Editors.

Wycliff went to the *Tribune* in September 1990 from *The New York Times*, where he was briefly a higher education reporter after spending five years as a member of the editorial board. Earlier, he had worked as an editor in the *Times*'s "Week in Review" section and as a reporter or editor at several other newspapers, including the *Chicago Daily News*, the *Chicago Sun-Times*, the *Dallas Times-Herald*, the *Seattle Post-Intelligencer*, the *Dayton Daily News*, and *The Houston Post*.

He won the ASNE Editorial Writing prize in 1997.

He has served as a juror for the Pulitzer Prizes and as chairman of the ASNE Writing Awards Committee. He is a Texas native and 1969 graduate of the University of Notre Dame. He lives in Evanston, Ill., with his wife, Catherine, and two sons, Matthew, 16, and Grant, 14.

In "A Trust Bestowed, a Trust Betrayed," Wycliff gives fair airing to the range of opinion about the firing of longtime *Tribune* columnist Bob Greene. He then defends the newspaper by walking readers down a path toward his argument's trump card: "that most precious asset, credibility."

A trust bestowed,
a trust betrayed

SEPTEMBER 19, 2002

It would be impossible to explain better than my colleague John Kass did Tuesday the breach of trust involved in former *Tribune* columnist Bob Greene's contact with that teenage girl some years ago, the incident that, over the weekend, cost him his job.

As Kass summed it up: "Her parents trusted the *Tribune* enough to bring their daughter here to interview a top columnist. A bit later, the columnist and the girl were in bed together."

It's about trust. Trust bestowed. Trust betrayed.

That the breach goes beyond the principals in the case has been evident in the phone messages and e-mails that have flooded the public editor's office this week.

"I feel totally betrayed," said one reader, a woman, in a phone message. "After all these years of reading his column…that he was basically preaching. This kind of hits me even worse than the priest thing."

"I'm shocked about Bob Greene," said another caller, a man. "Here he was an advocate for children and he goes and does this."

But in truth, the predominant sentiment among the callers was in Greene's favor.

"We have all made mistakes in our life," a male caller said. "I would trust him with any of my family members."

"I am so opposed to what happened to Mr. Greene," said a woman who described herself as 76 years old and "not a prude." "He had an indiscretion. It's nobody's business but his and Mrs. Greene's."

And probably the most indignant and expressive of all the calls, from a 64-year-old woman in Glenview: "How could this happen? [Is] this paper…run by a bunch of virgins or something?"

Not likely, given that virtually all of us are parents. But beneath the humor of the lady's remark is a serious question: How to react to the moral frailty that has been part of the human condition since Adam and Eve?

How do newspaper readers react? How must newspaper editors react? Their responses may differ because, while they share certain interests, not all of their interests are identical.

A persistent theme among Bob Greene's supporters has been that the good he did in writing on behalf of abused and neglected children more than compensates for any bad he may have done, any yielding to temptation.

"He's done too much good for little boys, little girls and the *Tribune*," went a typical comment.

While there are legitimate grounds for debate both about the quality of Greene's journalism and the amount of good it actually did for children, the proposition that his good might outweigh his bad is not nonsensical on its face.

But the *Tribune*—in the person of editor Ann Marie Lipinski and her assistants—cannot confine its calculations to Bob Greene and the balance between his good work and his bad behavior.

What the *Tribune* sells to readers each day is a full menu of news, commentary, features, sports and advertising—a menu far bigger than just one columnist. More fundamentally, what the *Tribune* sells is a reputation for credibility, a conviction among readers that, if you read it in the newspaper's pages, you can depend on it to be true.

That covers everything from the spellings of names to the ingredients in recipes to grave assertions of fact ("John Doe was indicted Wednesday by a federal grand jury..."). The fact that we publish corrections almost every day on Page 2 testifies that we don't get everything right. But it also testifies that we try—and we do not take errors lightly.

Likewise, our editorial ethics policy—separate from and in addition to a companywide "Code of Business Conduct"—seeks to secure that most precious asset, credibility, against corruption by either intentional or inadvertent actions by reporters, editors and others involved in the newsgathering and writing process.

To outsiders, it often may seem as if we are merely being precious or self-important in our ethical agonizing. But it would astonish most outsiders to learn how much people contort themselves and go out of their way to please when they know they are dealing with a member of the press. Knowing that, journalists and the organizations they work for must act accordingly.

By comparison with some of the ethical problems editors face, Bob Greene's case was clear-cut. Trust bestowed. Trust betrayed.

Lessons Learned

BY N. DON WYCLIFF

By the time I sat down to write this column, I had been exposed to two full days of e-mails and phone calls from readers about Bob Greene's departure, and most of them were angry. They also were uncomprehending, for the most part, of the concept of a newspaper code of ethics that might be more rigorous than the legal code.

In reflecting on what I might write and in doing the actual writing, a couple of things became clear to me.

Sometimes the most useful thing you can do is help people understand what a thing is *not*. The Greene episode was not about lawbreaking, about having sex with an underage girl. The girl was not under the legal age of consent at the time and neither she nor Greene alleged that they had engaged in intercourse. Yet most of those who called in support of Greene assumed that one or both of those were the issues in the case. I alluded right away to John Kass's column because he had explained the facts better than anyone else to that point. And then I tried to crystallize the issue with the third paragraph: "It's about trust. Trust bestowed. Trust betrayed."

A big part of a public editor's job is to remind readers what is at stake each day with each edition of the newspaper. Most readers are not cavalier or uncaring about the ethics and credibility of the newspaper. But they sometimes don't see the connections between the actions of individual reporters or editors and the believability of the newspaper as a whole. They have to be reminded that our credibility is implicated in everything we do, or fail to do, and that our ethics codes are not just ornaments, but essentials. They also have to be reminded that the role of an editor like Ann Marie Lipinski is to safeguard that credibility. Greene's family and friends may be able to say, "All is forgiven. Now let's go on with life." But the editor doesn't have that luxury.

Writing this column was complicated by the fact that I was one of the "assistants" that Lipinski called on for advice. But my sense of the stakes involved and my ability to articulate them were heightened by that same fact.

THE PLAIN DEALER

Jim Strang

Finalist, Passion for Journalism

Jim Strang, an associate editor of *The Plain Dealer*'s editorial pages, has been in newspapers for 36 years.

Strang, 58, was born in Ashtabula, Ohio, and graduated from Kent State University with a bachelor's degree in journalism in 1969. Along the way, he wrote for the *Star-Beacon* in Ashtabula, Ohio, the *Record-Courier* in Ravenna, Ohio, and *The Cleveland Press*. For the past 30 years, *The Plain Dealer* in Cleveland has been his journalistic home.

With *The Plain Dealer*, he has been a general assignment reporter, rewrite man, national correspondent, assistant national editor, editorial writer, deputy editorial director, and national editor. As national editor he directed coverage of airline safety reporting that received the Polk Award in 1996. In 14 years as an editorial writer, Strang has received 18 state and national awards for his work.

Among his areas of opinion responsibility are the war against terrorism, Congress, the presidency, the Supreme Court, international trade, and Canada.

His wife, Margaret, is a fiber artist. Their children are Megan, 19, Amy, 16, and Ben, 14.

Strang's passion for the free flow of information to citizens resounds in "What Price Security?" He flags for readers the Orwellian, "total information awareness" aspirations of former convict turned consultant John Poindexter. The editorial is direct, thoughtful, and foreboding without being alarmist.

What price security?

NOVEMBER 15, 2002

Say hello to John Poindexter's giant know-it-all machine. If Congress allows it to be assembled, you can say goodbye to any thought of personal privacy, ever again.

You may recall Poindexter. He once was an admiral, first in his class at Annapolis, rose to become President Ronald Reagan's national security adviser. He was briefly adjudged a felon as the highest-ranking Reagan administration culprit in the Iran-contra arms-for-hostages outrage, until an appeals court determined he had been granted congressional immunity for the testimony that convicted him.

Poindexter has spent the last several years as a security consultant, thinking about information, computers and stovepipes.

Practically everything about all of us, as we have come ruefully to realize, is entered in databases somewhere: What we buy at the grocery store with our discount cards; the movies we rent; the medical records our doctors, insurance companies and hospitals keep; any police reports we ever filed—or complaints in which we were named. The property we own, the automobiles we drive. Our credit card receipts. And now, thanks to increasingly prevalent public surveillance technology, our fingerprints, our faces, even the gait at which we walk.

Until now, that information has been kept fairly private in "stovepipes," insulated from prying eyes short of a court warrant. But if it were all compiled in one colossal database, where ultra-powerful computers could sift it to identify behavioral patterns, well, then, perhaps the terrorists in our midst could be culled in a few milliseconds of searching.

Or, perhaps, anyone with access and a grudge, or just a proclivity to electronic voyeurism, could access the entirety of our existence.

The only thing that would prevent such abuse would be the integrity of the government's highest officials—

people like John Poindexter, immunized felon, who is again in the highest reaches of government as head of the Office of Information Awareness at the Defense Advanced Research Projects Agency.

Poindexter is campaigning to make his dream of "total information awareness" the unending nightmare of every American citizen.

He's perilously close to attaining that goal. It's written into the Homeland Security Department legislation now before the Senate. On the opposite page, *New York Times* columnist William Safire lays out the frightening details.

In a terrible echo of last century's greatest crime, Poindexter says it is his mission to develop the technology, not the policy that guides it. He will sire Big Brother, not control him. Orwell miscalculated. The year was not 1984. It promises to be 2002.

Lessons Learned

BY JIM STRANG

Get angry and write.

That's what I did the morning I read about John Poindexter's "giant know-it-all machine" and its Orwellian portent. And that's probably why the editorial that resulted is here for you to read.

Dispassionate, detached analysis surely has its place and its audience. Else, where would all those forbidding volumes of gray policy ruminations that fill our mailboxes each month get their arid manuscripts and their erudite readers?

But that place is not on the opinion page. I believe that editorial writing, like lovemaking, is best done passionately. Lightning should greet readers arriving at the pages; thunder should echo in their minds' ears.

Give the readers a reason to spend some time with the fruits of your creative labors. Give them cause to throw down the newspaper and curse your unknown name, or to leap from their chairs and exalt your like-minded wisdom. But, for all our sakes, give them something to stir their souls.

And sometimes, the best "something" you can serve them is a slice of your own anger, cut thick and still steaming, au jus, on the page.

That's a lesson I've had reinforced repeatedly during my dozen or so years among the anonymous band of opinion crafters who constitute *The Plain Dealer*'s editorial board.

The first time was the morning when the city council president told the biggest radio station in town that he just didn't understand why the electrocution of a homeward-bound baseball fan at a shoddily wired bus stop shelter was such a big deal.

The absolute arrogance of his prevaricating know-nothingism, after days of stories about the questionable construction contracts and unperformed maintenance that had led up to that death, had me seething in the rush-hour dash to the Inner Belt.

By the time I got to the office 10 minutes later, the editorial already was written in my mind. Before our morning meeting it was smoldering in the computer under the headline, "Here's why, Mr. Forbes"—a sarcasm-laced, coldly angry recitation of the damning facts for the "edification" of the purposefully ignorant public official. The readers—and later, the contest judges—loved it.

Then there was the afternoon when a 5-year-old girl plucked a daffodil for her daddy from her elderly neighbor's flower garden—and the old man, in a rage, ran out and shot her father. A child's gift of love turned to horror, and an editorial writer, who just happened to have a loving 5-year-old daughter himself, let the sorrow and anger welling up within him flow onto the page for all to feel.

No reader will ingest a steady stream of wrath, but sometimes, the situation demands no less. Thus it was when word of Poindexter's nightmare computer-mining project finally spread. We each know, at some level, that all aspects of our lives have been reduced to computer files. The fantasy we held was that no one would connect those files—that, whoever we are and whatever "secrets" we think we hold, we could remain anonymous.

Then came Poindexter, the crafter of "total information awareness," the immunized felon who promised to shatter that fantasy and lay bare all our records at the stroke of a few keys. And the anger welled, and the fingers moved, and the editorial gushed forth.

I felt much better afterward.

Dan Barry
Deadline News Reporting

When Dan Barry speaks of Sept. 11, it is with the breadth of a journalist who says he will "keep going back"—to keep uncovering its meaning, to keep explaining its reverberations, to keep pursuing the stories that build on what we know.

Part of his commitment is to stay informed; part is to pursue stories as yet untold; part is journalistic perspective shaped by personal experiences.

Storytelling drew Barry to journalism. But he shoveled a lot of dirt and sold a lot of deli sandwiches before realizing that daily journalism was an inviting opportunity for his passion to tell stories.

Barry, 45, has been a reporter for *The New York Times* since September 1995. He has served as city hall bureau chief, Long Island bureau chief, and acting police bureau chief. He has written extensively about city politics and police brutality. He is now a general assignment reporter on the metropolitan desk. It was from that post that he covered Sept. 11 and its aftermath and made his contribution to the *Times*'s Pulitzer Prize-winning coverage.

He is a native of Deer Park, N.Y., and he graduated from St. Bonaventure University in 1980 with a major in journalism and a minor in English. He earned his master's degree in journalism from New York University before becoming a reporter at the Manchester, Conn., *Journal Inquirer* in 1983.

In 1987, he joined *The Providence Journal-Bulletin,* where he covered state government and organized crime and wrote regular essays for the Sunday magazine. From January 1991 until July 1995, he was a part of that newspaper's six-member investigative team. In 1992, he and two other reporters won a George Polk award for an investigation into the causes of a banking crisis. In 1994, he and the other members of the investigative team won a Pulitzer Prize for a series about the state's court system; the series led to various reforms and the criminal indictment of the state's Supreme Court chief justice.

Barry lives in Maplewood, N.J., with his wife, Mary Trinity, and their daughter, Nora.

As you read his ASNE prize-winning deadline story, "A Day of Tributes, Tears, and the Litany of the Lost," notice the depth of emotion, the unadorned language, the imagery and details that mark Sept. 11, the anniversary. Notice the tone—quiet and respectful. Notice the adeptness of Barry as observer—informed, watching, sensing the day, the people, the mood. The result is a story that belongs to the individual reader—that nurtures private thoughts.

—Pam Johnson

[Editor's Note: The Jesse Laventhol Prize for Deadline News Reporting is funded by a gift from David Laventhol, a former Times-Mirror executive, in honor of his father.]

A day of tributes, tears, and the litany of the lost

SEPTEMBER 12, 2002

They followed one another down, down into a seven-story hole in Lower Manhattan yesterday, thousands of them, filling with their sorrow the space where their husbands and wives, mothers and fathers, sisters and brothers, sons and daughters, had died a year ago to the day. Some left cut flowers on the hard earth; some left photographs; some left whispered words.

They lingered for a long while; a few even collected stones. And then the people who have become known as the "family members"—as though they belonged to one international family—trudged back to level ground, to the living.

There, a city and a country were commemorating a date so freighted with emotion and imagery that simply uttering it seems to say everything: Sept. 11, 2001. The day that as many as 3,025 people died in terrorist attacks that destroyed the World Trade Center, damaged the Pentagon and crashed a jetliner in rural Pennsylvania.

With moments of silence and recitations of familiar speeches, with the tolling of bells and the lighting of candles, with peaceful music and vows of military retri-bution, the United States observed that day's anniver-sary, joined by countries around the world that honored the date in their own, distant ways.

President Bush led the country in a moment of silence at 8:46 in the morning, Eastern time—the moment of the first strike, when American Airlines Flight 11 cut into the trade center's north tower at more than 400 miles an hour. Then, visiting the repaired Pen-tagon, the president spoke of a renewed commitment to the war against terrorism.

"The murder of innocents cannot be explained, only endured," Mr. Bush said. "And though they died in tragedy, they did not die in vain."

A short while later, in Lower Manhattan, Governor George E. Pataki read Lincoln's brief but powerful Gettysburg Address; Mayor Michael R. Bloomberg succinctly described the dead—"they were us"—and former Mayor Rudolph W. Giuliani began the invocation of the names of every one of the 2,801 victims on the city's official list.

It was Lower Manhattan that held the unfortunate claim as host to the largest, most elaborate observance, with foreign dignitaries—including Hamid Karzai, the president of Afghanistan—paying their respects. On a day almost as clear as the early Tuesday morning of a year ago, tens of thousands of people surrounded a 16-acre pit and watched the wind spin eye-stinging twirls of dust from the place where two 110-story towers once stood.

All the while, they listened in virtual silence as a riveting, two-and-a-half-hour story was read to them. The story, whose words leapt from loudspeakers to ring through surrounding streets, had no verbs or adjectives; in a way, it was one epic paragraph. It began with "Gordon M. Aamoth Jr.," ended with "Igor Zukelman," and in between contained the names of 2,799 other people— bond traders and secretaries, firefighters and assistant cooks.

They have been dead, now, a year.

A year may seem an arbitrary measure, but experts in the human condition say that first-year observances of cataclysmic events are fitting, even necessary. "The date itself is emblazoned in memory," said Robert A. Neimeyer, a professor of psychology at the University of Memphis. "The same ritual that allows us to remember also releases us to live."

Yesterday's ritual began in the first hours of this Sept. 11, in the darkness. In each of the city's five boroughs, teams of bagpipers began their miles-long march toward the disaster site, the wail of their instruments summoning city residents to their apartment windows for pre-dawn reflection.

As the Manhattan contingent made its way down Broadway, people in Washington Heights raised flags, fists and candles; some held their hands over their hearts. James Leyden of Yonkers was at the corner of West 96th Street well before 5, in time to see the lights in a nearby apartment building flick on as the loud procession passed. It gladdened him, he said, because he lost a nephew in the trade center calamity.

"I just liked the notion of marching down all the boroughs, and basically waking people up," he said. "It's just such a bad day, a bad day for families to relive."

The bagpipers, all employees of various city agencies, were slowly marching through a changed Lower Manhattan, part of a changed city. Those changes go beyond the 89-year-old Woolworth Building reclaiming a dominant piece of the city skyline. They are also in the unclaimed pairs of re-soled and polished shoes, dozens of them, at the Shoetrician shop on Fulton Street. The manager said he keeps the shoes because what else can he do.

The bagpipers converged like skirling streamlets into a sea of people already gathered at the bottom of Manhattan to honor the dead. By 8 a.m. the people were four deep along Church Street to the east, a dozen deep along West Street to the west, and thick through every alley and side street. Gone, for now, were the vendors selling mass-produced photographs of the World Trade Center in distress; in their stead, family members—distinguished by their ribboned pins—holding aloft photographs of their lost loved ones.

The photographs of the dead bobbed upon the swells of the living. Over here, one of Charlie Murphy, with the reminder to "Remember Me"; he had four older sisters, a fiancée and a deft sense of humor, and he was 38. Over there, Shannon Fava; her son is 4 now, and she would have been 31.

Then, suddenly, it was time: 8:46. Silence settled over Lower Manhattan and other corners of the world. In London, thousands paused during a memorial service at St. Paul's Cathedral, while in Dublin, the government asked for a minute of silence in factories, offices and schools.

At the Dallas Market Trade Center, employees held a moment of silence around a reflecting pool surrounded by votive candles for each victim. At Logan International Airport in Boston—where the airplanes that struck the trade center took off—operations halted for one minute.

That minute of silence, in a section of Manhattan not accustomed to silence, was followed by Governor Pataki's reading of the Gettysburg Address. Then up stepped Mr. Giuliani, who has been applauded for his leadership in the weeks after the terrorist attack and who a day earlier had attended the funeral of his 92-year-old mother, Helen.

"Gordon M. Aamoth Jr.," Mr. Giuliani said, reading the first name on a list of 2,801 that would take the rest of the morning to read. Mr. Aamoth, of course, was more than just the first name: he was an investment banker, just 32, and there is now a football field named after him in Minnesota.

Mr. Giuliani was the first in a long line of dignitaries, city officials and family members to invoke names, while Yo-Yo Ma and other musicians played "Ave Maria" and other selections in the background. Now and then, the wind would blow so hard that it would rumble like thunder through the microphones; now and then, brown billows would rise from the pit to anoint listeners with dust.

David Hochman, a master electrician who a year ago lost more than a dozen friends and co-workers, watched quietly from a raised vantage point in the World Financial Center's recently restored Winter Garden. Then, pointing his hard hat at the scene, he said: "You see that tremendous hole? That was New York."

The invocation of names paused at 9:04 so chiming bells could mark the moment that United Airlines Flight 175 hit the south tower, when, everyone present knew, a year earlier thousands were fleeing for their lives while hundreds of firefighters and emergency workers were filing in.

Family members would later say that it was important to hear the names of their loved ones read, though they could not say exactly why. Monica Ianelli, dressed in black and with head bowed, held a portrait of her fiancé, Joseph Ianelli—whose name she took—close to her body, now and then wiping away the dust. When his name was read at 9:53, she looked up and smiled.

At 10:29, the moment when the second tower collapsed, the readings paused again, while bells chimed and the fog horns of boats on the Hudson sounded. An hour or so later, the last name was read; Gov. James E. McGreevey of New Jersey read the Declaration of Independence; and family members began filing down a ramp and into the pit.

They went down together to be alone, it seemed, as people symbolized their grief in individual ways: a funeral wreath here, a photograph there. Many built small, almost primitive memorials by propping up photographs with mounds of pebbles; many took pebbles or fistfuls of dirt to bring with them.

Kathleen Shay, of Staten Island, later said that the death of her 27-year-old brother, Robert J. Shay Jr., a bond broker at Cantor Fitzgerald, did not really sink in until she had descended into the pit. Her sister, Leanne, said that in building a small memorial there, they "tried to figure out where his office was."

Remembrances and services and seminars continued throughout the day in New York City, ensuring that year-old memories remained fresh. At St. Patrick's Cathedral in Midtown, for example, Cardinal Edward M. Egan concluded a memorial Mass by introducing four brothers who had served as altar boys—all sons of Firefighter Vincent Halloran, killed in the trade center collapse.

Meanwhile, in Brooklyn, the Arab-American Family Support Center sponsored a silent vigil at Borough Hall to honor the victims, as well as to highlight what it said were the difficulties that the Arab-American and Muslim communities have faced in the last year.

In the late afternoon, President Bush and the first lady, Laura Bush, paid their respects at the disaster site. Mr. Bush seemed at ease amid the crush of grieving family members. He listened, occasionally smiled, rubbed the back of the neck of a father of a dead police officer. Someone handed him a palm-size photograph; he tucked it in a pocket.

As dusk came to the city, dignitaries representing the dozens of countries that lost citizens began to file into Battery Park, at the bottom of Manhattan, for a memorial service that would include the lighting of an eternal flame in front of "The Sphere," a battered sculpture that once graced the trade center plaza. Aaron Copland's "Fanfare for the Common Man" was performed; Mayor Bloomberg read the Four Freedoms speech of Franklin D. Roosevelt; vigil candles were clutched.

Meanwhile, back at ground zero, all of the dignitaries and invited guests had left. It was dark now, but the wind was still gusting, and throngs of people were still lingering. They snapped photographs, trying to capture the emptiness of it.

A petite woman named Marianna Dryl pressed her face against the chain-link fence along Liberty Street and looked north into the pit, set aglow by stadium-style lights. She said she was 53, an accountant from Kew Gardens, Queens; she said she had not been to the site since the first weeks after the disaster.

"When I first came, it was such a horrible pile," she said. "I thought they could never take it all away. Now it looks so empty and clean. It is almost beautiful."

A conversation with
Dan Barry

PAM JOHNSON: Your story, "A Day of Tributes, Tears, and the Litany of the Lost," was the lead-all for *The New York Times*'s coverage of the first anniversary of Sept. 11, 2001. What kind of discussion did you and your editors have about the story's purpose or style?

DAN BARRY: The *Times* took this day very seriously and on the day of the anniversary, the paper did a special section and had a lot of stories and photographs. This story benefits from all the people who could be brought into play. How do we tell this story with the benefit of omnipresence? How do we make it different from all the other stories written about Sept. 11 and the commemorations that followed? I happened to have written a lot of the previous stories. There was the Twin Towers of Light; that was a very moving moment. In late May there was another ceremony for the removal of the last girder from the site. And so now, here we were at the anniversary.

I had written a story for the special section about death as a constant companion; this idea that there's a need to recognize death, a need to memorialize. It's part of who we are as human beings. You have a moment when you address it, and then, as a society, you move on. So this was going to be an important day in the psyche of the city and of the country in terms of saying, "Okay, now we go to the next step of wherever we're going." But the day before, our mission was to make sure that we were as covered as possible and to make sure that all of us were looking for the little moments, for the little details that are not clichéd, that are true, that bring the story to a higher, truer plane.

And so where were these points? We said we wanted someone with the bagpipers early in the morning, walking with them and picking up what people said. We wanted someone to be with family members as they gathered, listen to what they said, and see what they looked like and be a part of it. Respectfully, always respectfully. We were very aware of not being intrusive. I was going to write the story. I was to get there as early as I could, and roam and then watch, roam again, and then go back and start putting together something. So that was the plan: Everybody be aware of what we're trying to do, make it as good as we can, make it as true as possible, and be alert for the small details and the small bursts of language that might make the story blossom.

As you approached the assignment that day, what do you recall about your own feelings or experiences—having been part of the coverage for a year?

Well, there were a couple of things. First, as a river of mourners and family members are flowing past as they're going around and then down into the pit, a lot of them are holding photographs of loved ones—large photographs, some of them in frames. I'm watching these heads of the dead flowing past. Your eyes are drawn to their faces and you wonder who they were and what happened. And one of the faces bobbing by was a guy I went to high school with. I recognized him immediately. It was Eddie Perrotta. I wasn't particularly close to him and I knew that he had died, but there's Eddie Perrotta floating past me at the ceremony.

Also, for many months the collapse of the twin towers was all I wrote about. For example, seven or eight days after the disaster, Chris Chivers, who had been camping out with the National Guard in Battery Park, wanted to rotate out. He had written wonderfully about what he had seen. So I went there and slept for two nights in the park with the National Guard and, with the photographer, walked around the pit many, many times. It wasn't a pit. I shouldn't say that. The "pile" they called it at that time.

So I had an intimate feel for the place—seeing the recovery efforts up close; going into a hotel and seeing on the wall "AON Corporation Breakfast Meeting at 9:30" and you know that a lot of those people from AON died in the building across the street. I kept going back, going back. Four months after the collapse, I spent a night at the Marriott Hotel, which is just south of the site, and I wrote a story about listening from my hotel room to the sounds of the machines digging and the lights—ballpark-like—

shining all night. I tried to imagine what it would be like
to be a hotel guest hearing and seeing this all night and
knowing what it was. And through my window I could
see the heavy machinery looking like dinosaurs as they
walked across this mess.

So by the time of the anniversary—after going back
again and again—I felt very intimate with the place for
so many reasons.

**The day of the anniversary, a lot of people were
working on stories and you all were identifying
things that were going to be important somewhere in
the total picture.**

Right. And the people who were out there weren't necessarily only contributing to my story in terms of calling
and saying, "Hey, Dan, I just heard a great quote" while
I sat at the desktop. They might have been writing stories of their own but were on alert for other things that
might not fit into their assignment but might fit into a
lead-all. Or they might have been assigned to help
someone else. For example, I think there was a separate
story on President Bush's visit. Some things might have
fed into that story, or they might not have been appropriate for that story and they might have come to me. There
were a lot of things coming in and out.

So how did the day unfold for you?

I got up at 4:30 in the morning. I live in New Jersey, so I
took the ferry from Hoboken to Lower Manhattan. That
was good in its own right because, as I was drawing closer by water to the scene, I could see the entire cityscape—
the changed cityscape—now absent those two towers. It
helped me begin to get my thoughts together. I tried to anticipate what would happen, but the idea was to just be
open to it. I had no idea what the lead would be or how
the day would progress. I knew there would be speeches,
and I knew that they were going to be reading names. I
don't think we knew that people would literally get on
their hands and knees and pick up fists of dirt. That hadn't
occurred to me.

So I got to Lower Manhattan near the site about 6 and

just walked around for an hour and watched people gather and reminded myself of buildings and where I had been over the previous year—in front of the Deutsche Bank Building or in front of this hotel or whatever—and then just found a spot within the rim. They had bleachers for reporters on the west side within the fencing and between the actual hole and the street. I had covered city hall previously, so I knew some of the mayoral aides in charge. You were supposed to stay in one spot, but they let me wander around and that was good for me.

Did any reporters go down into the hole when the family members went?

I know of at least one, Leslie Kaufman. There were thousands of people who almost organically began to flow south while the names were being read—after 8:46, which marked the first strike—and they began flowing and at some point were allowed down into the pit, and Leslie was with the families and just went with the crowd. I don't remember if we knew that they would be allowed into the pit. But she wisely went with the flow.

The reference to people picking up the dirt. Did she see that, or could you see that from where you were stationed?

I think I could see it from where I was stationed. We also had photographers right over the site; and Ruth Fremson, a great photographer, and Jim Estrin, another great photographer, were right at the lip, and I was going back and forth at times to talk to them. I can't remember if I saw it then or if I saw it through their photographs or if I saw it on television. I remember being struck by it. I didn't see the detail of people piling rocks on top of one another making these little memorials. But I did see it in the photographs that came back. While I was writing, someone dumped rough photographs on my desk and those helped me visualize as well.

What was on your mind as you approached the writing?

When I got back to the newsroom, I knew that something true and primal had happened that day that was beyond the trappings placed upon it. There was a structure to the ceremony that had been agreed to by heads of state. Then, when the ceremony was taking place, the sorrow was so great and the emotions were so raw that they broke through the structure, not disrupting it, but transcending it and becoming truer still.

Having witnessed this, having felt it and having seen the disembodied face of a high school classmate of mine float past, I just wrote what I felt in the first couple of paragraphs and, you know, waited to see if the editors would buy it. I always see the job as me pushing the envelope as much as I can, and the editors pushing back, so that we find the line. I figured the story would go on the front page, where there are all sorts of different rules for stories. But that wasn't my concern. My concern was to tell the story as best as I could and as fresh as I could, because by morning most people would have seen footage of it on television. Because it was such a staged event in many ways, I had to bring something new to it or to elucidate, illuminate. So the story became more essayistic in tone and then at times it had to be newsy.

I wanted to write something that would make people feel what it was like there. I wanted to bring out things like the dust—without saying "ashes to ashes." When the swirls of dust occurred, what else could you think? And the trick, then, is how do you convey that to the reader without making it sound overdone? And so I was conscious throughout of trying to do it subtly.

What has led you to this point in your writing—that awareness to check yourself?

There are a couple things. At times I'm not sure whether I'm going over the top or whether I'm killing the message with my writing. We could do a separate interview with my wife on how many times I call her on deadline and say, "Mary, let me read you this lead. Does this work?" She'll stop what she's doing, and she'll hear me recite. And I have an urgency in my voice because I'm on deadline, and she'll say, "Dan, you're going too far. You've got to tone it down." Or, "Dan, it made me cry," or "Dan, it made me laugh." That's one check.

And the other thing is in 20 years of doing it, you've done things wrong so many times that you begin to recognize what works. It's trial and error, trial and error. Lastly, it's ear. It's listening. I read aloud everything I write, which causes some odd glances sometimes, and if it doesn't sound right, if it doesn't have this kind of rhythm to it, then I'll go back at it. I do think a lot about that, about going too far or trying to find just enough without going too far.

Did someone suggest that you read aloud, or did you just come to that yourself?

Someone suggested that a long time ago. I think it was an English teacher at St. Bonaventure named Rick Simpson, who was teaching Romantics and poetry and composition—not journalism. It's writing and trying to listen to what you're saying. Simpson is a jazz musician, and there is a jazz that you sometimes try to adopt when you're writing. Here I am thinking that I'm writing jazz when I really ought to be informing people, but, to me, it's a synthesis of information and trying to write in a literate style so that it rises, it transcends the ordinary.

It's one thing to have information and put it on a page. It's another to make it mean something or bring some emotion to it that makes people stop and have an experience reading.

Right, right, right. So here I am, I'm bearing witness, and this is unfolding before me. I'm standing there and people are walking past me and people are reading the names in front of me and the wind is crackling over the microphone and the dust—you could see the dust popping up from the pit—and you look to your right and there's the Deutsche Bank covered in this black shroud and you look across and you see the Woolworth Building—well you're not supposed to see the Woolworth Building from this vantage point, but now you do—and it's a fairly sunny, warm day in September and it's Sept. 11. You just have to open yourself up to all those things and then say, "All right, how do I convey why I was choking up at the scene myself? What struck me the most?" The people flowing past me with those photographs and signs and then going down into the pit.

At that point, did you recognize that as the lead?

Yes. When I'm writing, I usually try four or five different approaches, pick one, and then try to hammer it down. I spend much, much more time on leads than almost anything else because that's how you grab the readers' attention and that sets the tone for the rest of the piece. On this one, I just went with what was foremost in my head. The challenge was whether I could get it across to someone else with words—the idea, down, down, going down into the hole and then coming back up. The city and the country had gone down for a year into this thing, and now, after a year, we come back up to the living. So that was on my mind when I was writing.

That's why I used family members in quotes and then said "as though they belonged to one international family" to signal to you, reader, you're part of this, too. We call them family members. What does that mean? Well, on this day we can at least invite ourselves into what that must have felt like.

The tone of the article is straightforward—almost quiet. How did you achieve this effect?

In terms of the tone, it was almost like a eulogy, and if it's established in the first two or three paragraphs, then that is the tone I want to keep throughout—straightforward, plain language. The whole thing was very biblical in a way. I'm not talking about the writing, but the day—the way it wound up, and with the dust, and the thunder of the wind blowing the microphone, and the people. The way people responded was, to me, so primal and so nakedly human, that it was humbling.

That's the tone: to stand there and record what happened and make it come alive, but be careful with the language. That's why the lead is so important, because it helps establish the tone throughout. I was very aware of using images and having the images speak for themselves—the eye-stinging twirls of dust. Eye-stinging can go many ways, and I wanted it to. I don't want to overdo it, but it was kind of holy. Jim Estrin took a photograph before the family members were allowed down into the pit. A huge human circle formed in the center of the pit. Then suddenly this wind kicked up, and it is like a mini-tornado, and you look at it and you see through the dust these people standing with their heads bowed. The photograph says it all.

Could you talk about the ending and the surprising turn it took?

Deadline was approaching, and my editors were telling me that I had to reflect what was happening elsewhere in the city and in the country in the late afternoon and evening. Reports were coming in from St. Patrick's Cathedral and Battery Park and Brooklyn, and I knew that these had to be touched on, but I was determined to have the story end back at the site. In our planning discussions, I had suggested that a reporter return to the site at night—just to see what it was like. We had taken a similar approach earlier in the year, when the last girder was removed from the trade center site and carted away. I had thought, "Wouldn't it be neat to be at the Manhattan Bridge as the truck carrying that girder rumbles along Canal Street and leaves Manhattan"—to capture that moment.

Now the idea was to go back to the site after all the media and dignitaries had left and reflect the quiet—to bring the reader back to the place where all this awfulness began. It worked well, I think. Just as I was coming to the end of the story—stalling, really—a reporter named Lydia Polgreen called from the site. I asked her to describe everything she saw and everything she heard. She described the wind gusts, the eeriness of it all. And then she told me what Marianna Dryl had said. "Now it looks so empty and clean. It is almost beautiful."

I took this to mean a kind of tragic beauty, the beauty found in the quiet of a cemetery at dusk. A humbling beauty, really. And when I heard it, I knew that's where the story would end.

It's an incredible stretch of time and coverage on

your part. What attracted you to journalism?

It's basically the chance to tell stories. I just like to tell stories. My mother was born in Ireland, and she came to the States when she was a teenager and had been orphaned. She came with this real sense of storytelling and things that she had learned in rural Ireland. She met my father, who also is a good storyteller—a Depression-era kid raging against the big oppressors of the little man. And so from them, it was almost destiny to go into journalism because here's a way to tell stories and to hold accountable the people in power and, therefore, to do justice to my parents in a way.

What a great way to make a living. You go and talk to people, then you come away and try to craft a story in a way that's interesting to others so they could share the experience. I've always, always, felt like, "How lucky can you be if you can get a job like that?" and by the same token, honoring my parents or learning from my parents or expanding upon the experiences of my parents in terms of telling stories and engaging people. The idea that you could write a story and hold a government official accountable or change something or even put someone in jail if they deserve to be because of some story you had written or some investigation or inquiry you had made. That's what my father would rage against and would want. I don't live simply to please my parents. My mother has passed away. But that is where it comes from.

How do you challenge yourself to keep progressing in your writing?

In terms of being challenged, I'm very, very, hard on myself. I'm motivated by fear of failure. I fear failing the moment. I fear failing the story—not delivering something that captures the worth of the story. So, I'm challenged just by trying to get it right, making sure that I'm telling the readers something that they might have known, but that I'm telling them in a new, different way that adds nuance or brings another layer of meaning to it.

I'm still challenged by the idea of going out and over-reporting something and then coming back and trying to figure out a way to grab readers anywhere in the country with a sentence or two and then convincing those readers, in this day and age, to read it all the way through to the end because at the end I hope to have another surprise for them.

I'm challenged by having topspin in the story. How do you keep the topspin in the story? In the anniversary story, I was worried about those things that the story had to carry in addition to the moments at the pit, and I massaged it and tried to rewrite it so it was in the same tone and so you could come to the end and feel something.

In writing a story, I try to anticipate where readers might say, "I'm going to turn the page." "I'm going to bail out." "I'm going to turn on CNN." "I'm going to do something else." I want to anticipate that point and figure out a way to keep them until they get to the end, because I want them to finish the story. I still live to do that.

In terms of editors, I want an editor who will challenge me, who gets what I'm trying to do. I don't want whatever I write to go through. I want someone to say, "Dan, what about this word?" or "Why don't we try this?" I like that. Sometimes you'll think that you did it right and you'll get upset, but I like the signal from an editor that she is a careful reader and is trying to figure out how to make the product or the story better. That means that they're paying attention.

I did a Sept. 11 story last year in Skaneateles, N.Y. I wrote it one way and Jon Landman, the metropolitan editor, looked at it and said, "Well, you're giving away the punch line in the beginning." And you know why I did that? Because the story was being thought of for Page One and there are standards about the nut graph appearing on Page One. Jon said, "Why not save that until the end?" When he said that, my head exploded; it was like an epiphany. So I rewrote it and it winds up being like an O. Henry story where the surprise is at the end. Sometimes people say the *Times* has its own formulas, and some of that's true; but they also will push the envelope in writing.

What was your path to *The New York Times*?

I grew up on Long Island, got my journalism degree from St. Bonaventure, and wanted to be like Hunter

Thompson—a contributing writer to *Rolling Stone,* where you could be sassy in your writing. There was no market for a young guy coming out of college with that attitude, and so I dug ditches and worked in delis around Long Island. I applied to the NYU journalism graduate school and got a poor-boy scholarship where they pay you a stipend but you have to work in the office. I'm glad I did that, actually. It helped me understand New York and the lure of daily journalism.

I got a job at the *Journal Inquirer* in Manchester, Conn., and it was a great job. I covered prisons, and who knows how many planning and zoning meetings, and the murder of the week. I was there for four years before joining *The Providence Journal* in 1987. For a while, I was the bureau manager in West Warwick, R.I. After a couple of years, I joined the investigative team and wrote about the mob and the decline of organized crime in New England. I was on the team when we did a series of stories on the court system and it won the Pulitzer in 1994.

I got hired by the *Times* in 1995, and I've been here ever since. First, they sent me to Long Island because I was fluent in Buttafuoco. I was there when TWA Flight 800 went down, and then I was brought into the city and covered police brutality issues and became the city hall bureau chief at the height of the Giuliani years.

Then in 1999, my life took a turn. I was diagnosed with a nasty kind of cancer. I went through all sorts of chemo and radiation for several months. The *Times* really took care of me. They made sure that I got the best attention at Sloan-Kettering; and Joe Lelyveld, who was the executive editor, took a personal interest. I'll always be grateful because it was a rough time.

But I kept working. I wasn't in city hall anymore, but I would come in just to work and be the bald guy in the corner doing odd little things. Then I wound up getting a clean CT scan. Every six months now I go and get scans. I'm not out of the woods, but it's much, much, much better than it looked in the beginning.

Since 2000, I've been general assignment on the metro staff. Sometimes I do national stuff and sometimes I do a quick foreign thing, but mostly I'm on metro—and Sept. 11 has pretty much been my focus since it happened.

One of the themes that emerges in talking with you is the commitment to "going back" to a story, a scene, an issue. Why is that important to your work?

I wrote maybe 20 stories through the remainder of 2001 and a good number more than that in 2002. When the focus began to shift in 2002 to other important stories, I wanted to stick with Sept. 11. I was insistent that you can't blow a hole in the bottom of Manhattan and then just accept it, and so I kept going back. I went back to the landfill in Staten Island six months later when everyone else had moved on. I went back to Ground Zero, looking in the pit when just two months earlier you still had the remnants of one of the smaller trade center buildings. I talked to family members about what it's like now. I went back to the medical examiner's office and did a big story on what that was like for those people. That was unbelievable work being done in the examiner's office in the first few months after Sept. 11.

So all that going back and going back informed the way I wrote when it came to Sept. 11, the anniversary.

When Sept. 11 happened, I strongly felt the need to bear witness and to get it down, get it down now—to tell the story. Did the cancer figure into my perspective? There's something about that experience that gets your attention and reminds you of fragility and mortality.

One of the first stories I did was about when the buildings collapsed, this creamy dust was spread all over downtown. I walked around with a photographer and then wrote a story about all the things that were written on the sides of the buildings—you know, people writing in the dust on the sides of buildings asking for loved ones, writing their loved ones' names. They'd scrawl, "Where are you?" "I love you," "I miss you." I knew that that stuff would be washed away by power-hoses in a few days, and I felt this need to get it down. I felt that about the whole thing, about the landfill, about the medical examiner's office, about the site, and I felt it about this day, too.

I learned you can get emotional and you can stand there and get choked up, even if you are supposed to be detached as a journalist. Then when you get back to the newsroom and you have to write the story, how do you funnel that emotion in the best journalistic way, to tell the truest story that captures, as best as you can with words, the emotions of the day without a preponderance of adjectives, without a preponderance of adverbs, with real words to convey to someone else what it was like to stand there when this happened. If I didn't feel moved by what I saw, just even on the anniversary day, I don't think I belong in the business, because if I don't feel the emotion of that, then I can't possibly convey it to someone else. It was a very moving event. I thought the day would suffer from those structures applied to it—the Gettysburg Address and other things. But if you strip away that stuff and someone is standing up there reciting names—just reciting names and Yo-Yo Ma is playing in the background and he's having trouble because of the wind and then these people are going by—it's so raw, it's so in front of you. The trick is to go back and balance being dispassionate, yet putting emotion on the page.

When you think back over the time since Sept. 11, what insight would you share with other journalists as a result of your experiences?

I don't know if I have any great bits of wisdom, really. In the case of this deadline story, I guess it would be to anticipate, and to open yourself up to all that is going on around you in bearing witness. Put all your senses to work; be a sponge.

Personally, though, I like to revisit an event or an incident after all the other reporters have gone on to the next one, because I think that is where our opportunities —our responsibilities—are: to give context; to explain the repercussions of an event like Sept. 11 in people's lives; to slow it down. That's what Tom Heslin, a great editor of mine at *The Providence Journal*, used to say: Slow it down.

Writers' Workshop

Talking Points

1) Dan Barry talks about the effort he puts into leads and endings. In one instance, he wrote a story one way because the *Times*—like many newspapers—strives to get key information on Page One before the jump. Then the metro editor asked Barry a simple question that flipped the story and pushed the punch to the end. Think of standards, rules, or preferences you've experienced. How do they contribute to—or detract from—the work of the writer?

2) For a year, Barry covered the aftermath of the Sept. 11 attacks. He talks about going back to key places and people to keep telling the story. Think about ongoing stories you've covered. What could you learn from Barry's examples?

3) Read the first two paragraphs of Barry's story. Think about your reaction to the description of people going down into the pit and re-emerging among the living. What mood did those images evoke? Did that mood hold up through the entire story?

Assignment Desk

1) After Barry finishes a story, he reads it out loud. Take one of the stories you've written and read it aloud. What kinds of changes do you identify from this exercise?

2) Read the part of the interview in which Barry talks about starting the Sept. 11 anniversary day by riding a ferry in the early morning hours from New Jersey to Lower Manhattan. He talks about his impressions. What do you learn about preparation, context, and familiarity with settings? Take those lessons and apply them to an assignment, or experiment by arriving early just to observe, note details, and watch people interact. Note the insights you gained.

3) ASNE judges described Barry's writing as straightforward. The writer says he avoids overusing adjectives and adverbs. Scan his winning story and count the adjectives and adverbs. Scan one of your stories and count them. On the next story you write, check your use of adjectives and adverbs.

Star-Telegram

Deanna Boyd

Finalist, Deadline Reporting

Deanna Boyd is a senior crime reporter at the Fort Worth *Star-Telegram*. She was born in Chicago and graduated in 1994 from the University of Texas at Austin. While in college, she served an internship at the *Billings* (Mont.) *Gazette*.

She then served a yearlong internship with Capital Cities/ABC, spending four months each at the *Albany* (Ore.) *Democrat-Herald*, and the *Belleville* (Ill.) *News-Democrat* before joining the *Star-Telegram* in 1995, first as intern, then as a full-time reporter.

Her reporting work was recognized by the Texas Associated Press Managing Editors in 2003 (for the article reprinted here) and in 1996 (both awards for spot news, second place) and by the Association for Women in Journalism in 1999 for an inside look at a battered women's shelter.

Boyd, 30, is engaged to marry *Star-Telegram* reporter Anthony Spangler.

She appears in this book for telling the bizarre tale of an accident in which the victim died after apparently spending several days lodged in the windshield of the car that the driver parked in the garage. Boyd delivers powerful, purposeful quotes and a clear, compact narrative from what was a complex set of facts.

Bizarre details
of man's death revealed

MARCH 7, 2002

FORT WORTH—When Gregory Glenn Biggs' body was found in October in Cobb Park, evidence pointed to a hit-and-run.

But in the past two weeks, police have learned that Biggs lived for two or three days after he was hit, lying on a car hood in a southeast Fort Worth garage, his body trapped in the windshield.

Despite Biggs' pleas, police said, the driver refused to help and left him to die. Afterward, the body was dumped in the park.

"I'm going to have to come up with a new word. *Indifferent* isn't enough. *Cruel* isn't enough to say. *Heartless? Inhumane?* Maybe we've just redefined inhumanity here," said Richard Alpert, a Tarrant County assistant district attorney.

What happened to the 37-year-old Biggs, police said, was not a simple case of a driver's failure to stop to help an injured man. It was homicide, they said.

"If he had gotten medical attention, he probably would have survived," traffic investigation Sgt. John Fahrenthold said.

Wednesday, police arrested Chante Mallard, a 25-year-old nurse's aide, basing their case primarily on Mallard's confession about four months later of what happened on an October night as she drove near the East Loop 820 split with U.S. 287.

Mike Heiskell, Mallard's attorney, called the woman's arrest on a murder warrant premature.

"I think this is overreaching on the part of the prosecution and the police, and in the end, I believe the law will shake out that this was simply a case of failure to stop and render aid," Heiskell said.

By Mallard's account, as told to police, she had been drinking and using Ecstasy that October night and was driving home when she struck a man. The impact hurled him headfirst through the windshield, his broken legs protruding onto the hood.

She panicked, she said, and with the man lodged in the windshield, she drove a few miles to her home. There, she parked her 1997 Chevrolet Cavalier in the garage and lowered the door.

Biggs pleaded for help, she told police.

He got none. Not then, or for the next two or three days, as he remained lodged in the windshield, bleeding and slowly going into shock, police said.

Mallard told police she periodically went into the garage to check on the man. She said she apologized profusely to him for what she had done but ignored his cries for help.

When the man died, several of the woman's acquaintances helped remove his body, putting it into the trunk of another car and driving to Cobb Park, where they dumped it, police quoted the woman as saying. Two men found the body Oct. 27.

"This goes so far beyond failure to stop and render aid because she did more than not render aid," Alpert said. "She made it impossible for anyone else to do so."

Mallard first surfaced in the investigation last month when police received a tip that she might have been involved in a hit-and-run accident, Fahrenthold said.

Mallard had recently told a friend "bits and pieces" about an accident when questioned at a party about why she was no longer driving her car, Fahrenthold said.

"Within the next day or so this girl came forward and told what had happened because she couldn't live with that," he said.

On Feb. 26, police obtained a search warrant for Mallard's house in the 3800 block of Wilbarger Street. Inside her garage, they found the damaged Cavalier. Blood, hair and other trace evidence was visible inside and outside the car, he said.

The car's seats had been removed and were found in the back yard, one of them burned, Fahrenthold said.

Mallard agreed to go to the police station for questioning. There, she gave a statement and was arrested for failure to stop and render aid.

She was free on bail when officers arrived at her home Wednesday morning and arrested her on the upgraded warrant charging her with murder. Later in the day, she was released on a $10,000 writ bond.

The Tarrant County Medical Examiner's Office has told police that Biggs suffered no internal injuries and apparently died from loss of blood and shock, Fahrenthold said.

The investigation is continuing and other arrests are expected, he said.

"We think there are other people involved, at least after he had passed, in taking the body and putting it in the park," he said.

Biggs' mother, Meredith Biggs, said she and her son had been estranged for several years. Medical examiner's records listed Gregory Biggs' address as 1415 E. Lancaster Ave., a homeless shelter.

Meredith Biggs said she and her daughter, Janeen, had recently begun looking for him. They were frightened when a search on an ancestry Web site a couple of months ago indicated that he had died. They prayed it was a hoax.

Wednesday, she learned it was not, and was told the details about her son's death.

"How could she just leave him like that to die?" she sobbed. "Drugs and alcohol wear off, so why didn't she get him some help?

"I should have prayed more."

Lessons Learned

BY DEANNA BOYD

The e-mails flooded in from all over the world.

"This is unbelievable. You are yanking our chain here with a new urban legend, aren't you?"

"This sounds like a Stephen King novel."

"As a retired 30-year veteran police officer, I thought I'd heard it all. A definite death penalty candidate. I'll pull the switch!!"

"I'm a local criminal defense attorney. Before that I was a cop for 15 years…and not much gets me excited. Your story today takes the cake on hideous human (or should I say inhuman) behavior. When I got to court this morning, in the lounge all the lawyers were talking about the article and clamoring to read the only copy in the room."

The skepticism and shock came as no surprise. A day earlier, when I had heard about the ghastly allegations against a Fort Worth woman, I thought the traffic sergeant was pulling my leg. I made him swear, numerous times, that he was telling the truth, then congratulated him for shocking a reporter who thought that she had seen and heard it all.

Here are the lessons I took to heart:

■ **Be mindful of the clock.** It was already midafternoon when I learned about Chante Mallard's arrest, so I focused on the urgent phone calls first. Lawyers usually leave work at 5 p.m.; family members typically don't arrive home until the evening. Don't waste time tracking down family until you've got all the details you need from police, prosecutors, and defense lawyers.

■ **Don't assume homeless means lifeless.** Although they create a bigger challenge, homeless victims have histories that deserve to be uncovered and shared. Start with the obvious. For example, try the directors of local homeless shelters, whose numbers are a staple in the Rolodex of any reporter who has written a cold weather story.

■ **Master the Internet.** When the shelter director

couldn't give me information on Biggs, I turned to the Internet. Too many reporters never bother to learn how to use people-tracking programs, such as Autotrack. Using only Biggs's name and date of birth, I tracked a long list of possible relatives, then made about a dozen calls before I finally reached his mother.

■ **Tread carefully.** My relief at reaching Meredith Biggs was short-lived. Her cheerful phone greeting and confused response when I identified myself as a reporter made it quickly evident that she had no idea what had happened to her son. Gregory Biggs had been estranged from his family for several years. After his body was found in a Fort Worth park in October, authorities tracked down his teenage son, but no one had reached Meredith Biggs or her daughter, Janeen. The pair had long been searching for Biggs. An ancestry website had indicated that he had died, but they had hoped it was a mistake. My phone call confirmed that it was true.

■ **Don't keep a victim's family members in the dark.** Meredith Biggs, of course, had no idea how her son had died. I had no choice but to share the horrific details. Hearing such news from a reporter would surely be a softer blow than reading about it the next morning. After I was sure her daughter was by her side to offer support, I took a deep breath and painfully told her the details that, hours later, would be on the paper's website and front page. I would like to say that I delivered the news with the compassion of a police chaplain. In reality, I stammered, stuttered, and struggled to find the most gentle words. I was far from the calm, professional journalist; but I was honest, and Meredith Biggs appeared to appreciate it. She thanked me profusely for giving her the answers, albeit painful, that she had been seeking over the past few years.

■ **Don't over-sensationalize the sensational.** The biggest struggle in writing the article was choosing the right words to describe the indescribable. Words such as "impaled" were quickly nixed by helpful copy editors, who reminded me that you could be impaled on a pole but not in a windshield. Think simple. A story such as this is astonishing on its own; it doesn't need to be drowned in overwriting.

Top: Joel Engelhardt, Elizabeth Clarke
Bottom: Christine Stapleton, Gary Kane

The Palm Beach Post
Team Deadline News Reporting

Religion reporter Elizabeth Clarke said she knew something wasn't right with the Catholic bishop in the Diocese of Palm Beach, Fla. Since he'd been installed three years earlier, Anthony O'Connell had been accessible and easy to interview. Suddenly he no longer answered his cell phone. He was "unavailable," the diocese spokesperson told her. On Friday, March 8, 2002, Clarke figured it out.

A story in the *South Florida Sun-Sentinel* detailed Bishop O'Connell's sexual encounter with a teenage seminary student 25 years earlier.

Post metro editor Carolyn DiPaolo read the story at home. "I knew what the day was going to be like," she said. The east coast of Florida is one of the most competitive newspaper markets in the country with *The Miami Herald*, the *Sun-Sentinel*, and the *Post* encroaching on one another's circulation. From home, DiPaolo began calling editors and planning coverage. She tapped staff writer Joel Engelhardt as the lead reporter. She got online to find the original version of the story, published that day in the *St. Louis Post-Dispatch*.

Deputy managing editor Bill Rose arrived in the newsroom that afternoon. "We knew we were behind and we could not abide that in our county," he said. "So we threw the whole newsroom at that story, and we were determined to cover every aspect of it."

Database editor Christine Stapleton spends most of her time on computer-assisted reporting projects. As a former court reporter and a Catholic, she was amazed that a second bishop would leave the Palm Beach Diocese because of a sex-abuse scandal. She was the first reporter of many across the country to interview Chris Dixon that morning.

Editors pulled reporters John Pacenti, Kevin Thompson, Eliot Kleinberg, Pat Moore, and Pilar Ulibarri into the day's work. Researchers Monica Martinez, Madeline Miller, and Sammy Alzofon also contributed to the effort.

DiPaolo also drafted investigative reporter Gary Kane. Using the Internet, Kane turned up details of a program O'Connell had started at his previous diocese that required each Catholic clergyman to swear he had never been accused or convicted of sexual misconduct. Suddenly there was another front-page story.

As the religion reporter, Clarke became the safety net. She worked the phones, gauged the reaction of the flock, and researched how the broader church hierarchy could have let a second sex offender become the leader of an already wounded diocese.

By the end of the day, the team produced a package of articles that tells an almost mythic story of a powerful and charismatic leader brought down by the revelation of events that had been suppressed for decades. The stories detail the conflicting emotions of the clergy and the congregants, torn between adoration and devastation. Finally, the package offers insight into the power structure that allowed the bishop to keep his secret for so long.

—Kelly McBride

[*Editor's Note: The Jesse Laventhol Prize for Team Deadline News Reporting is funded by a gift from David Laventhol, a former Times-Mirror executive, in honor of his father.*]

Bishop offers his resignation

MARCH 9, 2002

By Joel Engelhardt and Elizabeth Clarke

PALM BEACH GARDENS—In the same forthright style that endeared him to the priests and parishioners of the Palm Beach Diocese, Bishop Anthony J. O'Connell admitted Friday to two cases of sexual misconduct 25 years ago and announced his resignation.

"I want to apologize as sincerely and as abjectly as I possibly can. I am truly and deeply sorry for the pain and hurt and anger and confusion as it will result from all of this," O'Connell said at a news conference at the Cathedral of St. Ignatius Loyola.

An apologetic O'Connell verified that he tried to counsel a victimized teen in the late 1970s by going to bed with the boy, as reported Friday in the *St. Louis Post-Dispatch*. They were naked, but both the victim, Christopher Dixon, and O'Connell said they did not engage in any sexual activity beyond touching.

O'Connell, 63, said an additional victim from the late 1970s could come forward but never has.

His resignation came the day after he and Florida's nine other bishops pledged to report, investigate and root out sexual abuse from their churches.

A row of 27 priests stood vigil behind O'Connell as he explained his decision to resign and leave his fate to Rome. In a meeting earlier, the priests begged O'Connell to stay, said the Rev. Seamus Murtagh, the diocese's vicar general. O'Connell remains bishop until the Vatican responds, perhaps as early as next week.

Stunned parishioners expressed anger and disappointment Friday, both with O'Connell and the leadership that brought him here. Many were embarrassed for their church, one they feel faces such problems far too often. They lauded O'Connell's spiritual leadership until now and many, although not all, offered support for him to stay in his job.

O'Connell came to the five-county diocese in January

1999 to replace another disgraced bishop, the Most Rev. J. Keith Symons, who left after admitting to molesting five altar boys in the 1950s and 1960s. O'Connell's gregarious and straightforward style is credited with restoring the confidence of the diocese's 250,000 members.

Unlike Symons, who quietly left town only to turn up 11 months later at a Michigan convent, O'Connell stayed to address the members of his diocese, which stretches from Boca Raton to Vero Beach.

His 10-minute statement echoed the conflict that rages in a church that believes firmly in forgiveness but is ravaged by allegations of misconduct by its most holy and exalted members.

O'Connell said the people who selected him to succeed Symons didn't know about the allegations even though the church paid Dixon $125,000 to settle allegations against O'Connell and two other priests in 1996.

"When I asked why they wanted me to come here, the papal nuncio at the time said, 'You have the gifts that we're looking for,' and he named them off," O'Connell said. "I had to agree with him that I had those gifts. And I thought that this incident was settled to everybody's satisfaction.

"While…it would always color my approach to things, nevertheless, I didn't bring it up at the time. So nobody who made the appointment knew."

Two key players in O'Connell's selection—the Most Rev. John C. Favalora, archbishop of Miami, and the Rev. Robert N. Lynch of St. Petersburg—issued statements Friday grieving at the news but did not address whether they knew about O'Connell's misconduct.

For no one to know isn't surprising, said Jeff Anderson, a St. Paul, Minn., attorney who has made a career since 1984 of suing the church over sexual abuse by priests.

"The way the Catholic Church in America operates, it is to keep the secret," Anderson said. "They are effectively fugitives from the truth because they continue to deny that there is an enormous problem."

The bishop in the Jefferson City, Mo., Diocese, which paid the settlement, had no reason under church rules to tell the Palm Beach search committee about the charges, Anderson said.

Church law requires silence in instances of misconduct by priests, Anderson said. In a practice that dates back centuries, only bishops have access to records of misconduct, he said. And typically, they don't share them with other bishops, he said.

O'Connell said the secrecy surrounding his settlement convinced him to remain silent.

"My understanding was that he (Dixon) made the settlement with the diocese...he asked for confidentiality for his own reasons and I thought that brought all of that to a conclusion," O'Connell said.

Dixon, a former priest, said he came forward publicly in light of other charges against priests in Boston and the St. Louis area.

Only recently has the Vatican outlined a change in policy that encourages leaders to report sexual misconduct to church courts but does nothing to encourage the notification of lay courts.

The issue has raged in Boston, where 90 priests or former priests face accusations of molestation dating back 50 years, including one former priest accused of abusing nearly 200 children.

O'Connell submitted his resignation within the past two days to Archbishop Gabriel Montalvo in Washington, the apostolic nuncio or pope's ambassador to the United States. Montalvo, who could not be reached Friday, cannot accept the resignation, however. Only the pope can do that.

That's because Pope John Paul II appointed O'Connell as he appoints all bishops. But he doesn't make those decisions alone. Typically, a diocese seeking a new bishop begins by requesting recommendations from that diocese's lay leaders, priests and other employees.

Ultimately, the prospects are reviewed by the archbishop, the papal nuncio and the Vatican Congregation for Bishops in Rome. Three finalists are forwarded to the pope.

No matter what happens, O'Connell said he remains haunted by his past.

The bishop asked his diocese to pray for him and said his heart bleeds for Dixon. He described the relationship as an experimental therapy that looked better in the context of the 1970s than it does now.

Dixon, who is now 40, came to O'Connell as a ninth-grader trying to cope with previous molestation by a priest. O'Connell was the rector of the school, the St. Thomas Aquinas Seminary in Hannibal, Mo.

O'Connell started at St. Thomas upon his ordination in 1963 and said he left the school reluctantly in 1988, when he was called to be bishop of the diocese in Knoxville, Tenn.

Calling his approach stupid and naive, O'Connell, who was then in his 30s, said he let the tenor of the times dictate. He cited the sexual studies of Masters and Johnson and new approaches in Catholic theology at the time.

"I've always been one who thought you could change things. I think that's part of my strength. But I also preach that in our strength always lies also the potential for our greatest weakness, the shadow side. I was as wrong as I could be in taking that kind of approach with him and I am so sorry," O'Connell said.

The relationship involved only fondling, both O'Connell and Dixon said.

"There was nothing in the relationship that was anything other than touches....There was nothing beyond that," O'Connell said.

However, Dixon, who left the church in 1996, said O'Connell's approach went beyond therapy. Once O'-Connell came to Dixon's home and undressed him, Dixon said Friday.

O'Connell's remarks show he's beyond denial but indicate he is minimizing the effects of his behavior, a classic response, said David Clohessy, national director of the support group Survivors Network for those Abused by Priests.

Clohessy, who said he once was abused by a priest, knew O'Connell in the 1960s when O'Connell was at St. Thomas.

"He fits a certain profile of abuser in that he's very warm and charismatic and outgoing and gregarious," Clohessy said. "To rob a bank you need a weapon, and to molest a child you need charm and charisma and all those other traits, which he has in abundance."

Such traits are often overlooked in a world gripped by misguided stereotypes, Clohessy said.

"Even in this day and age when we ought to know

better, we still cling to that dangerous illusion that the molester is the obvious social misfit," he said.

Staff writers John Pacenti and Christine Stapleton and staff researchers Monica Martinez, Madeline Miller, and Sammy Alzofon contributed to this story.

Memories won't leave him alone

MARCH 9, 2002

By Christine Stapleton

It started in the fifth grade.

Chris Dixon remembers it "like it was yesterday." His Catholic church in Hannibal, Mo., had just introduced "face-to-face" reconciliation—confessing your sins in the open to a priest instead of in the secrecy of a dark confessional. Dixon, an altar boy who also played the organ for school Masses, wanted to check it out.

"I came up with whatever sins a fifth-grader has and he asked me, 'Do you kiss your father?'" Dixon recalled. When Dixon explained that he not only kissed his father but also his mother "10 times before going to bed every night," the priest, the Rev. John Fischer, asked him if he wanted to kiss Jesus. Then, Fischer pulled Dixon toward him and kissed him on the lips, Dixon said.

"I knew it wasn't right, but I trusted him because he was a priest," Dixon said. "This is the classic example of a wolf in sheep's clothing."

That began eight years of sexual abuse in the 1970s by three priests in Missouri, including Anthony J. O'Connell, now bishop of the Diocese of Palm Beach, Dixon said.

Dixon met O'Connell when he entered high school at the St. Thomas Aquinas Seminary, also in Hannibal. O'Connell was the rector of the school. Dixon wanted to tell someone about what the priest had done to him in elementary school.

"I was a relatively naive and honest boy," Dixon said. "I told him what had happened to me under the guise of wanting to come to terms with adolescence, going through puberty, being a teenager, and he said he wanted to help me."

"We talked and talked, and he thought helping me come to terms with my body was to lie in bed naked with him," Dixon said. "He pressed his body against mine and hugged me." That happened three or four times over four years. O'Connell also went to Dixon's home one summer day when Dixon's parents were at work. "He had me take down my pants," he said. All of the incidents involved fondling, not penetration, Dixon said.

Dixon said the abuse began when he was in the ninth grade and continued through the 12th grade, according to The Associated Press.

For nearly 20 years after the abuse, Dixon, now 40, hid what had happened to him. During those years, he finished the seminary and became a Catholic priest. The church first assigned him to the Cathedral of St. Joseph in Jefferson City, Mo., where he served as an associate pastor and teacher. Then, in 1993, he was reassigned to St. Thomas Aquinas Seminary in Hannibal—the same school where he says O'Connell had abused him. By then O'Connell had been transferred to Knoxville. But the new rector, the Rev. Manus Daly, also had abused Dixon when he was a student there, Dixon said.

"As a result of the stress, I became depressed," Dixon said. "I woke up one morning and said I'm either going to kill myself or get help."

Church officials recommended he get treatment in St. Louis, Dixon said. O'Connell learned of Dixon's troubles and wrote him a letter.

"There's an extra weight in my heart because of your suffering," O'Connell wrote in the Nov. 19, 1995, letter. "I keenly remember how tough relationships were for you. If I could relive those days again, I would surely have recommended better help for you than I was able to give. To the extent, Chris, that through my own misguided help or failure to respond in a way that would be more helpful to you, I am profoundly sorry and abjectly apologize."

O'Connell went on to praise Dixon as a priest, and said he had always "loved him like a brother" and would keep Dixon in his prayers.

"Again, for anything I've contributed to your present cross, whether by omission or commission, I beg your forgiveness," O'Connell wrote, then signed the letter, "with prayer and warmest wishes, love, Tony."

The letter infuriated Dixon.

"I thought, you know, this is just another masterful way of him to love up to me so I can't see what went on," Dixon said. "I was fooled for many years. I knew in my gut it wasn't right, but he was a man so loved and respected by so many, including my family. Here I am, a little boy. Who's going to believe me? They're going to think I'm making it up."

Dixon wrote back.

"I said to him, 'Do you remember when,' and then I outlined every 'when,'" Dixon said. "I wanted him to admit what he did, get help, and I wanted restitution. I got a response that was cold as ice, at least compared to the earlier letter."

At that point, Dixon decided to leave the priesthood and hire a lawyer. In 1996, with the threat of a lawsuit looming, the Jefferson City diocese settled out of court for $125,000, Dixon said. The diocese did not admit any wrongdoing, and Dixon promised not to pursue further claims against the diocese, O'Connell and two other priests, The Associated Press said.

He got a job working as the operations manager of a housing agency run by Catholic Charities in St. Louis.

Dixon, who today speaks openly about the abuse, remained quiet about the settlement and what happened to him until this week. The recent sex scandal in the Boston diocese and the church's reaction to it, coupled with the removal of Daly from a Marceline, Mo., church this week, prompted him to speak out. Fischer was removed from the priesthood in 1993 after allegations involving other children.

"Wow," Dixon replied when learning Friday afternoon that O'Connell had submitted his resignation. As for O'Connell's explanation that "it was the '70s" and sexual therapy, such as "Masters and Johnson," were popular, Dixon said: "That's so sick. He used to say that, that these were the premier sex studies of the time."

Although Dixon wasn't aware of any other victims, he wasn't surprised to learn that O'Connell admitted "there may be one more."

"It makes me feel better, to know I'm not the only one, to know I'm not alone, but I can't really feel good about it," Dixon said. "I've exposed him for who he really is. I wished I had done it sooner."

What still makes Dixon angry is his belief that church officials knew of O'Connell's history when they appointed him bishop of the Diocese of Palm Beach in 1998. He was bishop of Knoxville before that.

"That's what makes it smell and taste like such a conspiracy," Dixon said. "I'm not accusing everybody, it's just a conspiracy of secrecy."

Dixon hasn't lost his faith in God. But he has no faith in "institutionalized religion."

"They are the epitome of hypocrites," Dixon said.

Staff researcher Sammy Alzofon contributed to this story.

Bishop says past 'always hung over me'

MARCH 9, 2002

By Gary Kane

WEST PALM BEACH—Moving to Palm Beach County three years ago spared Bishop Anthony J. O'Connell the question he hasn't had to publicly answer until today.

Had he remained in Knoxville, Tenn., the bishop would have been expected to sign an affidavit declaring that he had never been accused or convicted of any sexual misconduct.

"The policy was promulgated by the bishop and then he left," Knoxville Diocesan Chancellor Rev. Vann Johnston recalled Friday. "The bishop did not sign those papers."

One month after establishing the Knoxville Diocese Policy and Procedure Relating to Sexual Misconduct, O'Connell received a call to comfort and lead the Diocese of Palm Beach, which was reeling from a sex scandal involving its own bishop. The Most Rev. Keith Symons had resigned in disgrace after admitting inappropriate sexual contact with young boys early in his 40-year ministry.

The church turned to O'Connell to ease the hurt and confusion caused by the Symons affair. The bishop pledged to devote all his energies to healing his new diocese. And though he felt most were ready to move past the scandal, he said he would be careful "not to brush it under the rug."

Even in his role as healer, O'Connell wrestled with his past.

"It always hung over me," he said during a news conference Friday. "I don't think I've ever preached without being conscious of it and especially in these recent times."

Earlier in the week, O'Connell offered his resignation. He knew the *St. Louis Post-Dispatch* would disclose his long-held secret. A former priest had told the newspaper that O'Connell and two other priests had sexually abused him as a student more than 25 years ago. The paper published the story Friday.

The 63-year-old bishop discussed the revelations with several diocese priests, who stood behind him at the news conference. Many of the same clergy marched in the procession that opened O'Connell's installation as the diocese's third bishop on Jan. 14, 1999. O'Connell celebrated a Mass of thanksgiving that day and became spiritual leader of 250,000 Roman Catholics in five counties.

Taking a cue from Pope John Paul II, O'Connell traveled extensively to establish himself as a presence in both the church and secular community. He logged 30,000 miles in his first year in the diocese.

His high-energy style became his hallmark. For example, in November 1999, O'Connell traveled to Gambia, Sierra Leone and Senegal as a board member of the Catholic Relief Services, rushed to Washington to attend the U.S. Conference of Catholic Bishops and capped the month by celebrating Mass at St. Jude Church in Boca Raton, where the reliquary of St. Therese of Lisieux concluded a 117-city tour of the United States.

The bishop also has been very active in recruiting young men for the priesthood, sometimes hosting dinners for dozens. He said Friday he took "severe exception" to the insinuation by the St. Louis newspaper that there was an ulterior motive for the dinners.

O'Connell said he accepted his appointment to the Diocese of Palm Beach as an act of obedience, not choice, just as he had done in 1988 when he became the first bishop of the new Diocese of Knoxville. He received the papal appointment to Tennessee while teaching physics and chemistry at St. Thomas Aquinas Seminary in Hannibal, Mo.

The seminary was O'Connell's first assignment after his ordination in 1963. In his 25 years at the boys' high school, he served as dean of students, spiritual director, principal and rector.

It was there he encountered Christopher Dixon, a young student who went on to become a priest in 1995. Dixon says O'Connell, who was the school's rector at the time, invited him into bed under the guise of counseling. He maintains that the abuse continued throughout his four years at the seminary.

O'Connell moved to Knoxville believing he had left

behind his "stupid and foolish" mistake.

"My understanding was that he made the settlement with the diocese, he signed off, he asked for confidentiality for his own reasons and I thought that brought all of that to a conclusion," he said Friday.

The Jefferson City Diocese in Missouri did reach a $125,000 settlement with Dixon in 1996, in which he agreed not to pursue further claims against the diocese, O'Connell and two other priests. The diocese did not admit to Dixon's allegations in the settlement.

Meanwhile, no one in Knoxville knew of the settlement or the allegations.

"I've just heard about this today," said Johnston, the diocese's chancellor. "It will be received with great sadness and total surprise."

The faithful in rural east Tennessee remember O'Connell as an incredibly caring leader, who donned a Santa Claus suit for the poor children from the mountains and marched arm in arm with black clergy in the annual Martin Luther King Jr. Day parade. Though the diocese is in the heart of the Protestant Bible Belt, it grew more than 50 percent during his stay.

"He was beloved. Everyone just thought that he walked on water," said an employee of the Cathedral of the Sacred Heart of Jesus in Knoxville.

O'Connell was born in Lisheen, County Clare, on the west coast of Ireland. He left home when he was 12 to attend boarding school with the Presentation Brothers, a religious order of laymen in Cork. He later attended a Jesuit college and was convinced he would not teach but be a priest.

He began applying to bishops for acceptance as a candidate for priesthood. He was turned down 36 times, he said.

He went to Birmingham, England, when he was age 20 to teach in a Catholic high school. Within four months, a letter came from a friend telling him that a new diocese was starting in Missouri and the bishop was so desperate he would take anyone. He left for Jefferson City, Mo., in 1959 and was accepted into a seminary in St. Louis.

On Friday, O'Connell spoke as though he was again leaving a place where he found love, respect and trust.

"I'm truly and deeply sorry."

Recalling deadline with
The Palm Beach Post

KELLY McBRIDE: How did you get involved in this story?

JOEL ENGELHARDT: The *St. Louis Post-Dispatch* had published an interview on Friday with Chris Dixon saying that 25 years earlier he had been abused by Bishop O'Connell, who was now our bishop. And they had a really telling quote in their story. Bishop O'Connell said, "I would say I was extremely ill advised and naïve in that approach. I thoroughly regretted it, and I apologized to him when he made his complaint."

I come in at 10 in the morning, and we have this quote, and we have news that our bishop is going to have a news conference. So we assumed that he was either going to admit to the problem and fight the charges, or he was going to resign. We were behind. At that time I was doing a lot of work on more in-depth general assignment stories. So the editors asked me to cover the news conference, which was at 3 that day.

The previous bishop in Palm Beach also resigned amid a sexual scandal. Did you work on that story?

No.

So you were pretty much new to this whole issue of sex scandal in the Catholic Church?

The reporter at the time was a guy named Dan Moffett. He had covered the heck out of the events in 1999, and he has moved to our editorial board. So one of the first things I did was contact him, and he gave me a list of the sources he still had from the '99 coverage. And that was really helpful. I got hold of two really good national people: Jeff Anderson, the attorney who sues dioceses all over the country, and David Clohessy, the national director of SNAP, the victims' group. And they were really helpful in giving me some contacts.

What else did you do prior to the news conference?

I started reading heavily about O'Connell, when he came, and about how the previous bishop had left. I also acquainted myself with a couple of stories from Boston that Anderson told me about.

After the news conference, what was on your list of things to do? How did you organize the rest of your day?

I remember driving back with Elizabeth Clarke, the religion reporter, so we had time to talk about the story. She was driving, so I was able to take notes on my way back. I started writing the story right away.

I remember having to waste a lot of time typing the transcript when we got back to the newsroom. I had gotten a tape recorder for Christmas the year before and I brought it with us, and we recorded the bishop's 10-minute statement. So we were able to get a verbatim transcript in the paper the next day.

You had to do the typing?

Well, I started to. And then as the night went on and I didn't get it all done, I asked a fellow reporter, John Pacenti, to help and he was very willing to help me out.

Other than that, how did you organize the rest of your day?

So we got back probably at 3:30, and I had to combine writing with finishing the interviews of the people I needed to reach. I talked to Anderson in St. Paul and Clohessy in St. Louis, who had actually known our bishop. And I had a list of four or five other national people to call whom I never got hold of. So I would type the transcript and then stop to do the phone calls, and then go back to writing. I just kept piecing it together as the day went on.

How did you coordinate the writing with Elizabeth?

Well, her office is on the other side of the building, and she was being dumped on with a whole bunch of sidebar type things. I think they wanted her to call Rome. They're kind of hard to get hold of, you know? But she had to piece together the way succession is determined; and she was supposed to talk to people in Washington, and, of course, she was striking out there. And I think she also had to do another side on the diocese's response, the laypeople, and the clergy's response, so she had that kind of major far-reaching sidebar to do. Plus, she had to feed me. So we worked together. I think I did most of the writing and then she fed me, because the stuff on the succession was dropped as a sidebar and was inserted into my story. And then I remember late in the night she finally moved over from her end of the building to mine so we were sitting next to each other so we could talk while we wrote.

At what point did you realize the magnitude of this story?

Probably when I opened the papers the next day and *The New York Times* had covered the same event I did. That's unusual.

Tell me how you decided on your lead. "In the same forthright style that endeared him to the priests and parishioners of the Palm Beach Diocese, Bishop Anthony J. O'Connell admitted Friday to two cases of sexual misconduct 25 years ago and announced his resignation."

On the way back from the news conference, we talked about his forthright style and gregarious nature, and that had to be part of the lead. The other thing was to put two cases in there because everybody was focused on Chris Dixon, but it was in answer to a question from the press that he said, "There may be another one out there ready to complain." So he admitted to a second one. We had to make a decision to go with two in the lead and explain it later on. And then I thought it was important to go right to the quote and get his voice out there because we were saying he was forthright, and we wanted to show it.

When you read the story, it does not seem like a news conference story. How did you avoid the appearance of simply reporting on a news conference?

We had a lot of facts. We were taking O'Connell from the news conference and Dixon from our interview. I guess I just looked at the news conference as my notes, as if I'd interviewed him. Plus, I was arguing that we should be running the transcript anyway for the faithful here who wanted to hear what he said.

What was the editing like?

One thing that I'm pretty sure deputy managing editor Bill Rose did is the paragraph that says, "Stunned parishioners expressed anger and disappointment Friday, both with O'Connell and the leadership that brought him here." Now that was from Elizabeth's reporting in the sidebar. "Many were embarrassed for their church, one they feel faces such problems far too often. They lauded O'Connell's spiritual leadership until now and many, although not all, offered support for him to stay in his job." That was a summary of a whole lot of stuff going on that I think came in the editing process.

Were there many changes during the editing?

In looking back on this, I don't think there were a lot. I think Bill added his nuances. I can't remember exactly what. But I do remember that paragraph. That is textbook Bill Rose. But, you know, it's awfully hard because you do a lot of daily stories and this one wouldn't have jumped out at me at all as anything unusual or different from what we normally do. I think it was the combination of all the stories together that made it great.

What tips do you have for reporters who need to get up to speed quickly on a deadline story that has both local and national angles?

Read heavily. I wouldn't waste too much time on the national clips because this was really a local story for us. This was our bishop, and getting to know our bishop a little bit was more important than finding out what was going on in Boston. Bishop O'Connell was a different kind of guy. He was very gregarious and warm with everyone. He had been brought in here to heal. So we wanted to have this story reflect the very different way he handled this compared to the previous bishop, who had left without a word. This man stood in front of all the television cameras and faced the press and even answered questions for a few minutes and admitted to everything. And then he walked off with respect.

Did you have any particular strategy for writing on deadline?

I think sometimes you try to do all the reporting and then start writing, and then that only gives you an hour, and you get crunched. I felt like I had enough ground covered, because I had all these other reporters running around doing all the hard work, that I could start writing early, and I think that was part of the strategy. So, at 3:30 or 4 when I came back, I had already started writing. And so I was able to go back and forth to it. The strategy, I guess, was to start early and rewrite often.

Any other tips on deadline reporting and writing that you can pass along?

I always emphasize rewriting. Even if you only have an hour, you've got to get done after 45 minutes so you have time to rewrite what you've been doing. It also helped to type up as much of his news conference as I could, getting my notes out in front of me.

Why?

Because that gives you a menu or a plate full of things you may want to use. It puts it in front of you in typewritten form so you can see how it looks on the page, and you get an idea of what looks like a good quote and what looks like something you really want to run. It just splashes it in front of you, so you can move quickly from one point to the next.

Elizabeth Clarke, religion reporter

I remember walking into the room where they had the news conference and I saw the diocesan spokesman, whom I talked to two, three times a week. We're friendly and I had never felt any sort of antagonistic relationship with him before. He came over and gave me a hug, and I remember feeling very strange about that. He was hugging all the other priests. And the fact that he felt comfortable enough with me to give me a hug was a good sign because it demonstrated that he trusted me. At the same time I felt very strange. I remember thinking, "I hope he knows that I'm a professional and my job is to tell the story and that's not going to change." So all that day I kept wondering, "Have I done something wrong this past year being friendly and cordial and professional?" In the end, he had no expectations that anything was going to change. He was very professional. But there was definitely a change in our relationship that day.

When you cover a beat like religion for the features section, it's very different from a regular newsroom beat. I do so many stories about the holidays. I'm not out there investigating every call I get about some minister doing something wrong. Somebody looks into that, but it's usually not me. I write a lot of positive stories just by the nature of the beast. Because it's so rare that I have to do this, it's that much harder.

When I first heard about this story, I thought, "Oh, my God, how am I going to do this all by myself?" There's also a tiny little part of me that thought, "Darn, I just want to do the whole damn thing myself." On that kind of day you can't do it all yourself. I felt like I spent a good bit of time talking. I tried to make sure that everyone knew that they could ask me questions about how the church works on this. I just wanted to make sure that I was open to answering questions, not that I'm much of an expert because I've only been doing it a year.

The number of people we had working on the story was definitely key. And I think it was good to devote people who don't normally cover this kind of stuff because they came into it with a fresh perspective.

Deadline Tip:

When faced with a negative story, talk to as many sources on your beat as soon as you can. I was really glad I put out a lot of calls to the people I knew. I don't think I actually got any of them on the phone before the news conference, but several of them called me afterward or I saw them at the news conference. I think some of them even told me afterward that they couldn't get back to me, but they were so glad that I'd called. That has been important in the year since this has happened. I was worried that I'd never be able to write about the Catholic Church again.

Carolyn DiPaolo, metro editor

When I found out about the St. Louis story, I immediately called our day editor, Holly Baltz, who contacted Joel Engelhardt and told him that he was going to be anchoring the story. I live close to the office, so I was probably in the office in about 10 minutes. Before I came in, I had gone to the *Post-Dispatch* website and pulled its story. It was still pretty early when I came in, and there weren't that many people in the newsroom.

But I knew that we needed to get to Chris Dixon as soon as possible. Christine Stapleton, who is our database editor, is a veteran reporter. She covered courts in Palm Beach County during the William Kennedy Smith trial. And she was just outraged because she happens to be Catholic and she also had endured the sad departure of another disgraced bishop. So she was sitting there saying that she couldn't believe that it had happened again.

At that moment the library director, Sammy Alzofon, had found the number for Chris Dixon in St. Louis. So I just looked at Christine and said, "Do you want to call him?" I don't even think she hesitated. In about 30 seconds she had him on the phone, and they had a very extended interview.

In the meantime, Elizabeth Clarke arrived, and I looked across the newsroom and saw Gary Kane. And we kind of reeled them all together. It was fascinating to watch because they operated almost as a self-directed team. They had a really good combination of experience. They all three decided that they wanted to be at the news conference, and off they went. In the meantime we just did the other typical things that you would do, which was to get people going on the react.

This sounds so corny, but there was no ego. There was no friction. I don't recall disagreements. I don't recall having to mediate anything. There wasn't an argument about what the lead was going to be. There wasn't an argument about who was going to be the top byline. It was just this great spirit of cooperating. And I don't know how an editor creates that.

I think one of the things that set this day apart was that we had the beginning and the middle and the end all wrapped up into one day. We were able to show how extraordinary that was.

Deadline Tip:

Get there early. Do whatever it takes to get there first, to get to people first. I know that Dixon's line was busy later or his phone was off the hook, so you cannot underestimate the importance of being the first one to talk to him.

Christine Stapleton, database editor

In my whole career, the interview with Chris Dixon was one of the easiest interviews I've ever done. I was brought up in a real Catholic family in the Midwest, and Chris came from a real Catholic family in the Midwest. And we're the same age, and we've had a lot of the same experiences. So I think it was easy for us to talk to each other. I've interviewed a lot of victims of sex crimes, and those can be really tough interviews. This was just a really easy interview.

Finding that common bond with the person you're interviewing is what makes the interview. It enables you to make contact with that person. I don't think I crossed any lines. There have been many times in my career when I've had very personal strong feelings about a situation. Because you have those feelings, you get a better interview.

This was a rare instance in which we were able to interview the victim first. In a lot of situations, the perpetrator tells his side of the story first, and then you try to track down the victim. But we had Chris's details, so when the bishop gave the news conference, it didn't really jibe with what Chris had said. So we called Chris back and said, "This is what the bishop said went down." Then we were able to get his reaction to the bishop's comments. That's what made it really more powerful, because the bishop was trying to say it was like a sex-ed class.

I believe there has to be something visual in the top of the story. Something that people can see in their minds, something that happened. I don't like to write about ideas in the lead. When Dixon described the transition from going to confession in a booth, where you slide a little door open and talk to a priest through a screen, and going to confession face to face, I knew that was powerful. For Chris, the sex started when those curtains came down, and we started having face-to-face confessions with the priest.

I wanted to leave people with the image of this little boy alone in a room with a priest confessing his sins. And I didn't want to just say "little boy," because I have a daughter the same age as he was when he was first molested. She's in the fifth grade. So I wanted to use "fifth grade." I wanted to leave the image of this little boy who's so inquisitive about his church. That image is central to the story because it shows the whole thing with the Catholic Church has been about the betrayal of these innocent children.

When you have a situation in which there are a lot of victims, sometimes you hear about it so much that you don't think about the individuals. So if you can plant an individual image in the reader's mind of one case—this is what it must have been like for this one person—you can get at something that's forgotten in the magnitude of the story.

Deadline Tip:

When interviewing victims, ask basic, open-ended questions. It's really easy to ask questions that have a yes or no answer. Make sure you're asking questions that require them to spit out an answer, because with victims, if you ask them questions that only require a yes or no answer, that is all they'll usually give you. They want to get out of the interview quickly. Your questions should begin in a very simple way: What happened? Who did it to you? How did it happen? Why did it happen?

Gary Kane, investigative reporter

I was deep into an investigative project when metro editor Carolyn DiPaolo asked me to write a quick profile of Bishop O'Connell. I was not happy, but I never say no to editors. I began with the online library, compiling a list of all the places the bishop had been.

God bless the Internet. The Diocese of Knoxville, O'Connell's previous post, had a website. And there was a story about a new policy requiring all priests to sign a document declaring they had never abused a child.

My jaw fell open a bit when I saw that. It was something we hadn't reported when he arrived. Keep in mind that he came here to replace a bishop who had to resign in disgrace, so in a way I was surprised we hadn't uncovered it previously. From there, my plan was to contact people who knew something about that, how it came into being, and what possible role the bishop might have had in formulating it, and to get their reaction to the bishop's resignation here in the context of that particular issue.

It was getting pretty late and I ran out of time in terms of contacting people. But I did manage to get at least one person from the diocese. That one person was close enough to give me some idea as to how that came about and why and recall the bishop's role in it.

Deadline writing is very much like driving a cab. You know the territory. You know shortcuts. You know the direct route. You know the scenic route. In deadline writing, you often choose to put the pedal to the floor and run the risk of either frightening the reader or exhilarating the reader. In this story, we kicked the reader right in the face with the fact that O'Connell could have been admitting this problem before he arrived and probably would have never been here to cause the pain and suffering that his flock had to endure.

Deadline Tip:

Organize your notes as you go. When I'm filling a note-book for a story that I'm going to be writing that same day, I try to highlight things I'm certain I'm going to be putting into my story. You can go to a news conference and take 15 pages of notes and possibly more, depending on your penmanship, and you can come back to the office with a tape recorder, too, and find that you don't have time to just sit around listening to the whole news conference again. So you'd better have some notations as to exactly what you know is critical to that story.

Bill Rose, deputy managing editor

I got here about 2 p.m. What typically happens, and what happened during that day, is editors work the room. Reporters would come back and the editors would be on them like a swarm of bees. Joel and Eliza-beth would come back into the room from the news conference, and Carolyn and other editors would imme-diately grab them, get them into Carolyn's office, and find out what had happened.

But that's just the beginning. As reporters report dur-ing the day, editors at this newspaper have a tendency to work the room. Carolyn would stroll back and ask, "How are you doing?" Maybe look over their head at the screen and pick up a clue from that. Maybe listen to a fragment of a phone conversation or a conversation be-tween reporters. All those things add to the body of knowledge that the editor has.

And if you're used to doing that, you can quickly de-termine whether things are headed in the right direction, whether some incredible new thing has been discovered that requires the use of another reporter, or whether to send a reporter in another direction. Working the room is real, real important. And at various times during that day, I can remember Carolyn doing it, I can remember John Bartosek, the managing editor, doing it. I can re-member me doing it.

I did some of the hands-on editing, but my editing was walking around and looking at what the reporters were doing and making suggestions. I have access to the stories even when they're working on them. I'd call them up on the computer on "read" and see where they were headed.

I would urge them to put this story in a broader context. I wanted people to know that this was not just a story of the Palm Beach bishop resigning; it was part of a much broader story that had to do with the national scandal in the Catholic Church and had to do with betrayal of an entire church. It was important to make that point, and I tried to make sure that in every story you got some sense that this was more than a local problem, because it was. It was a huge thing.

In Joel's story, the thing that amazed me was the fact that so many priests came and stood behind the bishop. And I wanted to make sure that that was way up high in the story because that showed that here was a man who had developed strong allegiances among his priests. And even in the moment of disgrace when he's resigning, some of them were there hoping that it wasn't as bad as it would later turn out to be.

I was a reporter for an awful lot of years. When you're on the road by yourself—and that's what I did, I traveled the South—you don't just run and do daily stories. You try to write what I call breaking perspective. We need to tell people not just that something happened. They can get that off the Internet. They can get it from television. They can get it from any number of sources. But what we can do is we can tell them why it happened. Or if we can't say specifically why, we can provide context and perspective and let the reader see what forces shaped the story. Things do not happen in a vacuum. Things happen for reasons. And stories are not just black and white. There are grays.

I think putting a story into a broader context and making sure that story is imbued with the very reasons for its existence are important. And they're too often ignored on deadline because people are in a hurry. That's why you have editors. The reporters already had the information. The editors needed to make them feel free to use the best parts of it.

Deadline Tip:

A lot of reporters on deadline freeze for some reason. What I tell people is, "Don't hold back." That's what editors are for—to restrain you. You know, don't do anything irresponsible. But don't hold back. When you've got something that has so much excitement, so much drama in it, milk it. Don't go over the top, but milk it.

Writers' Workshop

Talking Points

1) *The Palm Beach Post* made some key decisions early in the day that helped the newsroom catch up on the story. Editors assigned several staff members to the story and clearly divided the responsibilities. How can editors best divide responsibilities among reporters on a big story?

2) What techniques do the writers use to capture the telling images of Bishop Anthony O'Connell? How are those traits portrayed in the story?

3) The story about victim Chris Dixon begins with an image of him as a child that has very little to do with Bishop O'Connell. How effective is this image as a lead?

4) In the main story, readers are reminded that O'Connell is the second bishop in a row to resign after a past sexual indiscretion. Knowing that most readers would be thinking, "Not again!" does that timing work?

Assignment Desk

1) Using the Internet, Gary Kane found information about the bishop that took on greater significance in light of the scandal. Research a religious leader from your community on the Internet. Are there non-traditional places, such as church websites and seminary publications, where you might find important details?

2) Both Christine Stapleton and Elizabeth Clarke were raised Catholic. Is that a conflict of interest? Examine the last 10 stories you wrote or edited. Did you have a personal stake in any of them?

3) Joel Engelhardt spent much of his reporting time asking sources about Bishop O'Connell's personality and style. He factored those traits into the lead of his story. Print out a recent story about a well-known newsmaker in your community. How does that person's personality and character fit into the story? Now rewrite the lead, including some of those details. Does it make the story more or less readable?

The New York Times

Serge Schmemann

Finalist, Team Deadline Reporting

Serge Schmemann is the editorial page editor of the *International Herald Tribune*, a position to which he was assigned in the spring of 2003 by *The New York Times*, owner of the *Tribune*. Before then, he was a senior foreign correspondent and bureau chief in Moscow, Bonn, and Jerusalem. He also returned for a reporting stint on the metro desk before becoming deputy foreign affairs editor in 1999.

He is the author of *Echoes of a Native Land*, a book that traces two centuries of Russian history through one village. His writing about Germany's reunification won the 1991 Pulitzer Prize for international reporting.

Schmemann has covered some of the major events of recent history, most notably the last years of the Soviet Union and the rise of the new Russia. He covered the transition to majority rule in Zimbabwe, the nuclear catastrophe of Chernobyl, the fall of the Berlin Wall and the reunification of Germany, the assassination of Yitzhak Rabin, and the struggle for peace in Israel.

He was part of the *Times*'s team of foreign correspondents to chronicle the fateful push by Israeli military into West Bank cities as the Middle East rumbled toward anarchy. On April 10, the *Times* had veteran correspondent James Bennet, based at an Israeli stronghold, writing an overview of the day's events. Reporter Joel Brinkley wrote from Nablus, a city devastated by Israel's military.

In his story, Schmemann recounts what he calls a "spasm of destruction" by describing crushed homes and cars, an economic recovery obliterated by bombs, and a bleak future clouded further by an escalating and ever-spinning cycle of death, retaliation, and more death.

Attacks turn Palestinian plans into bent metal and piles of dust

APRIL 11, 2002

By Serge Schmemann

JERUSALEM, April 10—Thirteen days ago, Prime Minister Ariel Sharon sent Israeli forces into the West Bank to "uproot the infrastructure of terror." Since then, the uprooting inflicted by his tanks, bulldozers, helicopters and sappers has created a landscape of devastation from Bethlehem to Jenin.

The images are indelible: piles of concrete and twisted metal in the ancient casbah of Nablus, husks of savaged computers littering ministries in Ramallah, rows of storefronts sheared by passing tanks in Tulkarm, broken pipes gushing precious water, flattened cars in fields of shattered glass and garbage, electricity poles snapped like twigs, tilting walls where homes used to stand, gaping holes where rockets pierced office buildings.

Today, on the day after 13 Israeli soldiers were killed going house to house in the crowded refugee camp of Jenin, the D-9 bulldozer was sent in instead, erasing whole stretches of tightly packed concrete houses.

There is no way to assess the full extent of the latest damage to the cities and towns—Ramallah, Bethlehem, Tulkarm, Qalqilya, Nablus and Jenin—while they remain under a tight siege, with patrols and snipers firing in the streets.

But it is safe to say that the infrastructure of life itself and of any future Palestinian state—roads, schools, electricity pylons, water pipes, telephone lines—has been devastated.

Even in areas where there is no fighting, the streets are largely the realm of alley cats prowling overturned garbage bins, while residents huddle behind shutters and drawn curtains. Many residents have been without water, electricity or telephones for long stretches of time.

International aid and development organizations have managed to make only occasional forays into the besieged towns. Today, a convoy of cars and trucks with

United Nations flags carrying emergency supplies for refugee camps in Ramallah waited for an hour at Qalandria checkpoint, and were forced to turn back at the end.

The images and reports of damage and destruction have come largely from journalists who make risky forays into the towns, or from residents reporting what they see when curfews are briefly lifted so they can restock on supplies.

What they see is only the visible destruction. Untold damage has been done to the workings of the Palestinian Authority, which to Mr. Sharon has abided and even abetted terrorism. Officials of the World Bank said they had briefly visited the Ministry of Education, the Central Bureau of Statistics and some other offices of the Authority, and found computers stripped of their hard drives, files ransacked and taken away, safes blasted open.

Officials of the United Nations, the World Bank and donor countries met on Tuesday to plan their actions once the Israelis withdraw. Officials said all they could do was organize teams for each city, and wait.

Their task is enormous. The latest spasm of destruction has come on top of the ravages of 19 months of fighting that left countless families without income and 40,000 people hospitalized at one time or another.

Long before Mr. Sharon unleashed Israeli forces, he had regularly sent jets and helicopters to flatten police stations, jails, television facilities and buildings used by Mr. Arafat. He acted in response to suicide bombings by Palestinian terrorists that have come to haunt Israeli society.

Some, like the British-era police headquarters in Bethlehem, were bombed again and again. The Gaza airport was laced with deep trenches, the nascent seaport was destroyed, all part of what the Palestinians and donors took to be an assault on symbols of Palestinian sovereignty. "We started in 1994 with damage control after the occupation. In 1995 we moved to rehabilitation. In 1999 we were building new infrastructure, roads, apartments, a seaport, strategic projects," said Muhammad Shtayyeh, the director of the Palestinian Economic Council for Development and Reconstruction, PECDAR, talking of an era that now seemed ages past. "Then Sharon went to the mosque, God bless him, and we're back to damage control."

It is a matter of angry dispute between Israelis and Palestinians whether the visit by Mr. Sharon, then an opposition deputy, to the sacred site of Al Aksa Mosque in Jerusalem on Sept. 28, 2000, was the reason for the violence that erupted that day and has continued since.

Israelis contend that Mr. Arafat found it in his interest to fan the flames and has since supported the work of suicide bombers.

What is impossible to dispute is the calamitous setback to what had been a steady development of the Palestinian homelands. In 1999, the best year for the Palestinians, there were 20 million square meters of construction under way, $8 billion in private investment, 143,000 Palestinians working in Israel, each bringing home $30 a day, a 6 percent rate of growth.

The Palestinian budget actually had a surplus. The airport in Gaza was functioning, the private sector had created 3,500 new jobs, industrial zones were luring large new companies.

"The Palestinian administration was highly functional, and delivered good services," said Nigel Roberts, the World Bank representative for the West Bank and Gaza. "One of the good stories of the past 19 months was that they managed to maintain a functioning civil administration that delivered basic services, health, education, despite all the problems of delivering these services. Schools were running, municipalities were working, there was a government out there that was functioning."

All that has been crushed. Now, according to a World Bank report before the Israeli operations of the past 13 days, real incomes are below what they were in the late 1980s, the proportion of the poor—those subsiding on less than $2 a day—has doubled to almost half the population of the West Bank and Gaza.

Without support from international donors, especially the Arab League and the European Union, "all semblance of a modern economy would have disappeared by now," the report said.

Behind the statistics are the endless stories of lost income, lost investment and lost hope.

Before the current Israeli offensive began, Yasir Safadi, 31, stood in Gaza surveying a distant, muddy field that used to be his $3 million concrete works. The plant was near a road used by Jewish settlers living in Nissanit, and in January 2001 Israeli bulldozers flattened the entire factory to clear a buffer zone around the road. The same was done throughout the Gaza Strip, one of the most crowded patches of real estate on earth.

Mr. Safadi said the tanks took five days to destroy his plant. Fifty-five employees were laid off, depriving 385 Gazans of a source of income. Mr. Safadi himself was left with more than $1 million in debt. "Even if they leave," he asked, "how can I afford to rebuild? And if I do, how can I be sure they'll not destroy it again?"

In Jericho, a casino that had employed 2,000 Palestinians is closed. In Bethlehem, a grand Intercontinental Hotel that had employed 1,115 is being used by Israeli troops.

A few weeks ago, Sam Bahour, general manager of the Arab Palestinian Shopping Centers in Ramallah, handed over the glossy brochure for the grand shopping mall he was developing in neighboring Al Bireh. A native of Youngstown, Ohio, with an M.B.A. from Tel Aviv University, he had come to Ramallah in 1995, along with many other expatriate Palestinian businessmen who saw a golden future in the land of their ancestors. "We were fooled by Oslo," he said, referring to the treaty signed in 1993 that was to lead to an independent Palestinian state.

The $10 million mall was still under construction, but Mr. Bahour was not sure how long it would be before the building stopped, leaving the grand skeleton standing among other abandoned projects in Al Bireh.

Today, Mr. Shtayyeh of the Palestinian economic council insisted that "Palestine will be viable." But the Israeli bulldozers in Jenin and the Israeli dead from another suicide bombing suggested further destruction was more likely.

Lessons Learned

BY SERGE SCHMEMANN

This story began as an assignment to try to quantify the extent of damage to the West Bank a few days after Israel launched massive military actions against Palestinian towns and refugee camps. As with most conflicts, there was a massive amount of anecdotal material flowing in from reporters, witnesses, and officials. My assignment was to step back and try to give a broader sense of what was being destroyed, and with what potential consequences.

I spent a lot of time with United Nations and Palestinian officials trying to compile meaningful data, and also visited many of the devastated sites. But when I sat down to write, my mind was filled not with data, but with all the things I had seen or heard about. There had been a systematic assault on an entire system, which no catalog of losses or costs, and no amount of fancy writing, could convey.

One of the best editors I've worked for was the late Harris Jackson of the Associated Press. If your facts got all jumbled, or your prose too convoluted, he'd delete the story with a dramatic flick of the finger (there was always a copy in the system, of course) and bark at you to "call your mother and tell her what you're trying to say." The notion was that in a conversation with someone that close, you—the witness, the reporter—would cut to the heart of the matter and spell it out in the most direct and effective words. Many reporters who went through Harris's rough school still whisper to an imaginary parent when they're working on their lead.

In many years as a foreign correspondent, I've tried to build on that lesson, especially when describing conflict, violence, or other forms of chaos. When the story is stark and dramatic, the key is to put as little between it and the reader as possible. There's no need for drum rolls, flowery prose, or elaborate explanations. What strikes you, the reporter, should be allowed to strike the reader in the same way. So when you're out there in the field, my advice is to clear your mind and let the images direct your reactions and your reporting. Don't waste time trying to take elaborate notes; jot down the time, the names, and a few words to jog the memory when you're back at your keyboard.

I am not suggesting that reporting on conflicts should be purely anecdotal or subjective. Not at all. Nor am I suggesting that you *ever* call your mother from a battle-field. But I believe that if you walk into a chaotic scene and start counting, measuring, or writing, you will be distracted from what is really there. Things move quickly in times of upheaval, and you are likely to be scared, exhausted, and emotional. There's a temptation to hide behind a pen, to shut off the images by directing your mind to the comforting familiarity of writing. But there's not much you can write down at a time like this that will make sense later. What strikes you most powerfully at the scene is also what will strike your reader most powerfully, and your story will lack immediacy and force unless you keep your mind, your eyes, and your emotions open to what's happening around you. And when you start writing, don't bury your images under mounds of adjectives or clauses. Pretend you're calling in from the scene.

For a story like the one about the devastation of the West Bank, there is a lot of reporting that needs to be done, of course. The facts and details are scattered among agencies, witnesses, and many different places. But the data is never the true overall picture. It serves as supporting evidence, as illustration. As I started to write, I could hear Harris Jackson saying, "Don't tell me how many buildings have been destroyed. Call your mother and tell her what they look like."

That's what I tried to do, to open the story with a staccato series of raw images, in the way television might do it, with a minimum of adjectives or heavy breathing. I tried to keep it raw, creating a collage of devastation, and then letting the story develop from that. I found that all the interviews and data found their own places in the story.

I believe there is a lesson here that is equally valid for all newswriting. When I sit down to write a story, I am prepared to spend half the total time allotted me to the introduction—to the lead paragraph and the next three or four. This is not necessarily to seduce the reader into reading on—though that's an important side benefit—but because I know that if I get the top right, the rest will fall into place almost of its own accord. Whether this story worked is for others to judge (I thought there were a few extraneous sentences wedged in at the top by editors), but I can't think of any other way I could've done it.

THE COMMERCIAL APPEAL

Stephen D. Price

Finalist, Team Deadline Reporting

Stephen D. Price is a suburban reporter for *The Commercial Appeal* in Memphis, Tenn. He is a Cleveland native and graduate of the University of Toledo, where he received a bachelor's degree in journalism.

Price, 35, began his career at the *News Journal* in Mansfield, Ohio. He was a reporter at the *Chicago Tribune* and *The Times* of Shreveport, La., before moving to Memphis.

He has won a Scripps Howard award for deadline writing and the Ohio Rehabilitation Services Commission Award for disability coverage as well as an NAACP Image Award for minority coverage.

Price is married to Africa Price, managing editor of *The Jackson* (Tenn.) *Sun*. They have a son, Joshua, 6.

When news of a fatal shooting in a house in northeast Memphis reached *The Commercial Appeal* newsroom, reporters Yolanda Jones, Amos Maki, Mickie Anderson, and Stephen Price were dispatched to cover the carnage. Reporter Kevin McKenzie was assigned to write a sidebar on previous shootings in which local children had been killed or wounded.

Although police cleared reporters away from the shooting scene, they overlooked Price. He was able to get into the house and talk to witnesses, including two who had rushed in to offer help. Price opens his story with the heart-wrenching scene of a dying 3-year-old girl. He uses the recollections of several witnesses to piece together the final moments of Jessica Borner's short life.

Couple forget risk, rush in to see 'about those babies'

JUNE 13, 2002

By Stephen D. Price

As her eyes were fluttering, life was slowly fading for 3-year-old Jessica Borner.

Cornelius Green held her in his arms, telling her how God loves her and made her a vow.

"I promised her all the Popsicles she wanted if she would just open her eyes," Green said. "She then looked up at me."

The scene was part of what Green and his wife, Demetric, saw after they bolted across the street to 3448 Rosamond. The couple were in their bedroom Wednesday afternoon, when they heard about a dozen shots booming from the gray brick house across the street.

As they ran to their front door, they saw Jessica's mother frantically yelling in the street that her baby had been shot.

What they later witnessed were the results of what Memphis police said was a drug deal gone bad. Six children and three adults were either shot or hit by debris caused by the shots at the Rosamond address in the Jackson-Macon area of northeast Memphis.

Jessica later died at Le Bonheur Children's Medical Center.

Moments after the shooting, the couple ran to the house across the street.

There was no time to think of the danger.

"My mind was only thinking about those babies," said Cornelius Green, 35.

Demetric Green, 28, saw a young man in his teens, with a white T-shirt and blue shorts, running from the scene saying, "I got them, I got them."

The macabre scene they then witnessed stunned them. Blood and bullets, and victims strewn on the floor.

Beatrice Hobbs, 59, Jessica's grandmother, was shot in the chest. She shooed the couple away from her saying, "Go see about the babies," Demetric Green said.

Cornelius Green went to Jessica, who was lying on her face in a puddle of blood in a hallway. He said she was shot in the stomach, right forearm and left shoulder.

He held the girl.

"I kept talking to the baby to keep her alive," he said.

"I saw her eyes dilating," he said. "I kept telling her, 'God loves you, God loves you.' I didn't know anything else to say. I just kept telling her to say something to me. She just moved her mouth but nothing came out."

Meanwhile, Demetric Green went back to their house across the street and brought back white towels to mop blood off the victims.

She was consoling a 4-year-old boy who was balled up in a fetal position in the hallway, bleeding. A bullet was poking out of his arm.

A 13-year-old girl was on the floor on her back in a bedroom. She asked for something cool and Cornelius Green poured water on her.

Green then went to help the 4-year-old. The boy kept asking, "Am I going to be OK?"

"I had tears in my eyes. I told him he would be OK," Green said.

The couple and neighbors said they knew the boys who lived in the house were up to no good. Something bad was bound to happen.

"I would tell Mama (Beatrice Hobbs), why do you have those boys over there?" Cornelius Green said. He would frequently see boys outside the house smoking dope.

Standing in the front of his house, with yellow police tape snaking around his driveway, Green was thankful his 4- and 5-year-old children weren't out playing on this balmy afternoon.

"As soon as I get my kids, I'm going to the hospital and check and see how these children are doing," he said.

Lessons Learned

BY STEPHEN D. PRICE

Deadline stories can be the most challenging to write; but if they are approached the right way, they can be as fulfilling as any other stories.

When you cover shootings, there are usually plenty of media, residents, and confusion. When I first got to Rosamond, I knew I would have to get behind those walls before I could get to the real story.

Here are some of the tactics I used and how they helped.

■ **Get as close to the scene as possible.** By the time I got to Rosamond on that hot afternoon, there were already hoards of media, residents, and authorities. The police would give me the nuts and bolts of the story, but I would have to dig deeper to get the rest. Yellow tape snaked around the house where the shooting had occurred. The police herded everyone away from the scene. Residents huddled nearby talking about what had happened. I knew that's where I had to be. Those people would know more about what had happened than anyone.

■ **Be persistent.** I talked to scores of residents, taking few notes. I mostly listened. I wanted to know who knew the people who had been shot and who saw what had happened. Who called 911? The more people I talked to, the better my chances were to find a good story. And I did.

■ **Find the most compelling human element.** Once I found the neighbors who had come to the rescue, I knew I had found what I wanted. From there I wanted to write a story that would let the reader feel, hear, and see what they had seen. What were they thinking running into a house where shots had just rung out? I put myself in their shoes and thought of the danger and asked questions.

■ **Get detail, detail, detail.** It was time for me to do a lot of listening and writing and do little speaking. The more detail I got, the closer the reader would get to the scene. I needed to know how each person in the house was found and what Cornelius and Demetric Green did to help. I knew what had happened to Jessica Borner would be the most compelling, so I had Green detail what he did for the girl. We were both moved.

While I was writing the story, we got word that Jessica had died. I had to change my lead. The story began to write itself. I never met Jessica Borner, but the last moments of her life will stay with me forever.

Ted Jackson
Community Photojournalism

Ted Jackson, 47, was born in McComb, Miss., where he spent many carefree days on his grandparents' dairy farm. His dreams and goals centered on life in a small town.

After three years of college, Jackson pursued a career in graphic arts. With a growing freelance business and a growing family, he decided to use his artistic skills to communicate the human condition rather than to advertise merchandise. He returned to college and graduated with a degree in photojournalism from the University of Southern Mississippi.

His first newspaper job, at *The Daily Iberian* in New Iberia, La., introduced him to Cajun country. After two years there, he joined *The Times-Picayune* in New Orleans.

Jackson's geopolitical stories include the tearing down of the Berlin Wall, the 1991 Persian Gulf War, upheaval in Haiti, and life in Cuba. He also has covered the physical destruction and emotional trauma of earthquakes and hurricanes.

In the United States, he has produced photo essays on life in one of the country's worst housing developments, New Orleans' homeless population, and the U.S. tour of Pope John Paul II. In 2001, he documented Louisiana's Cajun culture, wandering the backroads, bayous, and swamps to photograph "Culture at a Crossroads," a three-day photo essay on the Cajuns' struggle to preserve their way of life.

Jackson's photographs have won numerous state and national awards. In 1997, he was part of the team that won the Pulitzer Prize for public service for "Oceans of Trouble," a comprehensive look at the impending collapse of the world's fisheries.

Jackson and his wife, Nancy, live in Covington, La. They have two grown sons, Chris and Jeremy. He commits much of his time to the leadership team and benevolence ministry at Tammany Oaks Church of Christ in Mandeville, La.

LEAP Year

In 1999, Louisiana began phasing in comprehensive tests at the end of fourth and eighth grades and made passage mandatory for promotion. But what has happened to the students who have been damaged by years of abysmal schooling and are forced to pay a humiliating penalty for failings that are recognized as institutional? To find out, *Times-Picayune* photographer Ted Jackson teamed up with reporter Brian Thevenot to spend a year with students gearing up for the big test. The upshot was a five-part narrative called "LEAP Year." It was a searing indictment and an irresistible drama. Page after page of photographs, as powerful and intimate as any the newspaper had published, put a face on the abstraction called educational reform.

The series generated an unprecedented flow of e-mails, letters, and phone calls as readers were shown the complexities of urban school reform. The story revealed truths that will be driven home across the nation as other states embrace the federal mandate for high-stakes testing. It also pulled away a veil that often stands between the media and public schools.

—Adapted from The Times-Picayune ASNE contest entry

A conversation with
Ted Jackson

KENNY IRBY: How did the concept for this story originate?

TED JACKSON: The project started with the writer, Brian Thevenot, who works on the education beat. Alphonse Davis, the school board superintendent and a former Marine, took a very strict position and locked out the media as one of his first moves of authority. We asked for full access to one class for one year. We played a long shot and wanted to see where it went. In the summer of 2001, we got our chance and the doors to the school were opened.

What was the greatest challenge for you as this story developed?

I was concerned from the start with kids posing, and I was reluctant to take pictures for fear of getting kicked out. So I was very careful about what I shot.

What did you do in your first week?

Well, in week one, I made little relationships. The kids were clowning around. But when they got bored with me, pictures started to come.

What was your strategy for when to go to the school?

In the beginning we randomly went there, but after the Super Bowl coverage ended in January, I went daily. I did not go to my office. I just went to school. The students did not even notice us after a while. A student-observer accompanying me said, "It's amazing. It's as if they don't even see you.'"

Did your relationship ever reach a point at which you were accepted by the kids?

Principal Sharon Clark pulls at one of Hayward Howard's braids to remind him they are prohibited at school. Clark was tough on the students and respected in return, but she could be as effusive in her praise as in her reprimands.

It sure did. One day, I got called down by the teacher for whispering in class. When the kids did not know answers, sometimes I would help them out, you know. Then one day after lunch I walked into the eighth-grade science class that had a substitute teacher. I introduced myself and explained what we were doing at the paper, and the kids were just doing their thing. They were really acting up and the substitute lashed out at them and said that she could not believe their behavior in front of a guest. Just then little Joseph Jones shouted back, "He ain't no guest, he's family!"

Family. How does one rise to that level of acceptance?

It was all born of the fact that I was there all the time. To begin with, they were aware and charmed by the fact that I outlasted them. They were going to be themselves regardless because I was not going away. I started to see kids sleeping in class, see their mixed emotions and competing needs. The teachers did not want to look bad, and the kids had a choice: pretending to be model citizens or being themselves.

I decided just to build little relationships by talking to them. And I liked getting down to an eighth-grade level.

Terrence Brooks, lower right, ducks as Justin Dyer throws a book at him during social studies class. A succession of teachers and substitutes never managed to establish control of the class.

What risks did you take as you worked on building relationships?

There I was, a 46-year-old man playing with kids on the playground. I gave them the simple answers and helped them whenever I could. I knew that they were in a vicious cycle, up against some serious odds.

What was the greatest problem that you observed?

Discipline, or should I say the lack of it. It was not that the teachers did not try to discipline the students; but many of the kids did not care. I witnessed detention slips being tossed back at teachers. Some teachers really cared, like eighth-grade math teacher Elzy Lindsey. He cared and talked their language.

What was the editing and support structure like for you while you were doing this project?

Doug Parker was the photo editor, and it was quite a challenge keeping me focused and figuring out what categories needed to be established. We had a good relationship with the reporter. I take that back. It was a marvelous relationship.

As the writing went along, our categories fell into place and we followed the school year: "Uphill Battle,"

At each table, taped-together manila folders form dividers that help students such as Timesha Gaines, left, and Krystal McGee avoid the temptation to cheat.

about the start of the school year; "Playing Catch-up," "Roadblocks to Learning" (I fought for this segment), "Countdown to LEAP," and "Judgment Day."

Tell me about how you worked with your writing colleague on this story.

Working with Brian Thevenot was great because he cared about the pictures and I cared about the story, and he was very focused and conscious of staying out of the pictures. He would run clear around the room to not be in the frame. We would have lunch together and have good conversations and give and take.

What made this story important?

I kept thinking about the intense pressure of the test preparation, and the kids were very emotional, and very few passed. Parents had to pick up the grades, and kids were crying. It was special because of the access and relationships. I don't recall anything quite like this story. My inspiration and motivation were to do right by the kids because people needed to know that kids were being punished by bad schools. What good comes out of this, I hope, is that more people will care and get involved and go beyond the statistics. I hope that people will look at where these kids' lives are headed.

David Pichon's mother, Cheryl Atkinson, arrives at Wright Learning Academy to pick up David's LEAP test scores. After finding his letter in the "unsatisfactory" box, she registered him for summer school. Then she had to break the news to David.

How do you find a story that only you can tell?

What made this story work so well for me was the fact that I really cared. We have to make connections and see the value of our work.

What were your research tools and how did you find the right situations?

Generally, there was no research, but I knew that the story was going to focus on the fear, anxiety, and struggle. There was not much on the Web other than looking at how others had approached kids in school. And I made it my purpose to document. I did not use creative lighting or different angles.

There has been lots of industry discussion about the difference between feature hunting and enterprise photography coverage. Could you explain your understanding of the difference and where your project fits?

I think that it is important for photographers to generate a fair amount of their own ideas and to contribute to the coverage of the newspaper.

David Pichon breaks into tears after reading the form letter containing his failing LEAP scores as his mother tries to console him. She reminds him that he can go to summer school and, with a lot of hard work, he can still get into high school next year.

What type of cameras did you use?

I started covering the story with film and finished with a Nikon D1H digital camera. The thing that I loved was the exposure latitude. The camera has a play-back feature that several students knew about, and I had to deal with what was good for me and bad for them. It was good because I could check my exposure and composition, and bad because they wanted to see themselves. Downloading was a tremendous benefit, too. I admit, I did not think that I was going to like digital, but I put the film cameras down in January 2002 and have not touched them.

What was your lens preferences?

I really love that 80-200mm, and I used the 14mm as well.

What might you share with other photographers from your experience?

First, never be afraid to ask for the impossible. Second, never rush the story. Let the images come to you and remember why you are there. And third, never underestimate the impact of documentary photography.

Los Angeles Times

Don Bartletti

Finalist, Photojournalism

Don Bartletti, 55, has been a photo-journalist with Southern California newspapers for 31 years and with the *Los Angeles Times* for the past 20. Except for a summer class in photography, he essentially is self-taught in the discipline. However, as an infantry officer in Vietnam, Bartletti honed the observational and survival skills that serve him to this day as a photojournalist.

During his professional newspaper career he has covered stories throughout Mexico, Central America, South America, and most recently in Afghanistan, Pakistan, and the Philippines. Hundreds of his photographs have appeared in the *Times* and other newspapers. Many are now held for historical preservation in museum collections, books, and scholarly studies. His work has been shown in exhibits throughout the United States and Mexico.

Bartletti has won more than 50 awards, most notably from the National Press Photographers Association, the National Association of Hispanic Journalists, the Inter American Press Association, Pictures of the Year, and World Press Photo, as well as the Ruben Salazar Award.

Bartletti won the 2003 Pulitzer for feature photography for his work on "Enrique's Journey," and accompanying stories by *Times*' writer Sonia Nazario won the 2003 Pulitzer Prize for feature writing.

"Enrique's Journey" touched Bartletti's photojournalistic passion like few other projects. It put him back on the immigrant trail where he has been chronicling change for 25 years.

Enrique's Journey

Don Bartletti credits his vision of photography to Dorothea Lange. "In documentary photojournalism, I believe the subject, not the photographer, should be the No. 1 author of the photo, and the viewer should be jolted to ask, 'How can such things be?'" says Bartletti.

Nowhere is this vision clearer than in Bartletti's photos for "Enrique's Journey." A boy is left behind by his mother and sets out on a perilous journey to be reunited with her. In the vast northward movement of people from Central America and Mexico, Enrique is one of 48,000 children who come to the United States alone each year.

Bartletti and writer Sonia Nazario took remarkable risks to photograph and report this story. Where Enrique walked, they walked, nearly 100 miles. They braved thieves, street gangs, and corrupt cops, just as he had. Where Enrique rode freight trains, Bartletti and Nazario rode freight trains, more than 800 miles. Most of the time Bartletti was on top of the train cars. Where Enrique rode buses or hitchhiked with truckers, Bartletti and Nazario did too, another 800 miles. They followed the route he took all the way into the United States.

Bartletti's pictures tell a story far beyond that of a single child, training a wide-angle lens on the hidden lives of tens of thousands of children who immigrate illegally and alone.

—Adapted from the Los Angeles Times ASNE contest entry

Photographers' Workshop:
An invitation to observe

BY KENNY IRBY

Don Bartletti's images demonstrate vision by extending the definition of community and vicariously exposing the viewer to remarkable risk. Each photograph embodies poetic tension, pulling the viewer from image to image.

"Every picture has a degree of difficulty of nine or higher," said the ASNE judges. "Every picture in his masterful visual narrative takes on a verb-like quality. And every picture brings the human heart to tears."

The following explores insights into Bartletti and his photographic philosophy.

KENNY IRBY: Why do you do what you do, and what makes it special?

DON BARTLETTI: My family, my home, and photojournalism are the loves in my life. In turn, I'm passionate about all three. As a newspaper photographer, not only do I get to see, smell, and feel the emotions of our world, I produce documents of visual information that preserve those moments for all time. I get additional satisfaction from exhibiting certain works in museums, making them available for scholarly works, and lecturing about my photo stories. My approach to photojournalism is somewhere between cultural anthropology and a scavenger hunt. Finding the meaningful subject is most of the job. But when I'm there, I take advantage of the courage and responsibility necessary to make an image that reflects the truth. I thrive on a careful, deliberate, and respectful interaction with my subjects.

Having spent some 20-plus years covering immigrant issues, how did you embark upon "Enrique's Journey"?

It began with the search for a minor who had fled Central America for the United States in search of his mother. As is the case with nearly every Central American immigrant, the subject on which I would base my photographs had to have traveled through Mexico on the freight trains. Sonia Nazario, my reporting colleague, and I spent five weeks on the Texas border searching for such a youngster. Most of the time was in Nuevo Laredo, a border town across the Rio Grande from Laredo, Texas, where northbound migrants arrive exhausted and broke. We found 17-year-old Enrique at a church shelter in Nuevo Laredo. He fit the characteristics and had a great story, but Sonia felt he looked too old. He admitted to using drugs and had left a pregnant girlfriend back home. He wasn't the "poster boy" of child migrants. Nevertheless, I photographed him off and on washing cars, living in a riverside camp, eating at shelters, and sleeping in abandoned houses. One night, Enrique made contact with his mother and was ready to cross the Rio Grande with a smuggler. I dearly wanted to go with him. Sonia was still uncertain if he was the one. He left. We stayed.

After another week looking for other youngsters, I suggested we catch up to Enrique. He had a good story and had shared his mother's phone number. We hopped a plane to North Carolina. Enrique had arrived only two days before. I photographed Enrique with his mom and working at his first job. Those pictures became the last chapter of the six-part series. While there, Sonia nailed down more details of his journey. With a phone call to Honduras and his grandparents' agreement, we flew to where Enrique was raised in Tegucigalpa. This became the first chapter in the series. I photographed the family that cared for him during the 10 years his mother worked in the United States. I also photographed street orphans, child laborers, and examples of conditions in Tegucigalpa that push thousands of Hondurans to go to *El Norte*. After a week in Tegucigalpa, Sonia and I began retracing Enrique's exact route northward through Mexico and eventually back to the Rio Grande, a distance of more than 2,500 miles.

How did you travel during this assignment?

I traveled very light with only two Nikon film cameras, two lenses, and a change of clothes. I carried the photo gear in a backpack that allowed me to run, climb, crawl, and quickly hide the gear during rainstorms or threatening situations. On assignments in Southern California I'd have a car loaded with eight different lenses, four cameras, a laptop, cell phone, and scanner. On "Enrique's Journey," the overriding concern was to be as unencumbered as possible and to keep up with the train-riding stowaways. In order to lessen the catastrophic results of losing important images if I were to be robbed, I shipped film and Xerox copies of my notes to the *Times* on a regular basis. I purchased film as I went along.

How did you develop relationships essential to the success of the project?

I never tried to be anyone but a photojournalist. With cameras and a *norteamericano* accent, I was obligated to explain myself. When confronted, I always requested from my subjects what I call an "invitation to observe." Whether in a town plaza, a riverside camp, a rooftop hideout, a church shelter, an immigration jail, or on top of a speeding train, I explained to my subjects something like this: "I am a newspaper photographer. I think *la lucha,* or 'the struggle,' you are experiencing is a life-changing experience. It's also an important part of the history of your country, and mine. If you'll let me watch, I promise my pictures will show the truth of your struggle. I'm sorry I can't help you with money or advice, but I won't interrupt your journey or cause you harm." I probably repeated all or parts of that a thousand times. It was essential for the success of the project. It helped eliminate mistrust among people who are literally running for their lives. Very few ran away from me. In fact, I think one man confirmed my sincerity by saying, "Up to now, the only people chasing us were priests and the police."

Please share insights on how you and Sonia Nazario worked as partners. What were some of the challenges between you?

During the best of times, Sonia and I worked side by side. During the worst of times, we were ready to kill each other. Understandably, Sonia needed to find the places and people Enrique told her about. But interviews seldom make interesting pictures. Things that happened to Enrique months before obviously couldn't be photographed. My mission was to find circumstances similar to those experienced by Enrique. Sometimes Sonia and I were on the same road, but in different lanes going at different speeds to the same destination. When I encountered a group of youngsters hiding out and waiting for a train, I had to stay with them. Sometimes I'd ride trains without her. After a couple of hundred miles, I'd jump off and catch a bus back. Upon my return, I shared anecdotes and observations with Sonia, backing them up with a hand-written account.

What were your greatest challenges?

Migrants rightfully call the Mexican state of Chiapas "The Beast." My biggest worry was trouble from train-riding gangsters who regularly rob and assault immigrants. We rode with a plainclothes force that patrols the train line to control violence against immigrants. Once aboard I struggled to balance atop the rocking roof as the train moved through the jungle. I quickly learned to pay attention when stowaways yelled the word *"rama,"* Spanish for "branch." Low-hanging trees could lacerate or knock one clean off the train. *Rama*! had me flat on the roof and firing the camera with my eyes closed for pictures of riders avoiding the lethal hazards. While photographing kids running to get on, I usually had less than a minute before it picked up too much speed for me to grab the ladder. I road atop about a dozen trains, from the broiling hot tropics to near freezing mountain tunnels— about 1,200 miles total.

Aside from these and countless other physical challenges, one of the hardest things to overcome was not offering assistance. I steadfastly adhered to the ethics of honest journalism. Although I gave not a peso to anyone, I knew they would make it. I realized I was among youngsters whose survival skills belied their age. Once I helped 15-year-old Ermis, who was experiencing more than discomfort. I bought him a package of Excedrin to lessen the suffering after he was clubbed on the head by a gang of local thugs.

What was your most memorable lesson during your time in the field?

One of the few moments on the trains when I felt I was safe, I was robbed! It was 2 a.m. and I was nearing the end of the entire train journey. I was riding alone in the second locomotive. As we rolled through San Luis Potosi, Mexico, I closed the doors and leaned on the engineer's window and watched the moonlit desert scrub roll past. For the first time in almost three months I was relaxed and enjoying the ride like a vacationer. Suddenly the rush of wind through the open door woke me up. A silhouette disappeared off the side of the train. My pack was gone! In spite of the loss of cameras and passport, the lesson was clear: I had prepared well. By shipping home a week's worth of exposed film earlier that day, the irreplaceable images were not lost.

Were there any major surprises for you while reporting this story?

Enrique's reunion with his mother was less than a storybook ending. I was surprised in some ways at Enrique's bitterness toward his mother. I have an image of Enrique and his mom embracing that shows their long-lost love. But there's another of him lounging on the couch as his mom cleans up after dinner. That hints at his discontent and simmering anger at having been abandoned so many years ago.

What are your thoughts on the need for photographers to be originators of ideas?

Photographers must find their own stories for at least a couple of reasons. Once you get going on a personal project, a more compelling proposal can be made. Second, I find I can work at my own pace for a while before bringing a reporter into it. I'm always storing away simple little picture packages and bigger project ideas. When I get them right, I make a proposal.

What advice can you offer younger photographers when it comes to working with editors?

After many years in the business, I realize the decency of sharing my vision and not being selfish about it. To be sure, images are your magic representations of reality. But in order to get that picture in the paper, it must first become a commodity of sorts. The photo credit proudly assigns the obvious authorship, but in reality it belongs to the subject, to the photographer, the photo editor, the section editor, the layout artist, the press operator, and the reader. There are many authors to your photo. Allow that, and your career will be long and fulfilled.

Austin American-Statesman

Rodolfo Gonzalez
Finalist, Photojournalism

Rodolfo Gonzalez, 33, has been a photographer for the *Austin American-Statesman* since October 2000. He previously worked for the *Denver Rocky Mountain News,* where he shared the 2000 Pulitzer Prize for breaking news photography for his photos of the Columbine High School shootings.

Gonzalez is married and the father of two children. He has been a staff photojournalist or picture editor since 1990, working at *The Times* in Shreveport, La., the *San Antonio Light,* Fort Worth *Star-Telegram,* and *The Providence Journal.*

Gonzalez was raised in San Antonio, Texas, and studied journalism, mass communications, and photojournalism at San Antonio College, where he worked for the student publication, *The Ranger.*

While growing up in San Antonio, Gonzalez found his passion for photography while carrying the video deck for his older brother, Jerry, a television photojournalist who now freelances primarily for ABC.

Gonzalez purchased his first camera at the age of 16, an event that began the "family photo feud" between him and his brother about which is the more powerful photojournalistic format. One thing they do agree on is the purpose of photojournalism. Gonzalez says he was inspired by his older brother to understand his job as "a privileged front-row seat to life that I cannot waste."

In "Chasing Hope," Gonzalez's unflinching pictures confront readers with the horrific effect of a car wreck on the life of Jacqui Saburido and reveal her inspiring struggle for command of her transformed life.

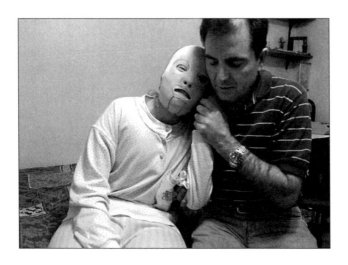

Chasing Hope

In "Chasing Hope," *Austin American-Statesman* photographer Rodolfo Gonzalez and reporter David Hafetz spent nearly a year chronicling the recovery of Jacqui Saburido, a young woman whose body and life were devastated by a fiery car accident.

The effect of "Chasing Hope" has been global. The Texas Department of Transportation made it a focal point of a campaign against drunken driving. Mothers Against Drunk Driving distributed the stories and photos at high school graduations. An emergency room worker at a Connecticut hospital revamped his alcohol presentation to showcase Gonzalez's photographs. The state used Saburido's image in posters and created a TV public service announcement that featured her speaking in English and Spanish about her accident. She has been on NPR and pursued by television news broadcasters in Italy, Germany, Japan, and Mexico and by those who wish to translate her story into other languages.

Gonzalez's photographs tell the inspiring story behind Saburido's horrific scars. His work shows us her passion for making a difference, the devotion of her father, and her struggle as a young woman who has soared beyond tragedy.

–Adapted from the Austin American-Statesman ASNE contest entry

Photographers' Workshop:
The hand of hope

BY KENNY IRBY

"Chasing Hope" and its true power come from the magic between Jacqui Saburido and her father, Amadeo, their passion for life, and their never-ending struggle to achieve Jacqui's independence. Jacqui's story invites readers to love life and dares them to take it for granted.

Since its publication, Rodolfo Gonzalez has received hundreds of e-mails from all over the world, "thanking not me, but Jacqui, for her strength."

KENNY IRBY: Recount the time that you first saw Jacqui Saburido.

RODOLFO GONZALEZ: I first saw Jacqui march past me and a wall of other photographers who lined the hallway leading to the courtroom where Reggie Stephey was on trial for two counts of intoxicated manslaughter.

What were your emotions during the trial?

Day after day as she paraded past with her father, Amadeo, at her side every step of the way, I would hear the whispers and notice the stares coming from passersby and members of the media, myself included. We would all flinch, squirm, and avert our eyes politely as she walked through our viewfinders.

During the early stages of the trial, what drew you to Jacqui and her plight?

She had survived the horrible car crash and the flames that claimed her physical body and took the lives of her two friends. As for myself, it was all of the suffering that the scars represented, not her appearance, that first made me uneasy. I thought the scars would be a constant reminder of all that was lost. It was heartbreaking.

Tell me about the first interaction that you had with

Jacqui and how your relationship developed.

When she walked into the room, Jacqui took my hand with both of her palms and smiled the way only Jacqui can. It was a gentle touch, one that I have since seen performed many times for other fortunate souls lucky enough to meet her. The spell she cast was a simple concoction: a warm smile and direct eye contact. The gesture told me, in its own subtle way, that it was okay to look and that she was fine. It was all I needed. I never looked at her or thought of her in the same way again.

How did you find the focus of the story in the midst of all those layers?

The interview that day went very well, but I knew that Jacqui's life of recovery deserved more attention. There was more to the story than just the outcome of the trial. She wanted to tell her whole story. Jacqui wanted to make sense of the accident. She believed that, by the grace of God, she had survived and was alive for a purpose. David and I were only a medium for her to share her story with all who dared to challenge their own inhibitions by reading "Chasing Hope."

How did the story transition from the office to her home in an effort to build the master narrative?

Following our interview I asked, with some reservation, if I could follow her home and document some of the trials and tribulations she and her father experienced on a daily basis. Without hesitation she simply replied, "Sure. If you want to come to Galveston, you can come."

How long did you work on the story?

In the next 10 months, I visited Jacqui and her father in different stages of their lives as they pursued any doctor or medical procedure that might add a little more independence to Jacqui's life.

This is a lot of time and commitment. Had you ever taken on a project of this magnitude before?

No, it is the first long-term story I have done. I was never exactly sure what would be made of the images, nor did I know exactly how they would be received. I just tried to be honest and hoped for the same excitement from the staff and, of course, to get enough space to give Jacqui's story its just rewards. Jacqui got both. In reality, I think that I knew deep down that I didn't have any control of the story at all. Jacqui's strong will and honesty did all of that for me.

What has been the reaction from others in the photo-journalism community to your work on this project?

In April 2003, the *Denver Rocky Mountain News* won its second staff Pulitzer for its coverage of wildfires that nearly engulfed Colorado this past summer. This was my former staff. A friend from the *Statesman* said, "If you had stayed (at the *Rocky*), you would be a two-timer," referring to the possibility of winning a second Pulitzer there. The thought did cross my mind, but if I had stayed, I would never have met Jacqui Saburido. The newfound appreciation for life that I cherish so much with my family could never have been. What ifs? I think I made out like a bandit. What do you think?

What specific lesson did you come away with from this story?

That same magical warmth and openness that I felt when she took my hand so long ago is what I feel in the images of "Chasing Hope." That presence, like photo-journalism, resounds differently for different people. For me it was a blessing. That blessing was that it made me feel as if it's okay to look or even take pictures. It's okay to be grateful for what I have.

Annual Bibliography

BY DAVID B. SHEDDEN

WRITING AND REPORTING BOOKS 2002

Amster, Linda, and Dylan Loeb McClain, eds. *Kill Duck Before Serving: Red Faces at The New York Times*. New York: St. Martin's Griffin, 2002.

Bloom, Stephen G. *Inside the Writer's Mind: Writing Narrative Journalism*. Ames, Iowa: Iowa State University Press, 2002.

Brooks, Brian S., George Kennedy, Daryl R. Moen, and Don Ranly. *News Reporting and Writing*, 7th ed. New York: Bedford/St. Martins, 2002.

Clark, Roy Peter, and Cole C. Campbell, eds. *The Value and Craft of American Journalism*. Gainesville, Fla.: University Press of Florida, 2002.

Fellow, Anthony R., and Thomas N. Clanin. *Copy Editor's Handbook for Newspapers*, 2nd ed. Englewood, Colo.: Morton Publishing, 2002.

Gibbs, Cheryl, and Tom Warhover. *Getting the Whole Story*. New York: Guilford Press, 2002.

Goldstein, Norm, ed. *The Associated Press Stylebook and Briefing on Media Law*. Cambridge, Mass.: Perseus Publishing, 2002.

Houston, Brant, Len Bruzzese, and Steve Weinberg. *The Investigative Reporter's Handbook*, 4th ed. Boston: Bedford/St. Martin's, 2002.

Jackson, Dennis, and John Sweeney, eds. *The Journalist's Craft: A Guide to Writing Better Stories*. New York: Allworth Press, 2002.

Martin, Paul R., ed. *The Wall Street Journal Guide to Business Style and Usage*. New York: Simon & Schuster, 2002.

Meyer, Philip. *Precision Journalism*, 4th ed. Lanham, Md.: Rowman & Littlefield Publishers, 2002.

New York Times. *Portraits 9/11/01*. New York: Times Books/Henry Holt and Company, 2002.

Rich, Carole. *Writing and Reporting News: A Coaching Method*, 4th ed. Belmont, Calif.: Thomson/Wadsworth, 2002.

Ross, Lillian. *Reporting Back: Notes on Journalism*. Washington, D.C.: Counterpoint, 2002.

Schwartz, Jerry. *The Associated Press Reporting Handbook*. New York: McGraw-Hill, 2002.

Walsh, Bill. *Lapsing Into a Comma*. New York: McGraw-Hill, 2002.

Wells, Ken, ed. *Floating Off the Page: The Best Stories from The Wall Street Journal's "Middle Column."* New York: The Wall Street Journal, 2002.

Wilber, Rick, and Randy Miller. *Modern Media Writing*. Belmont, Calif.: Thomson/Wadsworth, 2002.

Wilstein, Steve. *The Associated Press Sports Writing Handbook*. New York: McGraw-Hill, 2002.

CLASSICS

Atchity, Kenneth. *A Writer's Time: A Guide to the Creative Process, From Vision Through Revision*. New York: W.W. Norton & Co., 1996.

Bell, Madison Smartt. *Narrative Design: A Writer's Guide to Structure*. New York: W.W. Norton & Co., 2000.

Berg, A. Scott. *Max Perkins: Editor of Genius*. New York: Berkley Publishing Group, 1997.

Bernstein, Theodore M. *The Careful Writer: A Modern Guide to English Usage*. New York: Free Press, 1995.

Blundell, William E. *The Art and Craft of Feature Writing: The Wall Street Journal Guide*. New York: Dutton/ Plume, 1988.

Brady, John. *The Craft of Interviewing*. New York: Knopf, 1977.

Brande, Dorothea. *Becoming a Writer*. Los Angeles: J.P.

Tarcher; Boston: distributed by Putnam Publishing, reprint of 1934 edition, 1981.

Cappon, Rene J. *The Associated Press Guide to News Writing*. Forest City, Calif.: IDG Books Worldwide, 2000.

Clark, Roy Peter. *Free to Write: A Journalist Teaches Young Writers*. Westport, Conn.: Heinemann, 1995.

Dillard, Annie. *The Writing Life*. New York: Harper Collins, 1999.

Elbow, Peter. *Writing With Power: Techniques for Mastering the Writing Process*, 2nd ed. New York: Oxford University Press, 1998.

Follett, Wilson. *Modern American Usage: A Guide*. Revised by Erik Wensberg. New York: Hill & Wang, 1998.

Franklin, Jon. *Writing for Story: Craft Secrets of Dramatic Nonfiction by a Two-Time Pulitzer Prize Winner*. New York: Dutton/Plume, 1994.

Garlock, David. *Pulitzer Prize Feature Stories*. Ames, Iowa: Iowa State University Press, 1998.

Gross, Gerald, ed. *Editors on Editing: What Writers Should Know About What Editors Do*. New York: Grove/Atlantic, 1993.

Harrington, Walt. *Intimate Journalism: The Art and Craft of Reporting Everyday Life*. Thousand Oaks, Calif.: Sage, 1997.

Hugo, Richard. *The Triggering Town: Lectures & Essays on Poetry & Writing*. New York: Norton, 1992.

Kerrane, Kevin, and Ben Yagoda. *The Art of Fact*. New York: Scribner, 1997.

Klement, Alice, and Carolyn Matalene, eds. *Telling Stories, Taking Risks. Journalism Writing at the Century's Edge*. Belmont, Calif.: Wadsworth Publishing, 1998.

McPhee, John. *The John McPhee Reader*. William L. Howard, ed. New York: Farrar, Straus & Giroux, 1990.

Metzler, Ken. *Creative Interviewing: The Writer's Guide to Gathering Information by Asking Questions*, 3rd ed. Needham Heights, Mass.: Allyn & Bacon, 1996.

Mitford, Jessica. *Poison Penmanship: The Gentle Art of Muckraking*. New York: Farrar, Straus & Giroux, 1988.

Murray, Donald. *Shoptalk: Learning to Write With Writers*. Portsmouth, N.H.: Boynton/Cook, 1990.

Perry, Susan K. *Writing in Flow: Keys to Enhanced Creativity*. Cincinnati: Writer's Digest Books, 2001.

Plimpton, George, ed. *Writers at Work: The Paris Review Interviews*. Series. New York: Viking, 1992.

Ross, Lillian. *Reporting*. New York: Simon & Schuster Trade, 1984.

Scanlan, Christopher, ed. *How I Wrote the Story*. Providence Journal Company, 1986.

Scanlan, Christopher. *Reporting and Writing: Basics for the 21st Century*. New York: Oxford University Press, 2000.

Sims, Norman, ed. *Literary Journalism in the Twentieth Century*. New York: Oxford University Press, 1990.

Stafford, William, and Donald Hall, eds. *Writing the Australian Crawl: View on the Writer's Vocation*. Ann Arbor, Mich.: University of Michigan Press, 1978.

Stewart, James B. *Follow the Story: How to Write Successful Nonfiction*. New York: Simon and Schuster, 1998.

Strunk, William, Jr., and E.B. White. *The Elements of Style*, 4th ed. Needham Heights, Mass.: Allyn & Bacon, 1999.

Talese, Gay. *Fame & Obscurity*. Reprint edition, New York: Ivy Books, 1971.

White, E.B. *Essays of E.B. White*. New York: Harper Collins, 1999.

Woods, Keith, Karen Brown, Roy Peter Clark, Don Fry,

and Christopher Scanlan, eds. *Best Newspaper Writing*. St. Petersburg, Fla.: The Poynter Institute. Published annually since 1979.

Zinsser, William. *On Writing Well: An Informal Guide to Writing Nonfiction*, 6th ed. New York: Harper Collins, 1998.

— *Writing to Learn*. Reading, Mass.: Addison-Wesley Educational Publishers, 1997.

— *Speaking of Journalism: 12 Writers and Editors Talk About Their Work*. New York: Harper Collins, 1994.

ARTICLES 2002

Banaszynski, Jacqui. "Why We Need Stories." *Nieman Reports* (Spring 2002): 41-43.

Birge, Elizabeth. "The Lost Middle Voice." *Quill* (April 2002): 15-17.

Block, Mervin. "Is Your Copy Crawling with Errors?" *Communicator* (March 2002): 45-47.

Brown, Fred. "Storytelling Vs. Sticking to the Facts." *Quill* (April 2002): 22-25.

Collins, Steve J., and Kimberly L. Bissell. "Student Self-Efficacy in a Media Writing Course." *Journalism & Mass Communication Educator* (Winter 2002): 19-36.

Franklin, Jon. "The Extraordinary Adventure That Is Science Writing." *Nieman Reports* (Fall 2002): 8-10.

French, Tom. "Serial Narratives." *Nieman Reports* (Spring 2002): 48-50.

Kirtz, Bill. "Local Stories Far From Home." *Presstime* (September 2002): 26-29.

Larocque, Paula. "Finding the Right Word." *Quill* (September 2002): 60.

Lehrman, Sally. "Better Sources Make Better Coverage." *Quill* (June 2002): 58-59.

McGuire, Patrick A. "Avoiding the Presumption Trap." *Quill* (December 2002): 10-14.

O'Brien, Meredith. "When the Story Is Personal." *Quill* (April 2002): 13-14.

Paulson, Ken. "Editorialists Are Leaders in Guarding First Amendment." *The Masthead* (Summer 2002): 5-6.

Scanlan, Christopher. "Writing Is All About Rewriting, Which Means You've Got to Get Something Down." *Nieman Reports* (Spring 2002): 24.

Shapiro, Michael. "The Curse of Tom Wolfe." *Columbia Journalism Review* (November/December 2002): 36-43.

Sherman, Scott. "Going Long, Going Deep." *Columbia Journalism Review* (November/December 2002): 48-57.

Smolkin, Rachel. "What Did He Say?" *American Journalism Review* (September 2002): 36-39.

Toolan, Brian. "Whatever Happened to Local Columnists?" *The American Editor* (January/February 2002): 14-17.

Wilkerson, Isabel. "Interviewing Sources." *Nieman Reports* (Spring 2002): 16-17.

Woods, Keith. "The Importance of a Risk-Taking Editor." *The American Editor* (May/June 2002): 23.

The Journalist's Toolbox

Here is a selective index that loosely follows the writing process developed by longtime columnist and author Don Murray. It references places in the book where journalists shine a light on the tools and techniques that helped make their work stand out.

Front: Kenny Irby, visual journalism group leader.
Middle row, left to right: Pam Johnson, leadership faculty; Aly Colón, diversity program director and *Poynter Report* editor; and Keith Woods, *Best Newspaper Writing* editor and reporting, writing, and editing group leader.
Back row, left to right: Kelly McBride, ethics faculty; Bill Mitchell, online editor/marketing director; Christopher Scanlan, senior writing faculty; and Roy Peter Clark, Poynter vice president and senior scholar.

The Poynter Experience

The Poynter Institute, which opened in 1975 as the Modern Media Institute, is a school dedicated to improving the quality of journalism in the United States and wherever the press is free. Each year, the Institute hosts more than 50 professional development seminars, two programs for college students, seminars for college professors, a year-round journalism program for Tampa Bay high school students, and summer writing camps for the area's elementary and middle-school children and their teachers.

Poynter.

The Institute coordinates and supports the National Writers' Workshops each spring, joining thousands of writers in a celebration of the craft. Poynter also has established connections around the globe with training institutes and the journalists they serve.

Through its publications and website, Poynter Online, the Institute connects journalists with their peers and promotes the notion that ethics is synonymous with excellence in all areas of the craft. Poynter faculty speak at journalism conventions, advise working journalists, consult in news organizations, and provide commentary on the everyday issues arising in the industry. Eight members of the Poynter faculty, pictured on the preceding page, played a part in producing this book.

Winners and Finalists, 1979-2002

1979
Richard Ben Cramer, *The Philadelphia Inquirer*, Deadline News
Mary Ellen Corbett, *The News-Sentinel*, Fort Wayne, Ind., Features
Thomas Oliphant, *Boston Sunday Globe*, Non-Deadline News
Everett S. Allen, *The Standard-Times*, New Bedford, Mass., Commentary

1980
Cynthia Gorney, *The Washington Post*, Features
Carol McCabe, *The Providence Sunday Journal*, News
Ellen Goodman, *The Boston Globe*, Commentary

Finalists:
Dudley Clendinen, *St. Petersburg Times*
Pete Dexter, *Philadelphia Daily News*
Richard Ben Cramer, *The Philadelphia Inquirer*
Francis X. Clines, *The New York Times*
Michael Daly, *Daily News,* New York
Mark Bowden, *The News American*, Baltimore
Bill Lyon, *The Philadelphia Inquirer*
W.D. (Zeke) Wigglesworth, *The Minneapolis Star*
Barry Bearak, *The Miami Herald*
Martin Bernheimer, *Los Angeles Times*
Paul Galloway, *Chicago Sun-Times*

1981
Saul Pett, Associated Press, Non-Deadline Writing
Richard Zahler, *The Seattle Times*, Deadline Writing
Thomas Plate, *Herald Examiner*, Los Angeles, Deadline Writing
Paul Greenberg, *Pine Bluff* (Ark.) *Commercial*, Commentary
Thomas Boswell, *The Washington Post*, Sports Writing

1982
William Blundell, *The Wall Street Journal*, Non-Deadline Writing
Patrick Sloyan, *Newsday*, Deadline Writing
Theo Lippman Jr., *The Baltimore Sun*, Commentary
Tom Archdeacon, *The Miami News*, Sports Writing

Finalist:

H.G. Bissinger, *St. Paul Pioneer Press*, Non-Deadline
    Writing

1983

Greta Tilley, *Greensboro* (N.C.) *News & Record*, Non-Deadline
    Writing

Rheta Grimsley Johnson, *Commercial Appeal*, Memphis,
    Commentary

Orland Dodson, *The Times*, Shreveport, La., Business Writing

Finalists:

Manuela Hoelterhoff, *The Wall Street Journal*, Commentary

Rushworth Kidder, *The Christian Science Monitor*, Commentary

1984

David Zucchino, *The Philadelphia Inquirer*, Deadline Writing

James Kindall, *The Kansas City Star*, Non-Deadline Writing

Roger Simon, *Chicago Sun-Times*, Commentary

Peter Rinearson, *The Seattle Times*, Business Writing

Finalist:

Joe Nawrozski, *The News American*, Baltimore, Deadline
    Writing

1985

Greta Tilley, *Greensboro* (N.C.) *News & Record*, Non-Deadline
    Writing

Jonathan Bor, *The Post-Standard*, Syracuse, N.Y., Deadline
    Writing

Murray Kempton, *Newsday*, Commentary

Richard Aregood, *Philadelphia Daily News*, Editorial Writing

Finalists:

Daniel Henninger, *The Wall Street Journal*, Editorial Writing

Mark Patinkin, *The Providence Journal-Bulletin*, Deadline
    Writing

John Carman, *The Atlanta Journal & Constitution*, Commen-
    tary

Jim Murray, *Los Angeles Times*, Commentary

1986

John Camp, *St. Paul Pioneer Press-Dispatch*, Non-Deadline
    Writing

David Finkel, *St. Petersburg Times*, Non-Deadline Writing

Bradley Graham, *The Washington Post*, Deadline Writing

Roger Simon, *The Baltimore Sun*, Commentary

Jonathan Freedman, *The Tribune*, San Diego, Editorial Writing

Finalists:
Larry King, *St. Petersburg Times*, Deadline Writing
Carl Schoettler, *Baltimore Evening Sun*, Deadline Writing
Tom Teepen, *The Atlanta Constitution*, Commentary
Les Payne, *Newsday*, Commentary
Daniel Henninger, *The Wall Street Journal*, Editorial Writing
Kenneth Ikenberry, *The Washington Post*, Editorial Writing

1987
Steve Twomey, *The Philadelphia Inquirer*, Non-Deadline Writing
Mark Fineman, *Los Angeles Times*, Deadline Writing
Craig Medred, *Anchorage Daily News*, Deadline Writing
Dave Barry, *The Miami Herald*, Commentary
Don Marsh, *The Charleston* (W.Va.) *Gazette*, Commentary
Jim Nicholson, *Philadelphia Daily News*, Obituary Writing

Finalists:
Tom French, *St. Petersburg Times*, Non-Deadline Writing
Cheryl Lavin, *Chicago Tribune*, Non-Deadline Writing
Belinda Brockman, *The Miami Herald*, Obituary Writing

1988
Blaine Harden, *The Washington Post*, Non-Deadline Writing
Bob Herbert, *Daily News*, New York, Deadline Writing
Jimmy Breslin, *Daily News*, New York, Commentary
James Klurfeld, *Newsday*, Editorial Writing
Carl Schoettler, *The Evening Sun*, Baltimore, Obituary Writing
Tom Shales, *The Washington Post*, Obituary Writing

Finalists:
David Finkel, *St. Petersburg Times*, Non-Deadline Writing
Elizabeth Rau, *The Providence Journal*, Deadline Writing
Henry Allen, *The Washington Post*, Commentary
Graham Dower, *The Plain Dealer*, Cleveland, Editorial Writing
Michael Pakenham, *Daily News*, New York, Editorial Writing

1989
James Lileks, *St. Paul Pioneer Press/Dispatch*, Non-Deadline Writing
Francis X. Clines, *The New York Times*, Deadline Writing
David Jay Remnick, *The Washington Post*, Deadline Writing
Michael Skube, *The News and Observer*, Raleigh, N.C., Commentary

Samuel Francis, *The Washington Times*, Editorial Writing
Mark Davis, *The Tampa Tribune*, Government Reporting

Finalists:
Tom French, *St. Petersburg Times*, Non-Deadline Writing
Ken Fuson, *The Des Moines Register*, Non-Deadline Writing
Arnold Markowitz, *The Miami Herald*, Deadline Writing
Lynne Tuohy, *The Hartford Courant*, Deadline Writing
Henry Allen, *The Washington Post*, Commentary
Pete Dexter, *The Sacramento Bee*, Commentary
Ann Daly Goodwin, *St. Paul Pioneer Press/Dispatch*,
    Editorial Writing
Robert Barnes, *The Washington Post*, Government Reporting

1990
Terrie Clafin, *Mail Tribune*, Medford, Ore., Non-Deadline
    Writing
David Von Drehle, *The Miami Herald*, Deadline Writing
Diana Griego Erwin, *The Orange County Register*,
    Commentary
Samuel Francis, *The Washington Times*, Editorial Writing
Linnet Myers, *Chicago Tribune*, Government Reporting

Finalists:
Wil Haygood, *The Boston Globe*, Non-Deadline Writing
Charles Wohlforth, *Anchorage Daily News*, Deadline Writing
Mike Levine, *The Times Herald Record*, Middletown, N.Y.,
    Commentary
Tom Kelly, *Sun-Sentinel*, Fort Lauderdale, Fla., Editorial
    Writing
Mark Pazniokas, *The Hartford Courant*, Government Reporting

1991
Rick Bragg, *St. Petersburg Times*, Non-Deadline Writing
Paul Moran, *Newsday*, Deadline Writing
Julie Sullivan, *The Spokesman-Review*, Spokane, Wash.,
    Short News Writing
Richard Aregood, *Philadelphia Daily News*, Editorial Writing
Jim Dwyer, *New York Newsday*, Commentary

Finalists:
Susan Ager, *Detroit Free Press*, Non-Deadline Writing
Paul Wilborn, *The Tampa Tribune*, Non-Deadline Writing
Mitch Albom, *Detroit Free Press*, Deadline Writing
Donald Kaul, *The Des Moines Register*, Commentary
David Warren, *The Whig-Standard*, Kingston, Ont., Commentary
David Prosser, *The Whig-Standard*, Kingston, Ont., Editorial

Writing
Geoffrey Tomb, *The Miami Herald*, Short News Writing

1992
G. Wayne Miller, *Providence Journal-Bulletin*, Non-
    Deadline Writing
Colin Nickerson, *The Boston Globe*, Deadline Writing
Russell Eshleman Jr., *The Philadelphia Inquirer*, Short
    Newswriting
John Fensterwald, *Concord Monitor*, Editorial Writing
Henry Allen, *The Washington Post*, Commentary

Finalists:
Paul Hendrickson, *The Washington Post*, Non-Deadline
    Writing
Carol Morello, *The Philadelphia Inquirer*, Non-Deadline
    Writing
Paul McEnroe, *Star Tribune*, Minneapolis, Deadline Writing
Doug O'Harra, *Anchorage Daily News*, Deadline Writing
Marianne Costantinou, *Philadelphia Daily News*, Short
    Newswriting
Tom Alex, *The Des Moines Register*, Short Newswriting
Adrian Peracchio, *Newsday*, Editorial Writing
Thomas Harvey Holt, *Richmond Times-Dispatch*, Editorial
    Writing
Peter Dexter, *The Sacramento Bee*, Commentary
Robert Jones, *Los Angeles Times*, Commentary

1993
Michael Jennings, *The Courier-Journal*, Louisville, Non-
    Deadline Writing
Sam Stanton, *The Sacramento Bee*, Deadline Writing
Dorothy Rabinowitz, *The Wall Street Journal*, Commentary
Richard Aregood, *Philadelphia Daily News*, Editorial Writing
Charles Klaveness, *The New York Times*, Headline Writing

Finalists:
Richard O'Mara, *The Sun*, Baltimore, Non-Deadline Writing
Randall Richard, *The Providence Journal*, Non-Deadline
    Writing
Martin Merzer, *The Miami Herald*, Deadline Writing
Diane Pucin, *The Philadelphia Inquirer*, Deadline Writing
Clayton Hardiman, *The Muskegon* (Mich.) *Chronicle*,
    Commentary
Roger Simon, *The Sun*, Baltimore, Commentary
Kenneth Knox, *Chicago Tribune*, Editorial Writing
Wayne Nicholas, *The Bolivar Commercial*, Cleveland, Miss.,

Editorial Writing
Jules Ned Crabb, *The Wall Street Journal*, Headline Writing
Gene Weingarten, *The Washington Post*, Headline Writing

1994
Anne Hull, *St. Petersburg Times*, Non-Deadline Writing
Joan Beck, *Chicago Tribune*, Commentary
Donna Britt, *The Washington Post*, Commentary
Michael Gartner, *The Daily Tribune*, Ames, Iowa, Editorial Writing
Ken Wells, *The Wall Street Journal*, Headline Writing

Finalists:
Craig Dezern, *The Orlando Sentinel*, Non-Deadline Writing
Hank Stuever, *The Albuquerque Tribune*, Non-Deadline Writing
Betty DeRamus, *The Detroit News*, Commentary
Paul Gigot, *The Wall Street Journal*, Commentary
Daniel P. Henninger, *The Wall Street Journal*, Editorial Writing
Rick Nichols, *The Philadelphia Inquirer*, Editorial Writing
Rose Jacobius, *The Washington Post*, Headline Writing
Beth Witrogen McLeod, *San Francisco Examiner*, Headline Writing

1995
Mark Fritz, Associated Press, Deadline Reporting
New York Newsday, Team Deadline Reporting
Gerald M. Carbone, *Providence Journal-Bulletin*, Non-Deadline Writing
Brian Dickinson, *Providence Journal-Bulletin*, Commentary
Susan Trausch, *The Boston Globe*, Editorial Writing
George Vecsey, *The New York Times*, Sports Writing

Finalists:
David Von Drehle, *The Washington Post*, Deadline Reporting
Knight-Ridder Washington Bureau, Team Deadline Reporting
Ron Suskind, *The Wall Street Journal*, Non-Deadline Writing
Michael Gartner, *The Daily Tribune*, Ames, Iowa, Editorial Writing
Dan Shaughnessy, *The Boston Globe*, Sports Writing

1996
Barton Gellman, *The Washington Post*, Deadline Reporting
The Miami Herald, Team Deadline Reporting
Rick Bragg, *The New York Times*, Non-Deadline Writing
Peter H. King, *Los Angeles Times*, Commentary
Daniel Henninger, *The Wall Street Journal*, Editorial Writing

Mitch Albom, *Detroit Free Press*, Sports Writing

Finalists:
David Cannella, *The Arizona Republic*, Deadline Reporting
Michael E. Ruane, Knight-Ridder, Deadline Reporting
The Washington Post, Team Deadline Reporting
The Dallas Morning News, Team Deadline Reporting
Ken Fuson, *The Des Moines Register*, Non-Deadline Writing
Tom Hallman Jr., *The Oregonian*, Non-Deadline Writing
Paul Greenberg, *Arkansas Democrat-Gazette*, Commentary
Robert Lipsyte, *The New York Times*, Commentary
Lance Dickie, *The Seattle Times*, Editorial Writing
Michael Gartner, *The Daily Tribune*, Ames, Iowa, Editorial
    Writing
Dan Shaughnessy, *The Boston Globe*, Sports Writing
Kevin Sherrington, *The Dallas Morning News*, Sports Writing

1997
Tom Hallman Jr., *The Oregonian*, Non-Deadline Writing
David Maraniss, *The Washington Post*, Deadline Reporting
Newsday, Team Deadline Reporting
Eileen McNamara, *The Boston Globe*, Commentary
N. Don Wycliff, *Chicago Tribune*, Editorial Writing
David A. Waters, *The Commercial Appeal*, Memphis, Religion/
    Spirituality Writing

Finalists:
Henry Allen, *The Washington Post*, Non-Deadline Writing
Julia Prodis, Associated Press, Non-Deadline Writing
John J. Keller, *The Wall Street Journal*, Deadline Reporting
Sebastian Rotella, *Los Angeles Times*, Deadline Reporting
Michael Specter, *The New York Times*, Deadline Reporting
Chicago Tribune, Team Deadline Reporting
Sun-Sentinel, Fort Lauderdale, Fla., Team Deadline Reporting
Teddy Allen, *The Times*, Shreveport, La., Commentary
Mike Deupree, *The Gazette*, Cedar Rapids, Iowa,
    Commentary
Murray Kempton, *Newsday*, Commentary
Ian Darling, *The Record*, Kitchener-Waterloo, Ont., Editorial
    Writing
Mike Foley, *The Laurinburg* (N.C.) *Exchange*, Editorial Writ-
    ing
Michael Gartner, *The Daily Tribune*, Des Moines, Iowa,
    Editorial Writing
Laurie Goodstein, *The Washington Post*, Religion/Spirituality
    Writing
David O'Reilly, *The Philadelphia Inquirer*, Religion/
    Spirituality Writing

Bill Tammeus, *The Kansas City Star*, Religion/Spirituality
Writing

1998
Ken Fuson, *The Sun*, Baltimore, Non-Deadline Writing
John J. Keller, *The Wall Street Journal*, Deadline Reporting
Pittsburgh Post-Gazette, Team Deadline Reporting
Mike Jacobs, *Grand Forks* (N.D.) *Herald*, Editorial Writing
Justin Davidson, *Newsday*, Criticism
Stephen Hunter, *The Washington Post*, Criticism

Finalists:
N.R. Kleinfield, *The New York Times*, Non-Deadline Writing
Irene Virag, *Newsday*, Non-Deadline Writing
Barbara Demick, *The Philadelphia Inquirer*, Deadline Reporting
Lynne Tuohy, *Hartford Courant*, Deadline Reporting
The Boston Globe, Team Deadline Reporting
Chicago Tribune, Team Deadline Reporting
Dale McFeatters, Scripps Howard News Service, Commentary
Tracey O'Shaughnessy, *Waterbury* (Conn.) *Republican-American*,
Commentary
Leonard Pitts Jr., *The Miami Herald*, Commentary
Lance Dickie, *The Seattle Times*, Editorial Writing
Alyssa Haywoode, *The Boston Globe*, Editorial Writing
Kate Stanley, *Star Tribune*, Minneapolis, Editorial Writing
Gail Caldwell, *The Boston Globe*, Criticism

1999
DeNeen L. Brown, *The Washington Post*, Non-Deadline Writing
Bartholomew Sullivan, *The Commercial Appeal*, Memphis,
Deadline News Reporting
The News Tribune, Tacoma, Wash., Team Deadline News Re-
porting
J. Peder Zane, *The News & Observer*, Raleigh, N.C.,
Commentary
Bailey Thomson, *Mobile* (Ala.) *Register*, Editorial Writing
Mirta Ojito, *The New York Times*, Covering the World

Finalists:
Erin Hoover Barnett, *The Oregonian*, Non-Deadline Writing
Seth Mydans, *The New York Times*, Deadline News Reporting
Peter St. Onge, *The Huntsville* (Ala.) *Times*, Deadline News
Reporting
Mike Vaccaro, *The Star-Ledger*, Deadline News Reporting
The Boston Globe, Team Deadline News Reporting
The Oregonian, Team Deadline News Reporting
Colbert I. King, *The Washington Post*, Commentary
Peter H. King, *The Sacramento Bee*, Commentary

Cynthia Tucker, *The Atlanta Constitution*, Commentary
Paul Greenberg, *Arkansas Democrat-Gazette*, Editorial Writing
Howell Raines, *The New York Times*, Editorial Writing
Eric Black, *Star Tribune*, Minneapolis, Covering the World
Rhea Wessel, *The Anniston* (Ala.) *Star*, Covering the World

2000

Mitchell Zuckoff, *The Boston Globe*, Non-Deadline Writing
Leonora Bohen LaPeter, *Savannah* (Ga.) *Morning News*,
    Deadline News Reporting
St. Petersburg Times, Team Deadline News Reporting
Cynthia Tucker, *The Atlanta Constitution*, Commentary
Dianne Donovan, *Chicago Tribune*, Editorial Writing
Michael Dobie, *Newsday*, Diversity Writing

Finalists:
Anne Hull, *St. Petersburg Times*, Non-Deadline Writing
Robert L. Kaiser, *Chicago Tribune*, Non-Deadline Writing
Jenni Laidman, *The Blade*, Toledo, Non-Deadline Writing
David Finkel, *The Washington Post*, Deadline News Reporting
Hugo Kugiya, *Newsday*, Deadline News Reporting
Chicago Sun-Times, Team Deadline News Reporting
The Virginian-Pilot, Team Deadline News Reporting
Gail Collins, *The New York Times*, Commentary
Colbert I. King, *The Washington Post*, Commentary
Mike Littwin, *Denver Rocky Mountain News*, Commentary
Verlyn Klinkenborg, *The New York Times*, Editorial Writing
Kate Stanley, *Star Tribune*, Minneapolis, Editorial Writing
Somini Sengupta, *The New York Times*, Diversity Writing

2001

Tom Hallman Jr., *The Oregonian*, Non-Deadline Writing
Leonard Pitts, *The Miami Herald*, Commentary
The Star-Ledger, Newark, N.J., Team Deadline News
    Reporting
Stephen Magagnini, *The Sacramento Bee*, Diversity Writing
Stephen Henderson, *The Sun*, Baltimore, Editorial Writing
Steven Erlanger, *The New York Times*, Deadline News
    Reporting
John Beale, *Pittsburgh Post-Gazette*, Community Service
    Photojournalism

Finalists:
Michelle Kearns, *Sun Journal*, Lewiston, Maine, Non-
    Deadline Writing
Charlie LeDuff, *The New York Times*, Non-Deadline Writing
Colbert I. King, *The Washington Post*, Commentary

Paul Vitello, *Newsday*, Commentary
The Miami Herald, Team Deadline News Reporting
St. Petersburg Times, Team Deadline News Reporting
Mark Bixler, *The Atlanta Journal-Constitution*, Diversity Writing
Paul Greenberg, *Arkansas Democrat-Gazette*, Editorial Writing
Bailey Thomson, *Mobile* (Ala.) *Register*, Editorial Writing
Darrin Mortenson, *The Virgin Islands Daily News*, Deadline
    News Reporting
Leigh Daughtridge, *The Beacon News*, Aurora, Ill., Commu-
    nity Service Photojournalism
Thom Scott, *The Times-Picayune*, New Orleans, Community
    Service Photojournalism

2002
N.R. Kleinfield, *The New York Times*, Deadline News
    Reporting
The Wall Street Journal, Team Deadline News Reporting
Jim Dwyer, *The New York Times*, Short Writing
Anne Hull, *The Washington Post*, Diversity Writing
Ellen Barry, *The Boston Globe*, Non-Deadline Writing
John McCormick, *Chicago Tribune*, Editorial Writing
Steve Lopez, *Los Angeles Times*, Commentary
J. Albert Diaz, *The Miami Herald*, Community Service
    Photojournalism

Finalists:
Jack Kelley, *USA TODAY*, Deadline News Reporting
John Bussey, *The Wall Street Journal*, Deadline News
    Reporting
St. Petersburg Times, Team Deadline News Reporting
Los Angeles Times, Team Deadline News Reporting
Michael Phillips, *The Wall Street Journal*, Short Writing
Peter St. Onge, *The Charlotte Observer*, Short Writing
Stephen Magagnini, *The Sacramento Bee*, Diversity Writing
Amy Waldman, *The New York Times*, Diversity Writing
David Finkel, *The Washington Post*, Non-Deadline Writing
Dexter Filkins, *The New York Times*, Non-Deadline Writing
Kate Stanley, *Star Tribune*, Minneapolis, Editorial Writing
Stephen Henderson, *The Sun*, Baltimore, Editorial Writing
Leonard Pitts Jr., *The Miami Herald*, Commentary
Connie Schultz, *The Plain Dealer*, Cleveland, Commentary
Gail Fisher, *Los Angeles Times*, Community Service
    Photojournalism
Brian Plonka, *The Spokesman-Review*, Spokane, Wash.,
    Community Service Photojournalism

Best Newspaper Writing Editors

Front row, left to right:
Dr. Roy Peter Clark, 1979–1984; 1985 co-editor
   with Dr. Don Fry
Dr. Karen Brown Dunlap, 1991–1992; 1990 co-editor
   with Dr. Don Fry

Back row, left to right:
Christopher "Chip" Scanlan, 1994–2000
Keith Woods, 2001–2003
Dr. Don Fry, 1986–1989, 1993; 1985 co-editor with
   Dr. Roy Peter Clark; 1990 co-editor with
   Dr. Karen Brown Dunlap

About the CD-ROM

Included with this volume is a CD-ROM containing all the images in the winners' and finalists' entry packages for the Community Service Photojournalism category. Each package is presented with the photo captions and stories that accompanied the images. We have included full-screen images that are printable at low resolution for classroom projects and an interactive cropping tool that allows for re-editing of selected photos.

In addition, the CD includes two parts of Amy Ellis Nutt's "The Seekers" series, "Faith's Place" and "Genesis," along with illustrated glossaries created by Andre Malok for each of the five stories in the series.

Parts 4 through 6 of Jonathan Tilove's series, "Along Martin Luther King: A Passage to Black America," and photos by Newhouse News Service photographer Michael Falco that accompanied the stories also are included.

The CD project was created by Poynter's design editor Anne Conneen and multimedia editor Larry Larsen using Macromedia Flash. Kenny Irby of the Poynter faculty worked closely with editor Keith Woods and publications director Billie M. Keirstead on the presentation of the Community Service Photojournalism category.

The CD will run on both Windows and Macintosh platforms. It is designed to open at full-screen size. The Flash Player and Adobe Acrobat Reader applications are included on the CD.

We hope you find this CD useful and enjoyable.